THE PERFECT SHOT, NORTH AMERICA

The Perfect Shot, North America

Shot Placement for North American Big Game

BY

Craig T. Boddington

ARTWORK BY

Laurie O'Keefe

SAFARI PRESS INC

Dedication

To my old friends, publisher Ludo Wurfbain and editor Jacque Neufeld, who have always had the really good ideas for books, and who, over the years, have made my work look so much better—and, most especially, to their son Rory, to whom the best wish I could offer is that he have as much fun hunting with his dad as I did with mine.

Acknowledgments

The author would like to acknowledge that excerpts were taken from *American Hunting Rifles,* his previous North American book by Safari Press.

****

The publisher would like to thank the following photographers for the use of the photos seen throughout this book and on the dust jacket: Dusan S. Smetana, Gary Kramer, Len Rue Jr., and Leonard Lee Rue III.

Boddington, Craig T.
O'Keefe, Laurie

First edition

Safari Press Inc.

2003, Long Beach, California

ISBN 1-57157-271-6

Library of Congress Catalog Card Number: 2002106911

10 9 8 7 6 5 4 3 2

Readers wishing to receive the Safari Press catalog, featuring many fine books on big-game hunting, wingshooting, and sporting firearms, should write to Safari Press Inc., P.O. Box 3095, Long Beach, CA 90803, USA. Tel: (714) 894-9080 or visit our Web site at www.safaripress.com.

Table of Contents

Foreword

In the hunter's world, Brig. Gen. Craig Boddington certainly needs no introduction, so I was deeply honored to be asked to write the foreword in Craig's new book, *The Perfect Shot, North America.* Craig provides the modern hunter with invaluable information on the planning and the taking of North America's big-game species, and his book overflows with respect for North American game. By respect I mean that Craig provides hunters with the knowledge on the various species to plan their hunts as well as giving fresh, up-to-date advice on the best hunting rifles and bullets available.

Craig Boddington is an expert on sporting firearms and gives advice zeroed at the bench and proven in the field. No outdoor writer, at any time, has hunted more globally than Craig Boddington, and this book, then, is chockfull of fundamental and esoteric information. Craig is thorough and detailed, and he combines his experiences in hunting and ballistics to provide rare insight into the hunting of North America's big game. He gives solid data on where and when to hunt, how to determine a trophy in the field, the latest measuring techniques, and absolute up-to-date information on ballistics.

I have shared hunting campfires with Craig for three decades, both as a hunting partner and as his hunting guide. In hunting and shooting, his interest is intense yet still full of human emotion. Several years ago, Craig and his dad came to Montana to hunt bighorn rams with me. A few days into the hunt, we found a really good ram. Our first stalk put us within 300 yards of the animal. The shot offered by the ram didn't feel quite right to Craig, so we backed away. This was a tough thing to do. It wasn't until late the next day that we relocated the ram. The light was failing, so there could be no stealth and cunning on this stalk . . . rather we needed a full bayonet charge to get that magnificent ram. The stalk went right this time, and we were in perfect range. Craig crawled into the stock and steadied for the shot. Suddenly he raised his head from the rifle, and I could see that Craig was shaking with excitement. Calming himself, he studied this magnum ram for a few moments. Just as suddenly, he was back at the rifle and made that perfect shot. Boddington's book, *The Perfect Shot, North America,* mirrors the taking of that ram. Look a little harder at the game you seek, then make "the perfect shot."

I have watched my friend work through the ranks of the outdoor publishing world and seen him make the rank of brigadier general in the U.S. Marine Corps. As I write this, Brig. Gen. Craig Boddington is overseas, not on a hunting trip, but serving his country. I salute him as a fine hunter and a protector.

Jack Atcheson Jr.
Jack Atcheson & Sons, Inc.
Hunting Consultants
Butte, Montana
April 2002

Introduction

A couple of years ago my friend Kevin Robertson, or "Doctari" as he is known to his fans, came out with an excellent book on hunting African game entitled *The Perfect Shot*. There are many good books that I wish I'd written, but in most cases I can look in the mirror and say with honesty that I lack the talent, imagination, knowledge, or experience (sometimes all four!) to actually have written them. In the case of Robertson's book I probably have most of the qualifications needed, so it's mostly a case of looking in the mirror and wondering, "Why didn't I think of that?"

As many of you probably know, I've written several books about African hunting, and I'd like to think they are of some value to the Africa-bound hunter. Robertson's *The Perfect Shot*, however, is an absolute must-read. And, in all honestly, Robertson was much more qualified to write it than I would have been. Not only is he an African by birth and a lifelong hunter of African big game, but he is also a veterinarian with professional expertise in animal anatomy. His book is extremely detailed, providing a tremendous amount of information for hunters unfamiliar with African game and African hunting conditions. His book deserves to be the success it is!

Since its publication, dozens and dozens of people have suggested that a similar book should be produced addressing North American big game, and a whole lot of those people have recommended that I should be involved in writing such a book. Fortunately, my old friend and longtime publisher, Ludo Wurfbain, got Laurie O'Keefe and me together on this project. I say "fortunately," because we really needed this book—"we" being the huge number of North American hunters who would find a book like Robertson's so very handy. Our continent does not have the tremendous variety of game found in Africa. But our game does run the gamut in size, from javelina to deer-sized game, on up to elk and moose, and all the way up to bison and walrus. We have genuinely dangerous game in our big bears, and occasionally dangerous game in our wild hogs, black bears, and muskoxen. We have numerous diverse families of mammals among our game, with bears, cats, deer, sheep, goats, wild cattle, and more represented—each with slightly different anatomy that changes the location for "the perfect shot."

Even more diverse than our game is the topography, terrain, and vegetation where these animals are hunted. North America holds every imaginable type of habitat, from dense forest to tundra, from open plains to high mountains, from swamp to desert. Some North American animals, like the whitetail and black bear, are found across huge chunks of North America, and thus are hunted in almost every habitat type. Some, like the Alaskan brown bear and Stone sheep, are found in relatively small areas, so the conditions under which they are hunted are more predictable.

More predictable, that is, if you've seen the country and know what to expect. If you haven't seen it, then this book will be of value not only in depicting the game animals and optimum shot placement, but also in describing the country, the hunting conditions, and the kind of shooting you might expect . . . and thus which rifles and cartridges are most suitable.

Mind you, there are no perfect answers. One of the exciting things about the great sport of hunting is that no two situations are exactly alike, and you never know exactly what any day afield might bring. But within the normal uncertainty that is part of the game you can be—and should be—as well prepared as is humanly possible. I do not expect this book to offer any revelations about white-tailed deer to the experienced eastern hunter who has pursued them all his life, nor do I expect it to offer great knowledge on elk or mule deer to the experienced western hunter. Rather, I expect it to be of great value to less experienced hunters, and of equal value to old hands who are headed into new country in pursuit of unfamiliar game.

Luck is important in hunting, and while hunting luck often seems whimsical, I do believe the adage that luck occurs when preparation meets opportunity. To find opportunity, you will have to do your homework in researching a good area, and, once on the ground, you will probably have to hunt hard, and you should definitely hunt smart. Preparation takes many forms: physical conditioning, practice in shooting, packing the right equipment, and, of course, doing the research that will enable you the opportunity should it arise. All of these are part and parcel to preparation. I believe this book will stand as an important reference in preparing you for future North American hunts, just as the original African version has become a standard reference for African hunting. So I wish you luck . . . and I hope this book will help you make some of that luck!

Craig Boddington
Camp Doha, Kuwait
April 2002

CHOOSING THE RIGHT ACTION

Since the self-contained metallic cartridge came into common use, back in the 1870s, we American hunters have gone through three major shifts in our preference of sporting rifle actions. In the black-powder era, the single shot was king; it was reliable, dependable, and affordable—and it was capable of housing the large-cased cartridges powerful enough to handle the full spectrum of North American big game. True, lever actions garnered a lot of glory, and some, like the Winchester '76 and '86, were big enough to handle large cartridges. But they were expensive and relatively few of either model were made. Through the end of the nineteenth century, serious hunters relied on single shots from Ballard, Bullard, Remington, Winchester, Sharps, and many others—not to mention tens of thousands of trapdoor Springfields.

With the advent of smokeless powder, the picture changed. No longer did a repeating action need to be as bulky because, due to the higher velocity, much more compact cartridges were now effective for larger game. In the early years of the twentieth century there were a few bolt-action fans, and there were more slide actions than there are today—but the lever action was America's darling. After World War I, the bolt action started gaining popularity, but clear up to the 1930s the top guns—certainly to the public if not the sporting press—were lever actions from Winchester, Marlin, and Savage.

It's hard to pinpoint exactly when the bolt action really started to take over. The availability of cheap surplus Springfields, Mausers, and others in the years following both world wars certainly helped. So did the availability of good commercial actions like the Remington 721 series and the Winchester Model 70. Regardless of when it started, by the latter part of the twentieth century the shift was almost complete. Today, without question, the bolt action is far and away the most popular sporting rifle action, not only in America but in the entire world.

BOLT ACTIONS

Like most American hunters of my generation and younger, I'm a bolt-action fan. Unlike my forebears, I grew up with a bolt action. I'm comfortable with it and have great faith in it. A bolt action has several distinct advantages, and no serious disadvantages. First is versatility. Depending on the length of the bolt (and bolt diameter and width of action), the bolt action can handle cartridges of any size, from the smallest varmint cartridge on up through the largest magnums. Its massive locking lugs can handle the pressures of the hottest cartridges, and it has the greatest camming power for extraction of any type of action. The bolt action is the serious rifleman's darling because, with its rigid lockup and customary one-piece stock, it is generally (though not always) the most accurate sporting-rifle action. Generally speaking, bolt actions also have the most readily adjusted triggers, a small nuance that is extremely important to those of us who are accuracy freaks.

Virtually every maker of centerfire rifles offers a bolt action. The list of available cartridges is almost limitless, and while out-of-the-box accuracy won't always exceed the accuracy of other production rifles, the bolt action lends itself best to the fiddling that serious shooters love to do. You can play with the bedding, adjust the trigger, and mess with the loads to your heart's content—and a bolt action is the most likely to respond. Bolt actions are the easiest to weatherproof, the least susceptible to freeze-up in extreme cold, and are available in the greatest variety of options. These options include not only different chamberings, but stainless steel and rustproof finishes, different stock styles and materials, and different barrel lengths . . . in short, the works.

This is not to suggest that the bolt action is the only choice, nor that it is everyone's

Although I am primarily a bolt-action fan, I also admire and often use single shots and lever actions, like this Winchester Model 88 in .308 Winchester. As a left-hander, I don't use slide actions or semiautos very much, but when chambered to the proper cartridges, any of the action types are suitable for most North American hunting.

choice, nor even that, under all conditions, it's even the best choice. Lever actions still have a sizable following, and the single shots, slide actions, and semiautomatics all have their loyal, and often outspoken, fans. While there are far more makes and models of bolt actions than everything else put together, American hunters do have the full range of actions to choose from. As I said, I have more experience with bolt actions than anything else, but I am also fond of lever actions and single shots. As a left-hander, I have relatively little experience with slide action and semiautomatic rifles. There are left-hand shotguns in these action types, but no mirror-image left-hand rifles. Since this means my face is on the same side as the ejection port, I have pretty much avoided these action types—but that doesn't mean I have anything against them or any of the action types. Some have disadvantages in some situations, but all are available chambered to cartridges suitable for all North American big game. We'll talk about these relative advantages and disadvantages, but none of the latter is overwhelming. It really comes down to whatever gives you the most confidence.

SINGLE SHOTS

The single shot was almost a dead duck when I was a kid, but nearly forty years ago Bill Ruger thought it might have some appeal to modern hunters. The result was the Ruger Number One, an American classic that is just one of William B. Ruger's many successes. The Number One is the most famous and most successful of all the modern single shots, but it certainly isn't alone. There are other falling-block actions, such as the Browning and Dakota, and there are break-open actions like the Thompson/Center and the Harrington & Richardson/New England Arms Handi-Rifle. The falling-block actions are much stronger than the break-open actions, but, characteristically, the single shots can be chambered to darn near anything. They're simple to operate and, if used properly, exceedingly safe: They're either loaded or unloaded! The two-piece stock creates significant bedding challenges that the bolt action doesn't have, but single-shot rifles can be exceedingly accurate.

The charm and mystique of having only one available shot is part of the allure of the single shot. It does make you more careful with that one shot, which is certainly a good thing. However, I don't think the single-shot rifle is necessarily well suited to all types of North American hunting. It is available in cartridges more than adequate for the biggest bears, but certain one-shot kills are fairly unusual on grizzly and brown bears. I wouldn't recommend a single-shot rifle for the hunter who is hunting alone. Even for guided hunters, it should be understood that choosing a single shot may be asking for a guide's assistance when it wouldn't have been necessary had a repeater of identical caliber been chosen.

An inherent inconvenience with the single shot is the fact that it is either fully loaded or fully unloaded. I don't carry cartridges in the chamber when my rifle is slung, or when I'm negotiating rough country. The single shot is totally out of action when its chamber is empty, while the magazine rifle requires just the working of a bolt or lever to put it into action. In the high mountains, this is generally not a problem; stalks tend to be well planned and there is quite adequate time to load the single shot and prepare for a careful shot. In timber, whether for deer, elk, moose, or whatever, I see a real disadvantage to the single shot. If it's cold and gloves must be worn, it's going to take altogether too much time to get an empty single shot into action should you encounter an animal unexpectedly. The temptation to keep it loaded is even worse. Rifles simply should not have rounds in the chamber while hunters are climbing, negotiating deadfalls, or moving around other obstacles—or at any time when the rifle is not under the hunter's complete control. This difficulty also exists with horseback hunting.

Under no circumstances should a rifle have a cartridge in the chamber while on horseback, whether slung or carried in a saddle scabbard. That gives a repeater a decided advantage for any horseback hunt. If a fine bull elk is encountered on the trail, a hunter can drop off his horse, pull a repeater from the scabbard, and jack in a cartridge. With a single shot, the hunter must first produce a cartridge from somewhere. The single-shot shooter will *always* have that cartridge readily available—but again, if heavy gloves are needed, fumbling is inevitable.

To my mind the single shot, as good as it is, is best suited to very deliberate hunting techniques where surprises are unlikely. This would include any form of stand-hunting and most spot-and-stalk hunting. Where I feel the single shot would be a handicap—perhaps even a serious one—would be for any form of still-hunting or tracking in thick cover and uneven terrain. If the hunting you're doing is such that you might encounter game at any time, but you can't predict when—and if the footing is uneven enough that you might need to sling the rifle or use one or both hands for support—then the single shot is not a great idea. It needs to be used in situations where you either *know* you can keep both hands on the loaded rifle and have it absolutely ready, or you simply won't need it to be loaded until a time of *your*, not the game's, choosing.

LEVER ACTIONS

To my thinking there are three types of lever actions. The first is the traditional (or nontraditional, like the new Ruger) carbine chambered to what are essentially pistol cartridges. Although popular in the growing sport of Cowboy Action Shooting, the lever guns chambered to .45 Colt, .44-40, and lesser cartridges have very little place in modern big-game hunting. They will take deer at close range (just like they did in the 1870s), but there are much better tools available. Such rifles chambered to .44 Remington Magnum and .454 Casull have a bit more utility. They are still very limited in range, but in close cover they are quite effective on deer and perfectly adequate for black bear and wild hogs.

The second type is also a traditional tubular-magazine lever action, but chambered to the "brush-busting" rifle cartridges like .30-30, .307 Winchester, .348 Winchester, .35 Remington, .356 Winchester, .375 Winchester, .444 Marlin, and .45-70. I use "brush busting" in quotes because *no* cartridge is particularly good at plowing through obstructions, and the testing I have done personally suggest that the blunt-nosed, slow-moving bullets from these cartridges aren't any better at brush busting than the fast, flat-shooting cartridges. However, there is great appeal to the slab-sided, easy-carrying, fast-handling lever action. Because of either low velocity or the flat-nosed bullets required in tubular magazines—or both—these rifles are limited in range. However, they are extremely effective. The big bores hit like freight trains, and even the modest .30-30 is far more effective than its paper ballistics suggest because its blunt bullets transfer energy very quickly. Provided shots can be kept fairly close, these rifles are extremely effective on deer, and the big bores—especially the great old .45-70—are just wonderful for close-cover use on black bears, elk, and moose.

The third type of lever action has a box magazine similar to that of a bolt action, which means that it can use aerodynamic sharp-pointed (spitzer) bullets. There aren't many to choose from, but Browning's BLR is available in both .308 Winchester-length and standard-length cartridges; and the great old Savage 99 is back in production as well. The two-piece stock common to most lever actions makes accuracy a bit irregular, and the factory trigger pull is usually something you just have to live with. Having said that, these rifles are perfectly suitable for any hunting for which their cartridges are adequate—which includes most North American big game under most conditions.

The only real limitation on lever actions is their lack of truly powerful cartridges for hunting our biggest bears. Sure, you could do it at close range with a .45-70 or perhaps a .348 or .358. And you can do it with a .30-06 and very heavy bullets. But there are better tools available for our biggest bears. Other than that limitation, the lever-actions can do the job from coast to coast.

SLIDE ACTIONS

Although slide-action shotguns remain extremely popular, today there are just two slide-action centerfires remaining on the market: Remington's Model 7600 and Browning's BPR. The former is offered in standard chamberings from .243 to .30-06, while the latter includes the 7mm Remington Magnum and .300 Winchester Magnum. This means that, again with the possible exception of the big bears, slide-action rifles are suitable, at least in power, for any North American big game.

Their primary following seems to be among close-cover whitetail hunters, but, in reality, there is no reason why a slide action can't be used almost anywhere. Like all the two-piece stock rifles, accuracy varies a bit—and this is made worse by the simple fact that the fore-end cannot be bedded since it's used to operate the action. However, I've seen a number of slide-action rifles that shot well enough for any big-game hunting . . . and, conversely, I've never seen one that wasn't good enough for *most* hunting.

I'm not particularly an advocate of firepower, especially as a substitute for shot placement, but one advantage the slide action has is that it is very, very fast. Despite the legend, I'm not convinced that a lever action is faster than a bolt action, properly operated by skilled hands. I am certain that a slide action is faster than either, and in extremely skilled hands can be faster than even a semiautomatic. Some slide-action fans cling to them because they're just like their favorite shotgun; others use them because they're fast. Either way, there's nothing wrong with this uniquely American action type.

SEMIAUTOMATIC

The semiautomatic has the obvious advantage of rapid repeat shots without moving one's hands, and of course the gas-operated guns have a bit softer recoil than other actions in identical calibers. The drawbacks are essentially the same as for lever actions and slide actions. Accuracy, though adequate, is generally not as flashy as the average bolt action will produce. Extraction is also not as positive. Today's semiautomatics are extremely reliable, and jams are very rare; however, semiautomatics by their nature are a bit more finicky about the ammo they digest. For those who handload, greater care is required. Shooters who use factory loads needn't worry, though; provided the semiautomatic is kept clean and properly lubricated, it should function.

My only real complaint about the semiautomatic is that it's noisy to load and unload. To ride the bolt home slowly is to invite disaster; there's a very good chance the bolt won't go fully into battery and the rifle will fail to fire. You really need to snap the bolt home, and that's a noisy proposition. For this reason, I think the semiautomatic is best suited to stand hunting. You get on stand, load the rifle, and you're all set to go. When it's time to leave the stand, you unload.

As with slide actions, the primary semiautomatic sporters are from Browning and Remington, the Browning BAR and Remington 7400. Chamberings are similar with one big exception: The BAR is also offered in .338 Winchester Magnum. This means there is a semiautomatic suitable for any game in North America, and if this is the action type that gives you the most confidence, there is absolutely no reason not to choose it.

SLUG-GUN ACTIONS

Slug guns have come a long way in recent years, with most manufacturers now offering models with good sights, fixtures for sturdy scope mounts, and rifled barrels that offer exceptional accuracy. As far as actions go, the rules are exactly the same as with rifles: The bolt actions will, on average, produce the best accuracy because of the one-piece stock and secure lockup. The slide actions and semiautomatics, on the other hand, are faster for repeat shots and, with rifled barrels and good sights, will be far more accurate than the smoothbore slug guns of yesteryear. Either way, even with modern projectiles and the most accurate guns, the slug is a short-range affair, limited to perhaps 125 yards at best.

I lean toward the bolt actions simply because I'm mostly a rifle guy and accuracy gives me confidence. However, given the inherent range limitation, it probably doesn't make a difference. As with centerfire rifles, the right action for you is the one that gives you the most confidence.

SCOPES, SIGHTS, AND ACCESSORIES

When I was a kid, the most popular scope in America was a fixed 4X. The variables were out there, but they were widely distrusted. There was reason for this: Back then variables were much more fragile than fixed-power scopes, and considerable changes in point of impact were common as you moved up and down in magnification. Times change, and change again. I grew up using telescopic sights, but just a decade or two earlier most hunters were still using iron sights. Today, knowing how to use iron sights is almost a forgotten art, and even the old reliable fixed 4X is rare. The variable-power scope rules the roost today, and hunters are shifting to more and more magnification.

This is both good and bad. Under *most* circumstances a telescopic sight is superior to any iron sight—not because it magnifies the image, but because it enables you to see *better*. In order to use an open sight effectively, the eye must work back and forth on three focal planes—at the rear sight, at the front sight, and at the target. This is extremely difficult, and it doesn't get easier as you get older. For me, the rear sight fuzzes out almost completely these days, so when I use open sights I have to rely on stock fit to ensure that the front sight is properly aligned with the rear sight. Aperture or peep sights are a bit better. With an aperture, the eye naturally centers the front sight in the middle of the aperture; you're looking through it, not at it. So the peep sight cuts it down to two focal planes, one at the front sight and one at the target.

The scope is better yet. If properly focused, the telescopic sight places the reticle on the same focal plane as the target. All the eye has to do is superimpose the reticle on the target and squeeze the trigger. This is the real strength of the telescopic sight. Of course it's a good thing that the image is magnified, at least up to a point. A larger image gives you a larger target, and a larger target is easier to hit. These days, however, it appears that a lot of North American hunters are going overboard in the magnification department.

HOW MUCH POWER IS ENOUGH?

The variable power scope has been fully perfected and absolutely reliable for many, many years. The flexibility it offers is wonderful. I grew up using a fixed 4X, and I'll never forget what a revelation it was when I switched to a "big scope," a 3–9X variable! Suddenly, at maximum power, a 250-yard shot seemed incredibly easy. For some time now the 3–9X and its cousins (there isn't really much difference between, say, 2.5–8X and

3.5–10X) have been the most popular scopes in America. To my thinking, the popularity of this class of scope is appropriate. Magnification between 8X and 10X is enough for almost all sensible shots, even in the most open country. At the low end, magnification between 2.5X and 3.5X is low enough for close-range work in fast-moving situations.

Why? The problem with high magnification is that, as power increases, field of view decreases. Lots of magnification is great at long range—but, despite the current popularity of "long-range shooting," there are few hunting situations in North America where you can predict a long shot with absolute certainty. So, while it's nice to have a lot of magnification if you need to reach out a ways, the last thing you want is to have a blur of hair in the scope should a close shot present itself.

These days an increasing number of hunters are gravitating to extremely powerful variables: 6–18X, 6.5–20X, and so forth. To my thinking this is more power than is really needed. There are special circumstances where long shots are likely and really close shots are unlikely, such as those for pronghorn, Coues deer, caribou, and certain setups for whitetails. Under these circumstances, a "medium-high" variable from 4–12X to about 5–15X might be useful. The rifles I have set up for serious long-range use wear 4.5–14X scopes; in my experience this range offers enough magnification for the longest shooting I'm likely to do, but I've also used them for close, fast shots on the lowest setting. To each their own, but for big-game hunting I don't see any need or utility in a more powerful scope.

Most of my rifles, however, wear scopes in the most popular 3–9X range. In truth, this is also enough power for the longest shots most of us have any business attempting. The other reality is that many of us don't need even this much power. It isn't harmful as long as you have a low setting of not much more than 4X—and you leave your scope on the low setting unless and until you need more power. However, variable-power scopes are more expensive than fixed power scopes—so why buy more magnification than you really need? If, like millions of American hunters, you spend most of your time pursuing whitetailed deer and rarely shoot much past 100 to 150 yards, you might be just as well served by a fixed 4X or a low-range variable (from, say, 1–4X to 2–7X). The rifles I use for close-range hunting, such as bear hunting and hog hunting—and my slug gun—wear scopes in this power range.

Another way of looking at it is that you can buy a fixed 4X of the very highest quality for about the same cost as a high-range scope of mediocre quality. Quality is extremely important in optics, since it's quality of lenses and coatings that give you the resolution to help you really see your target. And quality is a major factor in the other important attribute of telescopic sights: gathering light. Regardless of magnification, scopes of inferior quality do not gather as much light as the best scopes. More so than in most sporting equipment, you tend to get what you pay for in optics.

OBJECTIVES AND TUBES

This also applies to scopes with larger objective lenses and the larger 30mm tubes. All things being equal, a larger objective lens will gather more light, and a scope with a 30mm tube will gather more light than a scope with a one-inch tube. But this only applies if the quality of the products is equal. In other words, quality counts first, so I would take a one-inch-tube scope from one of the best brands over a cheaper 30mm scope.

Scopes, Sights, and Accessories

Again, all things being equal, larger tubes and objectives do gather more light. The drawback is that these scopes are more bulky, weigh more, and cost more. This is fine if you need the capability, can afford it, and you're willing to carry it—but think through what you really need and go for the capability rather than just following trends.

SCOPE MOUNTS

The greatest enemy to scopes and mounts is recoil. However, in North America we have no need for elephant guns. Every scope mounting system I'm aware of, if properly assembled, will hold up just fine at recoil levels at least up to .375 H&H, which effectively covers virtually all North American big game. The real key here is proper assembly. It's important to read the directions carefully (at least a couple of times!) before mounting a scope. Use LocTite or a similar screw-holding compound, and get all the screws nice and tight with hand pressure. Never overtighten with a torque wrench or you'll break a screw—and you might not know it until your scope goes haywire.

Mounts that I particularly like are the good old Redfield system, which is fine until you get into serious recoil. Leupold's newer dual dovetail is stronger, as is the good old Weaver crossbolt system. The Conetrol mount is wonderful, and there are several others. All will work just fine if you put them together correctly.

Here are some of my favorite hunting rifles. All of them wear variable scopes, ranging in power from 1.75–6X to 4.5–14X. This entire spectrum offers versatility, but there's a reason why variables in the 3–9X range are the most popular: They are well suited for almost any North American hunting.

A new fad in scope mounts is the detachable mount. There are several good systems, including the Talley, Warne, and two different detachables from Leupold. I like the detachables, but I'm not altogether certain why so many people use them. To my thinking they have two purposes: First, they serve a useful function in conjunction with iron sights. I see a lot of rifles, however, with detachable mounts and plain barrels (no iron sights), and I really don't understand this . . . unless you have the second purpose in mind. A detachable mount allows you to switch scopes back and forth from one rifle to another, and it also allows you to carry a spare scope all set up in rings. In either context a detachable mount makes sense—but they cost a bit more, and there's no sense paying for one unless you're going to get some use out of it.

IRON SIGHTS

You shoot better if you can see better, and you can see better with a scope. However, there are a couple of situations where iron sights are superior. The first is in the rain. You can and should use scope covers, because they will keep water off the lenses and, during a snowstorm or gentle rain, give you enough time to take a shot. But if it's raining hard enough, water droplets will quickly obscure the lenses of any scope, and there isn't a darned thing you can do about it.

While aperture sights are generally superior to open sights, this is not true in the rain because water will collect in the aperture and obscure it. In really wet country you need, at a minimum, good auxiliary irons on your rifle and a detachable scope mount. Note that I said "good" iron sights. Since most Americans today use scopes, the manufacturers pay very little attention to iron sights . . . and most iron sights currently supplied by the factories are flimsy affairs! In more than thirty-five years of hunting big game, I've had very little trouble with scopes—but I've had a number of supposedly rugged iron sights break, bend, or simply fall off the rifle! So if you think you might actually use your iron sights, check them out carefully. If they look flimsy and rudimentary, they probably are—and should be replaced before you need them!

The other situation where iron sights are superior to scopes is in hound hunting, whether for bears, cats, or wild hogs. Many houndsmen simply will not allow the use of scope sights when hunting over their dogs. If the animal is bayed on the ground (always with hogs, often with bears, and sometimes even with cougars), the hunter can only take the shot if the dogs are in a safe position. The problem arises from the fact that a scope does not allow you to see whether the dogs are safe since it's tunneling in on only the animal being hunted. Things are happening fast and there's much excitement, and a scope creates tunnel vision. This is dangerous under such circumstances, for you need to be able to look beyond the animal on both sides to make sure the dogs are clear. If I were a houndsman, I wouldn't allow scopes anywhere near my dogs!

REDUCING RECOIL

Recoil is a function of both caliber and gun weight. This last part isn't widely understood, but it's important because there are numerous very light rifles currently on the market. Everybody has a different pain threshold for recoil, but it isn't just a matter of cartridge power. Stock style and fit matters, but gun weight is a critical factor. We all know that a .300

magnum has quite a bit of recoil, but most people can handle the recoil of a .300 magnum weighing, say, nine pounds. Reduce the gun weight by a third, to six pounds (which is quite possible) and you've increased the recoil by a third. Now you have a really brutal beast of a rifle, too much gun for a whole lot of folks!

The bottom line is that, if you want it light, fast, and powerful it's gonna kick! A straight stock will bring the recoil back in a straight line, which helps. A good recoil pad made of modern shock-absorbent polymers, like Pachmayr's Decelerator pad, also helps. Then there are muzzle brakes.

I must admit that I don't like muzzle brakes very much—but they absolutely work. The various muzzle brakes and porting systems vent expanding powder gases, sort of like a rocket effect, and actual felt recoil reduction can be as much as forty percent. The reason I don't like them is that they *significantly* increase muzzle blast. I'm already getting deaf, and I don't want to lose what little hearing I have left, so I avoid muzzle brakes as much as I can. Having said that, I still keep a couple of rifles with brakes. One is a six-pound .300 Winchester Magnum from Match Grade Arms. It has a brutally noisy brake, but the brake makes the rifle shootable. Without the brake, it would be extremely unpleasant to shoot—and probably impossible to shoot as well as the rifle will shoot.

In defense of the brake, the muzzle blast is actually far worse for bystanders than it is for the shooter. So if you hunt alone, a muzzle brake isn't quite as obnoxious as it is with a partner. Just make sure you wear good ear protection on the range. Actually, very few of us wear ear protection in the field, but we

This .30-378 Weatherby Magnum wears a 4.5–14X scope, which I consider the most powerful scope practical for big-game hunting. This rifle also has a muzzle brake; the muzzle blast is severe, but without it the large-cased, super-fast cartridges have more recoil than most people can handle.

all should—and if you're shooting a rifle with a muzzle brake, you should definitely hunt with earplugs or earmuffs that cut out the sound above a certain decibel level.

SLINGS AND SWIVELS

It seems a small thing, but pay attention to your sling swivel stud. The most common type seems to be the screw-in kind—and they can become loose and unscrew. If that happens, or if your sling should break, the rifle will come off your shoulder and, following Murphy's Law, will almost surely land on the scope. I've had this happen, and it isn't pretty. Far better than the screw-in studs are the two-screw studs often seen on custom rifles. They aren't that expensive and any gunsmith can fit them, but the screw-in types will work just fine if they're installed correctly.

I believe strongly in detachable sling swivels. A rifle sling is a wonderful tool, not only for carrying the rifle but also for use as a shooting aid. However, in some circumstances, such as still-hunting or stalking in close cover, a sling is noisy and can catch on brush. On many occasions I've taken the sling off the rifle and stuffed it in my pocket to reduce noise and ease movement.

The sling itself is more than just a carrying strap. When used as a hasty sling, it is invaluable for helping you get steadier, especially in unsupported shooting positions. Any sling can be used as a hasty sling, and every hunter should know how to make the conversion. This is what you need to do: With the sling hanging free, put your supporting arm between the sling and the rifle, take the sling and wrap it once around your arm, and then snug your supporting hand up behind the sling swivel. When you raise your rifle into a shooting position, the sling will tighten across your chest, essentially causing isometric pressure that helps immeasurably to steady the rifle.

The only type of sling that is difficult to use in this mode, though not impossible, is the "cobra" sling that has a wide portion at the top. I avoid this type of sling because, to me, being able to make a hasty sling is more important than carrying my rifle comfortably! Most slings come in either leather or, even better, canvas webbing, if you can find them.

RESTS

There are a number of excellent bipods and other arrangements that either fasten to the forward sling swivel or can be carried on the belt (or in a daypack) until needed. You don't need something like this in all circumstances—but should you need it, you need it badly! Several of my friends carry Underwood Shooting Sticks all the time. These are sectioned rods that form "crossed shooting sticks" like the old-time buffalo hunters used. I don't carry anything like this all the time, but in extremely open country I will often attach a Harris bipod to the front sling swivel. And there have been times when I didn't bring one and wished I had! There are a number of great shooting aids like these, but, if you decide you want to use something like this, you'll need to practice with it first. They're all wonderful, but it takes time to learn how to use them both properly and, above all, quickly!

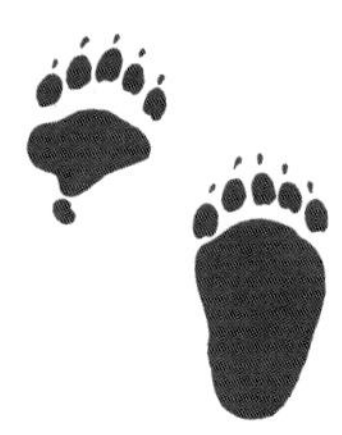

MATCHING THE GAME TO THE GUN . . . OR TO THE COUNTRY?

Depending on which record-keeping system you choose to follow, there are more than thirty varieties of North American big game. On the surface there seems to be such considerable diversity that you might wonder how you will ever be able to match the appropriate gun to the animal you wish to hunt. If you take a closer look, however, you will notice that, although there are several varieties of deer, caribou, moose, sheep, and elk, the different races and subspecies vary little in physiology. The size differences may be significant, as in the difference between the smallest and largest races of whitetail, but even these differences aren't pronounced enough to require significantly different levels of power as you choose your rifles.

We do have a few unique varieties of game, such as the pronghorn and mountain goat. But the requirements for hunting pronghorn aren't much different from hunting open-country deer, and the perfect gun for mountain hunting differs little from the perfect sheep rifle. We do have a few special situations, however, with the walrus, bison, and big bears. Even with these exceptions, though, there isn't a vast difference across the entire spectrum of North American big game in the sheer power required to take game cleanly. This is good news for those who truly believe in the concept of the "all-round rifle." You could (and at least a couple of people did—Grancel Fitz and J. Y. Jones, for example) take every variety of North American big game with a .30-06. If you could do it with a .30-06, you could probably do it more effectively with a .300 magnum. Come to think of it, if you were very careful you could do it all with a .270 Winchester . . . and, if you wanted a bit more margin of safety with the big bears, you could do it all with a fast .33 caliber.

Now, if you're a bit of a rifle nut, you probably have no interest in using just one rifle for every type of game and under every condition. Instead, part of the fun of the hunt is making sure you have exactly the right rifle, cartridge, and load for the job at hand. I am an unabashed rifle nut. When I discuss the rifles and cartridges for various types of game in the following chapters, it's in the context of what I consider absolutely ideal for both the game and the conditions under which that type of game is most frequently hunted. If you're a one-rifle hunter, you can take all this with a grain of salt. There are many rifles and cartridges that are at least reasonably well suited to hunting a tremendous variety of North American big game. And regardless of what I or anyone else tries to tell you, you should always use the rifle and cartridge that gives you the most confidence.

However, even by making a concerted effort to present what I consider to be the most ideal rifle and cartridge, you will find that there is quite a bit of overlap here and there. The perfect mule deer rifle looks a lot like the perfect caribou rifle, which looks a lot like the perfect sheep rifle, and so forth. This is good news for the hunter who wishes to own and use just one or two rifles.

On the other hand, the news isn't all bad for the serious rifleman who takes pride in selecting just the right tool and working up the perfect load for an upcoming hunt. North American hunting is extremely specialized, some of the most specialized hunting in the world. In contrast, look at the average African hunting situation, which does not call for a specialized setup. Africa holds at least four times the variety of big game as North America, well over 100 species, subspecies, and races from extremely small antelope all the way up to the giant elephant. These animals aren't all found in any one area, not by any means, but most African hunting areas will contain as few as a dozen to as many as twenty different varieties of big game. This is a wonderful place for a versatile, "all-round" rifle, but a very poor place for specialized

Guns for hunting white-tailed deer offer a good example of matching the gun to the country. The scoped 7x57 (top) will handle most situations—but in extremely open country a scoped .300 Weatherby Magnum (center) offers more flexibility. In close cover, however, a traditional .30-30 Winchester (bottom) remains extremely effective.

setups. There probably are different perfect rifles for at least a third, maybe even half, of the animals you might encounter on safari. You can't take six or eight rifles on safari, however, and even if you could you have no way to predict exactly what rifle you might be carrying when a certain animal pops up.

American hunting is much more specialized, partly because of our game distribution and partly because of our rigid system of hunting seasons and licensing. There are no North American hunting areas that hold a dozen varieties of big game; few spots hold even half that number. In the American West it is possible that a given area might hold elk, mule deer, white-tailed deer, pronghorn, black bear, Shiras moose, cougar, bighorn sheep, and mountain goats in reasonable proximity, but, even if the seasons overlap, there won't be tags available for all of them! In North America, a genuine "combination hunt" might mean sheep, caribou, moose, and bear in Alaska. In some spots in western Canada you could add mountain goat, and you can always throw in the wolves and wolverines that are always present but few people see. For most of us, a "combination" North American hunt means mule deer and pronghorn, or mule deer and elk, but the vast majority of North American hunts, from north to south and east to west, are for a single species of big game.

Versatility can be critical—especially if you aren't familiar with the conditions. On open, windswept Kodiak Island, I carried a .35 Whelen and didn't have the reach I needed. I borrowed my buddy's .300 Winchester Magnum and took this wonderful buck at long range.

This means that you rarely need genuine versatility in your hunting rifle; you can dream up the perfect rifle for a western deer hunt and carry it without undue concern about whether it would stop a charging polar bear. You can set up the perfect rifle for a spring black-bear hunt without concern about it not being able to reach out 350 yards for pronghorn. That is, if that's what you wish to do. Or you can choose an extremely versatile rig that will be perfectly acceptable in most situations. Neither course is right nor wrong; we have very little huge game to worry about, and in fact the majority of our game is similar in size.

However, I submit that there are differences in North American hunting that go beyond the size of the game. Elk hunting in the rain forests of the Pacific Northwest isn't the same as hunting elk in Colorado's timberline basins. Moose hunting in the forests of Maine or Manitoba isn't the same as hunting them in the mountains of British Columbia or along the edges of Alaska's tundra. To use the most classic example of all, whitetail hunting varies tremendously across this species' vast range. The ideal rifle in the southern swamps or the forests of the northern Midwest may not be quite so ideal if you need to reach out across southern soybean fields, Midwestern corn fields, Canadian wheat fields, or even down one of south Texas's endless *senderos*. So while there isn't always a strong requirement to match the rifle to the game (as we've seen, in many situations "one size fits all"), in North America it's wise to match the rifle to the country: to the terrain, vegetation, and thus the shooting distance most likely to be encountered.

In order to do this, you need to have some idea of what you're getting yourself into. I hope this book will help, but North America is a huge continent containing the full range of habitat types. I do not pretend that you will find in the pages of this book the perfect recipe, or complete description, for every North American hunting situation you might encounter. If you're headed into unfamiliar country, it's wise to do a bit of research. In the normal course of things, a smart hunter would try to find out what kind of weather might be encountered and what essential items of gear should be packed. The kind of shooting you can normally expect is another standard question, and, lest you think I have all the answers, it's a question I still ask!

I haven't made many mistakes in choice of hunting rifles, but I'll never forge a colossal one I once made. I was going to hunt Sitka black-tailed deer on Kodiak Island. My mental picture was one of lots of deer, heavy brush, relatively close shots, and the strong possibility of a close encounter with a brown bear. I chose a .35 Whelen, figuring it would give me plenty of reach yet enough power in the unlikely—but possible—event of a bear problem. Well, I hit fifty percent on my expectations! There were plenty of deer, and for sure there were bears around. But I went late in the season, and most of the brush had been beaten down by wind and weather, leaving the slopes wide open. Getting a close shot was almost impossible, not just because of the open terrain, but because there were so many deer that you couldn't get through them to get to the one you wanted!

My .35 Whelen was hopelessly outclassed by the distance! Fortunately the friend I was hunting with, Jake Jacobsen, was carrying a .300 Winchester Magnum. We saw a phenomenal buck (the best buck of the whole trip) standing on a bare ridge about 375 yards away. That is not necessarily an impossible distance for the .35 Whelen, but it was impossible for me because I had never contemplated such a shot and had absolutely no idea how much drop there would be at that distance. Jake was kind enough to offer me his rifle. I gratefully accepted, and the buck went into the Boone and Crockett book with plenty to spare!

There's a lesson to be learned here about cartridge choice. If you don't know exactly what you're getting yourself into, go with a versatile, flat-shooting cartridge! Remember that, with sensible bullet selection, a fast, flat-shooting cartridge will work up close as well as far away. A short-range rig, like that of a .35 Whelen or a .45-70, might hit harder up close, but it will make longer shots impossible.

That doesn't mean that the hard-hitting "brush cartridges" don't have a place. There are many whitetail setups where you absolutely know that a long shot will simply not be possible. The same can be true with hunting elk or moose in the timber, and is always true if you're hunting black bear over bait or with dogs. Under such conditions big, blunt-nosed, slow-moving bullets will anchor game with impressive finality, and I like to use the "brush cartridges" if I believe I won't be handicapping myself in the process. But, even though the results may not be quite as impressive, you can also use more

I used a fast, powerful Lazzeroni 7.82 (.308) Warbird to take this caribou in the Yukon. I would never argue that this level of power is needed for caribou, but in big, open, windy country there's never anything wrong with using a fast, wind-bucking, .30-caliber magnum.

versatile, flatter-shooting rifles for close-in work . . . and use the same rifle in more open country. So we're back to discussing your particular mindset: Do you prefer carrying the perfect tool for the job at hand, or do you prefer versatility? So long as you have enough caliber and bullet to get the job done, there is no right or wrong answer.

A WORD ABOUT SLUG GUNS

Literally millions of serious deer hunters don't have the luxury to choose what kind of rifle to take on a hunt. Across a broad swath of the United States, from the Northeast well into the Midwest—and in other patches of heavily populated country here and there—shotguns are mandated for deer hunting, and occasionally for other big game as well. The obvious reason for this is safety: A shotgun slug is a devastating projectile, but it's slow and heavy and sharply limited in range (which is the whole idea).

In years gone by most hunters obligated to use slugs simply loaded up their bird guns and let the Foster hollow-based "rifled" slugs or round "pumpkin balls" rattle down the bore. When I was a kid, buckshot was still fairly popular, and a lot of shotgun-toting deer hunters didn't even bother with sights. Things have changed, and definitely for the better. Buckshot is effective only at extremely short range, possibly as much as forty yards, but for sure lethality generally less. By now most deer hunters who use shotguns know this. Without sights a slug doesn't offer any more effective range than buckshot, but with good sights the old smoothbore slug guns were generally effective to maybe seventy-five yards.

You see, even though the shotgun slug is a short-range affair, the real limitation was accuracy, not effective range. Today virtually every major shotgun manufacturer offers slug guns with rifled barrels or rifled choke tubes. Couple these with new slug designs like the discarding sabot slug—and add in good sights or, better yet, a low-powered scope—and today's slug gun is effective to at least 100 yards. In some guns, under some conditions, this can be extended even farther. No, you can't shoot deer at 200 yards with any slug gun, but a modern setup can nearly double the effective range we had just twenty years ago, and that's a big improvement. If you're obligated to shoot slugs, you miss the fun of campfire arguments over which caliber and which bullet are the best. But if you set yourself up with a scoped shotgun sporting a rifled barrel and figure out which brand and style of slugs your gun shoots the best, you haven't given up much to your rifle-toting colleagues!

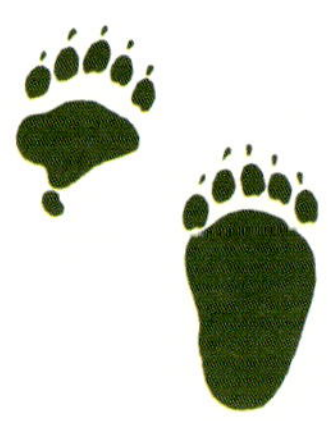

MULE DEER

Tough to come by . . .
but not all that tough!

If you're talking about really good trophy quality, I don't know of any North American trophy that is more difficult to come by right now than a really good mule-deer buck. This may seem strange, and for two reasons. First, hunters of my generation—and the generations that preceded me—grew up considering the mule deer a slightly retarded first cousin to the wily whitetail. Second, there are still millions of mule deer in the American West (which includes western Canada and Mexico). Let's examine both premises.

At one time the average mule-deer buck was indeed less wary than the average whitetail. Until the 1960s, and even later in some areas, the West's vast mule-deer country was lightly populated and lightly developed, and received very little hunting pressure. Mule-deer bucks lived and died without having a clue what those strange, orange-clad, two-legged creatures were up to.

Mule deer live in country that is often some combination of high, rugged, and arid, so they have always been subject to more radical population swings than white-tailed deer. Hard winters and drought have always caused die-off, followed by a rapid rebuilding when conditions improve. The good old days weren't always that good, but hunting pressure was usually not a factor. The expected percentages of the buck population would live to reach full maturity, and the adage that a mule-deer buck "would always look back" was generally true.

It is no longer true today. Much of the West is heavily developed—for recreation, for mining, for the myriad vacation and retirement homes that dot the hillsides. Hunting pressure is a major factor today, and so are ski slopes, roads, logging operations, and mines that either preclude usage by mule deer or block access to critical winter range. Other facts are sagebrush eradication; livestock overgrazing; rapidly expanding herds of elk in some areas; and, where the two species collide, increased competition from whitetail. Increased hunting pressure means that a much smaller percentage of the buck herd lives to maturity. All the rest means that mule-deer herds in much of the West are in a long-term decline. There aren't as many big bucks as there once were, and there aren't as many mule deer, period.

Despite all this there are plenty of mule deer. In several subspecies they range from the Great Plains to the Pacific and from western Coahuila to western Canada, with plenty of hunting opportunity throughout this vast range. It's just that I no longer know of any area where big bucks come easily—and there are lots of areas where the chances of finding a really big buck are virtually nil.

In terms of choosing the right rifle and load and making that perfect shot, what this means to mule-deer hunters is that you must choose wisely and shoot carefully. You'll work hard to get a shot, especially a shot at a really nice buck, and you cannot expect a whole lot of chances.

SHOTS AT MULE DEER

Mule deer are often considered "long-range game," especially by those who haven't hunted them a lot. It is true that mule deer often live in country that is big, open, and extremely rugged and broken. Any game that lives in this kind of country may sometimes present a very long shot. There are times when a cross-canyon shot is all there is, and there will be times when open ground or an unfavorable wind precludes a close approach.

The longest shot I have ever made on game was in Colorado about twenty years ago, on my second-largest mule deer. It was a cold, snowy morning, and the buck was bedded on a little knoll on the far side of a long, open valley, perhaps five hundred yards away. It was dead calm, but there was no way to cross the clean white snow of the valley unseen. It might have been possible to go around, but that little knoll was covered with dry, noisy oak brush. We

Mule deer are medium-sized animals and, in most cases, a relatively quick-expanding bullet will be ideal for an instantaneous kill. (Photo courtesy of Len Rue Jr.)

studied the ground hard, and we couldn't figure out how we could see the buck from a closer position without spooking it. So, in those days before laser range finders, we estimated and reestimated the distance, discussed the holdover, set up the equivalent of a benchrest on a flat boulder, and waited for the deer to stand up.

Eventually it did, offering a good broadside presentation. I was shooting a .300 Weatherby Magnum, always a good choice under such conditions, and I had all the time in the world. Even then I almost underestimated the distance and holdover; the bullet caught it very low in the chest, just at the bottom of the heart.

This is the kind of shot you may face with mule deer; but in my experience such a long shot is very rare, and I didn't have to take it. I could have waited until the buck moved. Maybe it would have moved to a location that allowed a closer approach, maybe not. In any case, shooting at that extreme distance is beyond the capability of most of us, and had there been even the slightest wind I wouldn't have attempted it. Note that, in the West, windy days outnumber calm days by a considerable factor.

The circumstances under which I took my best-ever mule deer were much different. In Sonora, Mexico, I was hunting desert mule deer by tracking with the local cowboys, who were without question the best trackers I have ever seen. We had followed a big set of tracks for a couple of miles, and, though I could not have followed

Even a large-bodied mule deer like this buck will easily succumb to a well-placed regular softpoint bullet if shot behind the shoulder in the heart-lung area. However, a better-constructed bullet is more appealing when a tough bone or a raking shot is offered or when the bullet needs to penetrate. (Photo courtesy of Len Rue Jr.)

them, I could tell by the way the spoor was winding and turning that the deer was looking for a place to bed. My guide, Beto Diaz, was moving slowly and carefully, and then he pointed ahead.

A huge set of antlers protruded from low brush in the shade of a mesquite, maybe sixty yards away. The antlers were connected to a head, fortunately facing straight away, and just under that head was a very small expanse of neck. We shifted to the left to find a slightly better angle, but the rest of the deer was hidden by brush. Perhaps I could have waited until the buck stood up, but it was nearing midday, when breezes become unstable and swirl. That small rectangle of stationary neck looked a lot better than my mental picture of the buck exploding out of its bed. So I wrapped into a tight sling with my .280 Remington, found the steadiest position I could, and shot the buck squarely in the center of that exposed patch of neck.

Obviously, bow hunters find ways to get closer to mule deer, but for rifle hunters both of these situations—coincidentally resulting in my best and second-best mules—represent the extremes. Most mule-deer hunts take place on ground that is broken enough to make close shots possible, or where there is enough vegetation, even if it is scattered. In most areas you might see deer at extreme distances, so very long shots are also possible. But most shots at mule deer come somewhere between the extremes. Over

This is a picture-perfect, side-on shot. Marked are the shoulder, heart, and lung shots. (Photo courtesy of Len Rue Jr.)

the course of thirty years of hunting mule deer under most conditions and in most habitat types, I believe most of my shots have come in the middle ground between 150 and three hundred yards.

The latter distance may seem very far for hunters accustomed to taking whitetail from tree stands in thick cover. Heck, for the millions of hunters obligated to hunt their whitetail with shotguns or muzzleloaders, even 150 yards may seem a far piece! In real terms I consider 150 yards a fairly close shot. A shot at three hundred yards is no longer close; it requires practice, skill, confidence, and a steady position—but the distance is not so great that it requires special equipment or a serious long-range rifle. Remember that a big buck may come out of a draw right at your feet. If you can handle any reasonable shot from point-blank to three hundred yards, then you are well prepared for almost any shot at a mule deer.

TAKING THE SHOT

I have never believed that mule deer were particularly tough. Although the average mule-deer buck is probably a bit larger than the average whitetail buck, the largest mule deer and the largest whitetail are probably about the same. However, I do not believe the mule deer is as tough or tenacious of life as the whitetail. By this I mean that a poorly hit mule deer is generally not as difficult to recover as a poorly hit whitetail.

Leica's Terry Moore and I took these two South Dakota mule deer on a memorable morning. Terry's rifle is a .280 Remington; mine is a .300 Weatherby Magnum; both are adequate for any mule deer under any hunting conditions.

The open country in which mule deer live perhaps contributes to this, but it should be a moot point. In the spectrum of big game, none of our North American deer are particularly large or particularly hard to kill. However, a mule deer lives its life roaming big, rough country. It withstands brutal winters and hot summers, and in many areas migrates vast distances from summer to winter range. Hit poorly, or with an inadequate cartridge or bullet, a mule deer can travel vast distances and can be lost.

Much as I hate to admit it, the only deer I have ever lost was a mule deer. The country was the high plains of eastern Wyoming, wide-open country where you might imagine that such a thing was impossible. The deer was bedded in the middle of a sagebrush flat, some distance away from a cottonwood bottom. The wind precluded a closer approach through the streambed, so I crept and crawled, using slight dips in the open sage, until I ran out of options at a bit over three hundred yards. I set my rifle up on a bipod and waited until the buck stood. Finally it did, and I took the shot with the buck quartering slightly to me. To my horror I saw the bullet impact not at the point of the on-shoulder, where I was aiming, but just inside the off-shoulder.

I missed the mule deer completely as it lurched toward the creek bottom. We found blood there and trailed it until the creek bottom petered out more than a mile away. Then we trailed it across the open prairie until the blood itself petered out. And no further trace of that buck was ever found.

I was shooting a very accurate 7mm Remington Magnum with a good 160-grain bullet, so the issue was not an inadequate cartridge or a poorly constructed bullet. It isn't an excuse but a statement of fact when I tell you that I learned, too late, that this rifle shoots to a different point of impact with a bipod than it does without one. This is not uncommon. I knew this, so it was altogether my fault, and it was avoidable. I should have either checked the rifle with the bipod, or I shouldn't have listened to that last-minute thought that, given the open country, the bipod was a good idea. But we can usually find excuses or reasons why a given shot didn't land in exactly the right place. The only way to avoid potential disaster is to place the shot correctly the first time!

As with all game animals, the various sensible options include brain, spine, shoulder/heart, and lung shots. For me the brain shot is out; except at very close range the target is too small to be certain, and even if you have the accuracy and the confidence, the trophy will likely be ruined. At normal shooting ranges for mule deer, the side-on neck shot is almost as risky. The target is very small; a high shot will only stun the deer, and a low shot will cause a terrible but not immediately fatal wound. Still, the central neck shot is deadly, and at closer ranges—with an accurate rifle and a steady shooting position—you should not rule out this shot.

A frontal shot is also not my preference. On a frontal shot, if you aim where the neck joins the chest, you have a huge margin for a ranging error; too high and you're somewhere in the middle of the neck; too low and you're in the center of the chest. However, your margin for a windage error is very small. Just a bit right or left, and if you're slightly high, you will miss the spine. If you're low, you will catch just one lung, or, far worse, your bullet will skitter along inside of the shoulder and do relatively little damage. On a frontal presentation it's far better to wait until the animal turns, the obvious exception being a very close and steady shot.

While I fully accept that a well-placed shot from the rear can be deadly, especially on deer-sized game taken with relatively tough bullets designed for penetration, the risks are quite high. They go up exponentially as the bucks get larger and the cartridges get smaller (or the bullets get lighter in weight and more rapid in expansion). I won't tell you that I wouldn't take a "Texas heart shot" with an adequate cartridge and a tough bullet, if that was my only chance at the buck of a lifetime—but I can tell you that I have never taken such a shot at an unwounded deer.

Given an adequate rifle and a well-constructed bullet, I don't mind strongly quartering-away shots, but my preference will always be to look for a presentation that is as close to broadside as possible, and I usually strive for a central lung shot. The aiming point will vary, depending on exactly how the buck is standing, but this means I'm trying to place the bullet just behind the shoulder and just under the horizontal midpoint of the body. This shot is not deadlier than a shoulder/heart shot, but is not less deadly. If the animal has just exhaled, a central lung shot will actually take effect more quickly than a heart shot; if the animal has just inhaled, then a final run of something less than one hundred yards is normal. The

I shot this good New Mexico mule deer with a 7mm Remington Magnum firing 160-grain Nosler Partitions. This buck was taken with a steep quartering-angle shot, but with that cartridge and that bullet, the buck dropped to the shot.

advantage of this shot is that it offers the most room for error of any fatal shot. Also, for game I like to eat, which includes all deer, less edible meat is wasted with the central lung shot than with any other body shot.

THE RIGHT BUCK

There are several subspecies of mule deer, with broad intergrade as one variety blends into another. The most widespread, most numerous, and largest subspecies is the Rocky Mountain mule deer (*Odocoileus hemionus hemionus*), found from the Great Plains to somewhere along the Sierra Nevada chain, and from Canada's western prairies to Texas's Big Bend country. The slightly smaller desert mule deer (*Odocoileus hemionus crooki*), distinguished in Safari Club's record book but not in Boone and Crockett's or Pope and Young's, are found from an almost indistinguishable point in west Texas through an equally amorphous line in central New Mexico and Arizona, down into old Mexico. In the Pacific Northwest, from northwestern California up through western Washington and Oregon to another amorphous point in western British Columbia you find the distinctly smaller Columbia blacktail (*Odocoileus hemionus columbianus*). Farther north the deer are the Sitka blacktail (*Odocoileus hemionus sitkensis*), larger in the body but smaller in antler development.

The extreme Southwest of North America is a grab bag, with the California mule deer (*Odocoileus hemionus californicus*) shading into the southern mule deer (*Odocoileus hemionus fuliginatus*) in extreme Southern California and northern Baja. In turn, the southern mule deer shades into the peninsular mule deer (*O. h. peninsulae*) in southern Baja. These subspecies, all smaller than Rocky Mountain deer but not so small as Columbia blacktails, are generally recognized by science, but not by any hunter's record book. All are (fairly or unfairly) lumped together with the Rocky Mountain mule deer. There are possibly a couple of other subspecies of mule deer in the Southwest—the so-called "burro deer" and "Inyo mule deer"—that scientists can't quite agree on.

With Rocky Mountain mule deer, the traditional standard for excellence has long been a "30-inch buck," a mule deer with antlers reaching 30 inches in extreme spread. This is a carryover from the good old days, when fully mature bucks were much more common than today—but it was, is, and always will be a silly standard. Boone and Crockett's *Records of North American Big Game*, the oldest record book with the highest standard, doesn't even use extreme spread; instead, inside spread is measured. This is only one of several criteria. Point length and beam length are actually far more important; the hallowed Boone and Crockett book is literally full of bucks that are not 30 inches, whether outside or inside.

So, although many mule-deer hunters tend to be "spread freaks," spread is really just one dimension. At full maturity the normal mule deer—of any subspecies—has bifurcated antlers (main beams that divide, then divide again) with four primary points per side. Eye guards are not as universal, nor as large, as on whitetail; very good bucks often lack eye guards altogether. Nontypical points are those that exceed the typical configuration of "four by four plus eye guards."

Bucks with spreads exceeding 30 inches—and with all the rest—do exist, but I'm not certain I have ever seen one. I know I have never shot a "30-inch buck"—but I have taken some very good mule deer by record-book standards. Although spread is the common yardstick of excellence, I think it's far more important to look at point and beam length, then look at the antler mass that denotes a fully mature buck, and the rest be damned. The elusive 30-inch buck is almost nonexistent today, but there are lots of beautiful bucks with heavy antlers and long points that have spreads in the class of twenty-four to twenty-eight inches. Today this is a good mule deer. Such a buck is very possible in many areas where Rocky Mountain and desert mule deer are found—and if the point length, mass, and symmetry all add up, such a buck can be a record-class specimen.

The other subspecies of mule deer are considerably smaller. Columbia blacktail and California mule deer do sometimes develop four-by-four antlers. Many good bucks are only three-by-three or even big forkhorns at full maturity, and this becomes more pronounced with all the other subspecies. Regardless of where you hunt and which subspecies you are hunting—and especially regardless of record-book score—the important thing is to know what kind of deer the area is capable of producing. If you find a buck that is above average for the area you are hunting—and if the buck pleases you—then you have a great trophy.

Left to right: 1) .270 Winchester 2) .280 Remington 3) .30-06 4) 7mm Remington Magnum 5) .300 Winchester Magnum. These are classic mule deer cartridges—flat-shooting and plenty powerful. The magnums aren't essential, but if they give you more confidence, that's all to the good.

RIFLES AND CARTRIDGES FOR MULE DEER

As is the case with most popular game animals, a big difference can exist between the deer you take on the last day to put in the freezer and the buck you might encounter if fortune smiles. The sad reality is that, even with the Rocky Mountain subspecies that is largest in both antler and body, the average buck taken is a 2½-year-old deer weighing little more than 150 pounds. But you need to be prepared for the buck you might encounter, not the buck you are most likely to encounter. The maximum body weight is as much as five hundred pounds, but a wise, battle-hardened old buck weighing 350 pounds is not exactly the same animal as a young buck weighing less than half as much.

You want to be prepared for the monster, and I suggest that you arm yourself accordingly. The 6mms and .25s are extremely popular in many areas, especially as "beginner's cartridges" for youngsters and ladies—but I submit that these are cartridges for experts. They lack the energy for long-range use, and lack the bullet weight to ensure penetration on the largest bucks. If you insist, the faster .25s (.25-06 and .257 Weatherby) are pretty darned good, but given the potential range and the size of the game I think serious mule-deer cartridges start at 6.5mm (.264-inch) and go on up to .30-caliber. This does not imply that magnums are necessary. Some of us will always prefer .270s, some of us will prefer 7mms, and some of us are .30-caliber fans—but I cannot imagine a better trio of deer cartridges than the triumvirate based on the .30-06 case: .270 Winchester, .280 Remington, and the grandfather, the .30-06 Springfield.

These three cartridges will all reach out as far as most of us have any business shooting at game, and all have plenty of power for any mule deer that walks. That said, many of us are somewhat overawed by the huge country that mule deer inhabit. It is important to have confidence in your cartridge, and, whether or not we really need the capability, many of us feel better if we have "magnum performance" at our fingertips. So I think the very best mule-deer cartridge in the whole world is the 7mm Remington Magnum. It really won't do much more than the time-tested trio just mentioned, but it shoots a wee bit flatter, and its larger case engenders all kinds of confidence.

Personally, I don't take much stock in this business about being "overgunned." There is nothing wrong with choosing a still faster .270, like the .270 Weatherby Magnum or the new .270 Winchester Short Magnum, or the 7mm Shooting Times Westerner (STW) or the new 7mm Remington Ultra Mag. Nor is there anything wrong with choosing any of the fast .30s. As I mentioned, I was carrying a .300 Weatherby Magnum when I took that extremely long shot in Colorado. I would not have attempted that shot with anything less than a fast .30-caliber. Which is not to say that an equally fast or faster 7mm couldn't have done it—it's just that my own comfort level wouldn't have been up to such a shot with a lesser caliber. As always, it's important to choose the cartridge that gives you the most confidence, whether it's a .25-06 or a .30-.378 Weatherby. Unless it's a pet rifle that you simply must use, there is no advantage to choosing a caliber larger than .30 for mule deer.

BULLET PERFORMANCE

This is a tough call. Deer-sized game does not require today's supertough, penetrating bullets like the Winchester Fail Safe, Barnes X-Bullet, and Swift A-Frame. When fired from an adequate cartridge, these bullets will exit from any angle, which is good. Bullets that expand more quickly, however, will expend more energy within the animal, will do more damage to vital organs, and will generally result in quicker kills. So for deer-sized game I tend to lean toward bullets that expand more quickly—fairly conventional softpoints like the Hornady Interlock, Sierra, and Speer, or

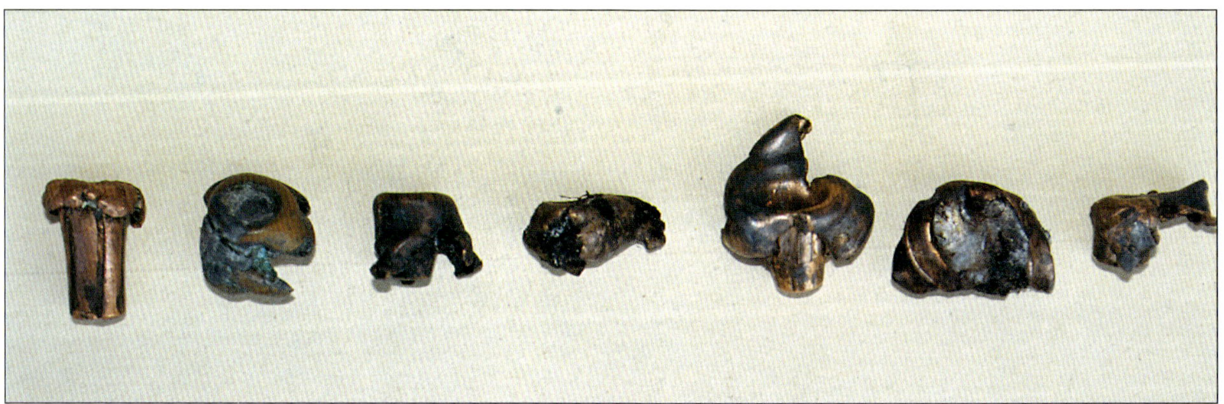

Bullet performance is very important, but on deer-sized game any hunting-weight bullet of adequate caliber should perform well. Some of these bullets look much better than others—but all were recovered from dead game, so all did their work just fine.

polymer-tipped bullets like the Ballistic Silvertip, Hornady A-Max, and Nosler Ballistic Tip.

There is one big exception. It is so difficult today to get a really big mule deer that you must be ready for any reasonable shot you can get. So I generally hedge my bets. I want a bullet that will expand, yet I also want a bullet that will penetrate should I draw a bad-angle shot. Historically, the Nosler Partition is one of the best bullets that combines both expansion and penetration in a single design. The front core, ahead of the partition, expands rapidly; the back core, protected by the partition, penetrates almost like a solid. Even today there are very few bullets that offer this combination. One that does is the new Swift Scirocco, combining a bonded core and heavy jacket for weight retention with a polymer tip for expansion.

Some time back I hunted mule deer on the Jicarilla Reservation, one of the few genuine hotspots for really big mule deer. I wasn't lucky; that year I was a bit behind the rut, and the weather was too warm. We saw very few bucks, and I was running out of time. Then we got a small snowstorm overnight and had one perfect morning. We came around a turn in the trail, and a good buck was leading its does almost straight away. It wasn't exactly a "Texas heart shot," because I could see a bit of flank—but it was close. Shooting a 7mm Remington Magnum with a 160-grain Nosler Partition, I put the cross hairs behind the last rib and squeezed the trigger. The bullet exited just in front of the off-shoulder, and the buck dropped in its tracks. I would not have taken that shot unless I was shooting a bullet that would ensure penetration.

SPECIAL CIRCUMSTANCES

Most of the foregoing concerns Rocky Mountain mule deer, or at least the larger subspecies of mule deer. Where I live in central California the deer are a mixture of California mule deer and Columbia blacktail, and they are small. The country is also patchy and tight, and longer shots are very unusual. Here the .243 is by far the most popular deer cartridge, and it's plenty of gun for our 125-pound deer. I tend to think other low-recoiling cartridges like the .260 Remington, 6.5x55mm, 7mm-08, and 7x57mm are even better. The point is that if you hunt smaller deer like Columbia blacktail, you don't need as big a gun.

One important exception is hunting desert mule deer in old Mexico. This is one of the very few opportunities for a really big buck, except that not everyone will get one or even get a shot. As I mentioned, most of the hunting down there is done by tracking. In four hunts I've taken two bucks, which is well ahead of the average. Even more unusual is that I've taken both bucks in their beds. It's more likely that you will jump the deer, and you'll have a quick, panicky shot at a fast-disappearing form. The deer are not large in the body, but the shooting can be exceptionally difficult, and you have little control over the shot you get. Under such circumstances you want a fairly powerful rifle—no less than .270—and a bullet that will surely penetrate.

The heart and a good deal of the whitetail's lungs are well protected by shoulder bone in a shot like this one. Also the margin of error either left or right is small at this angle. This is not a shot to take offhand or from a wobbly position. (Photo courtesy of Len Rue Jr.)

WHITE-TAILED DEER

Oh, so common . . .
and oh, so difficult!

The white-tailed deer is the most popular and most populous game animal in North America and on the entire planet. White-tailed deer are found in some thirty-eight recognized races from the Amazon Basin to Canada's tree line, and from the eastern seaboard to the Sierra Nevada. It is believed that more than twenty-five million white-tailed deer roam North America, and as many as ten million American sportsmen pursue them annually.

The whitetail is more than just a game animal; it is the basis for an entire industry designed to make its pursuit more successful. Camouflage; game calls; decoys; game care and recovery systems; special rifles, shotguns, muzzleloaders, and bows, and ammunition for each; and much more are manufactured, marketed, and sold with just the white-tailed deer hunter in mind.

In part, this industry arose because the whitetail is the most numerous and most available game for the majority of American hunters, who spend their time afield in pursuit of whatever game is locally available. The other aspect, however, is that, no matter how numerous it might be, the white-tailed deer is no pushover. It is an exceptionally wary creature, blessed with sensitive ears, sharp eyes, and a keen nose. By nature it loves cover, but it's also a homebody who knows its home turf intimately and doesn't need much cover to vanish completely. It is crepuscular, meaning it is typically most active during the twilight periods of dawn and dusk. It is also completely at home in the darkness and, with just a bit of pressure, can turn into a sort of antlered Dracula that is never seen in the daylight.

Part of the reason the whitetail is so switched on is simply that, in so much of its range, it has been exposed to man for centuries. It has adapted to life in hedgerows, wood lots, streambeds, and suburbs, and it has learned to deal with, and even thrive, in the midst of some of the most intensive hunting pressure on earth. This makes it one of North America's most challenging creatures to hunt. In trophy rooms of the rich and famous, you may see beautiful and exotic creatures from all over the world, but in relatively few of them will you see top-quality white-tailed deer. If you find a hunter who has the racks of several fully mature white-tailed bucks adorning his den, then you can put in the bank that he (or she) is a real hunter, regardless of any other trophies that might be present or absent.

It is not easy to characterize whitetail hunting; this depends on exactly where you hunt it. It is found in eastern wood lots, southern swamps, northern forests, southwestern mountains, cottonwood-lined streams in the Great Plains—and darned near every other habitat type you can think of. Given a choice, it loves edge habitat, the mosaic created by agriculture intermixed with small patches of cover. But it can be found where there is no agriculture at all.

In all of its subspecies, it's pretty much the same deer, developing antlers that have fighting tines rising from a main beam. Wherever it occurs, it leaves much the same sign—the tracks and droppings and rubs and scrapes we whitetail hunters argue about endlessly. But exactly how you hunt it varies considerably depending on where you hunt it.

The adage is that white-tailed bucks live and die within a mile or two of where they were born. This may be true in classic close-cover habitat, but it is not universally true. When I was a kid, whitetail hunters were still pursuing the remnant populations that had been pushed into the deepest, thickest, and most inaccessible habitat—the laurel thickets of the Appalachians, the southern swamps, south Texas's brush country, the forests of the northern Midwest.

With protection the whitetail increased, flourished, and adapted. Exactly when this happened varied with the region, and

Whitetails vary tremendously in size, but any decently constructed bullet in .25 caliber on up will kill with proper shot placement. (Photo courtesy of Len Rue Jr.)

exactly why it happened isn't altogether clear. But during the 1960s and into the 1970s, America's whitetail herds literally exploded. As the populations increased, whitetail moved out of the thick cover and into agricultural areas. In the West, in a trend that continues to this day, whitetail are following the river bottoms out into ranch country that used to be considered mule-deer range.

Regardless of where they occur, whitetail do have home territories, and during the rut they mark this territory with rubs and scrapes. In bigger, more open country, their home territories are much larger, almost certainly because the populations are less dense and there are greater distances between water, bedding cover, and preferred food. In the Great Plains, where I've done a lot of whitetail hunting, it isn't unusual for a given buck to range along seven or eight miles of river bottom and several miles out into the adjacent prairies.

Historically, taxonomists have been divided into "lumpers" and "splitters." Lumpers seek to minimize the number of races and subspecies within a given species; splitters separate whitetail according to the most minor physiological differences. The splitters held sway with the white-tailed deer; of the thirty-eight recognized subspecies of *Odocoileus virginianus*, thirty are found in the United States, Canada, and Mexico!

Wait till the deer stops, or lead the point of aim slightly. The heart, shoulder, and lung shots are marked. (Photo courtesy of Len Rue Jr.)

Generally speaking, we hunters have followed the splitters when establishing categories for our various record books. For just a half-dozen subspecies of mule deer, we have categories for three or four; of just four wapiti subspecies we have categories for three. Some of our categories for caribou are based entirely on regional groupings, with no biological basis whatsoever.

With the whitetail, however, the lumpers held sway. Safari Club International's record book subdivides the whitetail into seven regional groupings: northwestern, northeastern, southeastern, Texas, Coues, Mexican, and central American. It draws lines along political boundaries, and almost every regional category encompasses multiple subspecies. Boone and Crockett and Pope and Young are even more conservative. They each have just one category for all white-tailed deer. The one exception is a separate category for the small Coues whitetail (*Odocoileus virginianus couesi*) of the mountains of the Southwest.

The separation of the Coues whitetail is appropriate, because these small gray deer do look different from most other subspecies to the north and east, and hunting them in their mountain habitat is quite different. This separation is actually based on a mistake. When United States Army Quartermaster Elliott Coues "identified" the deer that bears his name, he thought he had found an entirely different species of deer!

A good Saskatchewan whitetail taken with a .30-06 and 150-grain Barnes X-Bullet. Although many cartridges are faster and flashier, the good old .30-06 is still a superb deer rifle almost anywhere.

The separation became traditional and remained so even after it was accepted that the Coues deer was just another of many subspecies of whitetail.

It is also appropriate to lump the rest into regional groupings or into one big category. For one thing, most of the subspecies are similar, especially in antler development. For another, there are broad intergrade areas between most of the subspecies, and it's almost impossible to draw definitive lines where one subspecies stops and another starts. A third reason is that, like most of our big game, whitetail were seriously depleted during our pioneering era. To speed the recovery process, many state game departments brought in and released whitetail from elsewhere. In many parts of the South, for instance, northern whitetail were released, and the northern woodland whitetail (*Odocoileus virginianus borealis*) is one of the largest subspecies, potentially much larger in both body and antler than the native southern subspecies.

SHOTS AT WHITETAIL

Unlike many types of game, most whitetail are relatively habitual, so to some extent you can control the shot you get through your hunting technique, and you can choose exactly where you set up. Even in the more open West, savvy bow hunters achieve considerable success by stand hunting along movement corridors between bedding grounds and feeding covers. The possible exception to this is Coues whitetail; they are thinly distributed in huge country and are generally less habitual than other whitetail. To this day archers have taken relatively few Coues deer, and they are considered one of America's most difficult game to bow hunt.

In the East literally millions of American hunters are obligated by law to use shotguns and/or muzzleloaders. Fully rifled slug guns and some muzzleloaders have enough accuracy to cleanly take deer out to two hundred yards, but for most of those hunters, the practical range limit is around one hundred yards. This is a handicap, but not so severe that it prevents hundreds of thousands of hunters from taking their deer every year. With such range limitations it doesn't make sense to set up over a feeding field. You can take a stand in heavy cover, where trails suggest deer are moving between feeding and bedding grounds. Or, in heavy or mixed cover, you can use calls or rattling antlers to lure deer to the gun. In many areas deer drives—whether with human or canine "drivers"—are the traditional technique, and buckshot-loaded shotguns are often the arm of choice. Whether by choice or by law, if you limit your range with a bow, shotgun, or muzzleloader (or, for that matter, a handgun), you simply need to choose ground and technique that are likely to yield a shot you can handle

Rifle-toting hunters have far more options, and indeed a shot at a white-tailed deer can take almost any form, from very close to very far. This spread occurs almost everywhere whitetail are hunted. I think my closest shot at a whitetail came while I was sitting on a tree stand in South Carolina. Off to my left were heavy woods with an active scrape line along the edge. Directly in front of me a rectangular food plot stretched for around 250 yards, so of course I was expecting a shot somewhere on its farthest edges. At dawn a few does drifted past, and then nothing. It was late morning and it was getting hot, so I figured the chances of anything happening were approaching zero. I started blowing a grunt call every twenty minutes or so, just to pass the time.

I'm not sure whether I heard something or saw movement, maybe both, but after the second series, I froze and swiveled my eyeballs to leafy cover at the near end of the tree line. After a few seconds a nice eight-pointer stepped out, and I slowly raised my .30-06 and shot it at less than ten yards.

Close encounters are most likely to occur from a stand, or while rattling or calling, but they can occur almost anywhere. Longer shots are also possible almost anywhere. The deep South is famous for its huge soybean fields that draw deer like magnets. It's this kind of hunting that gave South Carolina gunmaker Kenny Jarrett the name for his famous "Beanfield Rifle"—slightly heavy, flat shooting, super-accurate, and designed to reach out across those southern beanfields. It could well have been a "cornfield rifle," because wherever grain is grown, white-tailed bucks are just as likely to be standing on the far side as on the near side.

And one mustn't forget the power-line rights of way and logging roads that offer opportunities for longer shots even in the midst of heavy cover. One day in Georgia I was sitting in a tree stand overlooking a wide power-line right of way, with heavy conifers to my rear and on the far side.

In stand hunting, you control the shots you might get by where you site your stand. This Canadian deer stand offered a full range of shots from very close to very far, so a versatile rifle was the only sensible choice.

During a break in a heavy downpour, a buck stepped into the cut line to my right, and I shot it at about forty yards. A day later I shot another buck from the same stand—but this deer was slipping along the trees on the far side, and the shot was a bit over two hundred yards.

Very few whitetail habitats in the whole country are as thick as the famous brush country of south Texas. It's in this region that hunters developed the technique of calling rutting bucks by "horn rattling," simulating a fight between two bucks. If you're rattling antlers along the edges of the thick stuff, you may get a very close shot. But this country is crisscrossed by a grid of cut lines, the famous *senderos* of south Texas. It's always possible for a huge buck to walk under your stand—but you're much more likely to get a shot a couple of hundred yards up the *senderos*.

So it's almost impossible to categorize shots at whitetail. Several million whitetail are harvested annually, and it's probably fair to say that the average shot is well under one hundred yards. This is skewed by the fact that our greatest numbers of whitetail are found in the thick cover of the deep South, the Northeast, and the upper Midwest. It's also skewed by those millions of hunters who use short-range equipment. In the West shooting opportunities average a good deal longer, depending on how you hunt.

For several seasons, just for fun, I helped a buddy, an outfitter, guide hunters in the badlands and river-bottom country of eastern Colorado. During archery and black-powder seasons we mostly used deer stands set along the watercourses and overlooking natural funnels. It is difficult to get within bow range of plains deer, but it wasn't a great trick to set up shots within one hundred yards, ideal for muzzleloaders.

During rifle season we still used some stands, with increased vistas, but we hunted much more by spot-and-stalk tactics. Even though the country is wide open and there is always the possibility for longer shots, most deer are taken within two hundred yards. Another factor is that really big whitetail are just plain hard to come by. Big, fully mature bucks aren't exactly uncommon in all areas, but a buck that has survived several hunting seasons becomes so elusive and, often, so nocturnal that it is almost impossible to kill. I would never advocate taking any shot that you aren't absolutely certain you can make. But there is no telling when or where a big buck might present itself, and your chances of bagging it are much improved if you can handle the full range of potential opportunities, from very close to very far.

TAKING THE SHOT

White-tailed deer are amazing creatures. They have adapted to life in proximity with man, yet they have also adapted to the full range of harsh conditions, from the arid mountains of the Southwest to the bitter winters of northern Canada. All along the Rocky Mountain front, somewhat to our dismay, they are proving themselves capable of competing with mule deer! Pound for pound, I rate the whitetail as a fairly tough creature. Hit poorly, it is able to take a great deal of punishment, and it can cover a surprising amount of ground even if hit fairly well. This is a bit of a problem. Even fatally hit game can be hard to follow up and recover in the close cover that whitetail commonly call home—and many whitetail are hunted on relatively small properties, where recovering even a well-hit buck that "gets across the fence" can be fraught with difficulties.

Of course, the whole purpose of this book is to avoid these difficulties—to make the "perfect shot" that precludes a lengthy follow-up. Unless the range is very close and you have absolute confidence in your ability to place the shot, I don't like the brain, neck, or spine shots. They are immediately fatal, or at least totally disabling, if executed correctly—but there is just too much margin for error. My preference is the central lung shot. From a broadside presentation, divide the body horizontally into thirds: top third, middle third, bottom third. For a perfect lung shot, follow the back line of the rear leg up and shoot into the bottom half of the middle third. From various angles away from the broadside you must visualize where this area lies, but the good news is that, of all the surely fatal shots, the lung shot offers the greatest margin for error.

Whether the lung shot is immediately fatal depends a bit on luck. If the animal has just exhaled and is depleted of oxygen, a lung shot may well drop it in its tracks. If it has just inhaled, you may see very little initial reaction, but it should go down within sixty yards. The lung shot also offers the advantage of ruining less edible meat than the heart shot, but the heart shot is also a very good option.

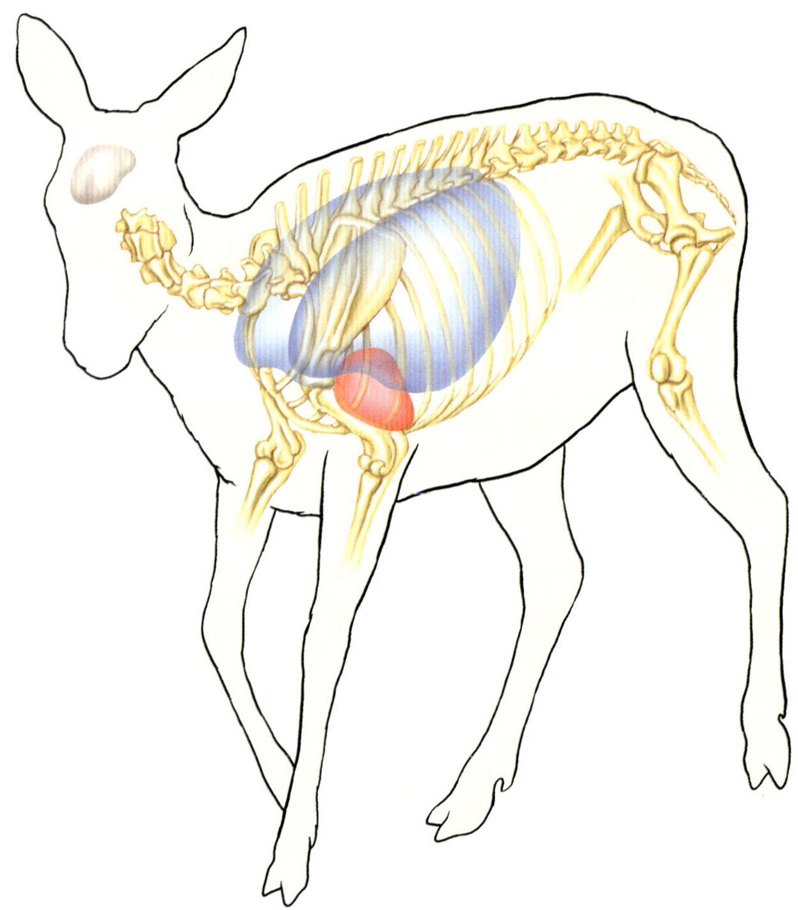

This illustrates a quartering-on shot. Note how the shoulder bones obstruct much of the heart/lung area.

White-tailed Deer

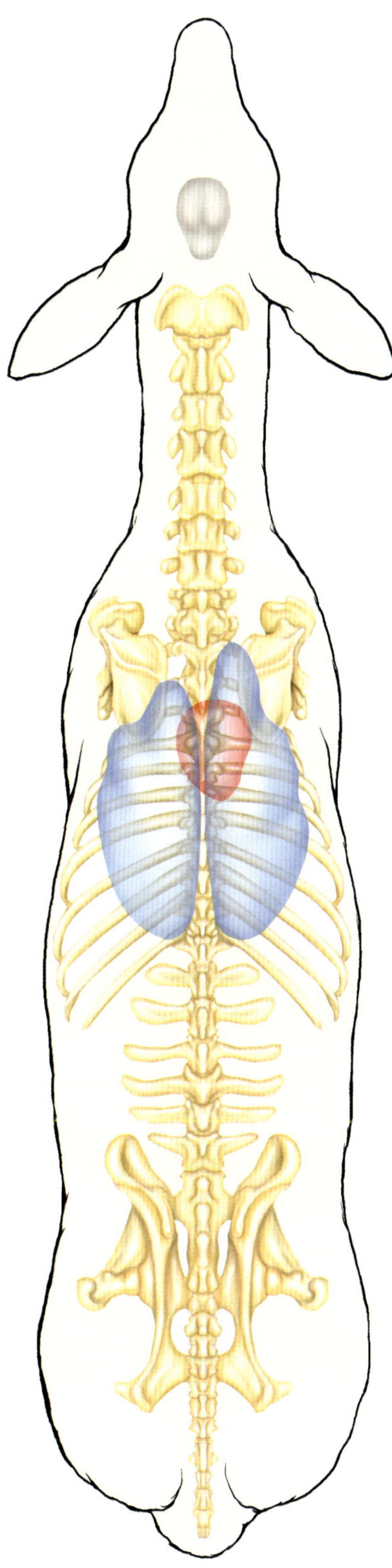

From this top view it really becomes obvious how small the heart and lungs are for a straight-on frontal shot. Also note, again from the top angle, how the heart is surrounded by the shoulder blades and the spine.

The problem with a true heart shot is that it's a bit tricky, and you must consciously shoot a bit lower than most people wish to. From a broadside presentation, again divide the body horizontally into thirds. Follow the centerline of the foreleg up to the center of the bottom third, and you have a heart shot. If you shoot high or you shoot a couple of inches too far back, you still have a fatal shot in the lungs. But you have very little margin for error if you shoot low or too far forward.

In terms of effect, anticipate a frantic final run of possibly seventy-five yards with a heart shot. However, you can expect your deer to go down in its tracks if you use a fairly powerful rifle with a tough or heavy bullet and you break both shoulders while transiting the heart. Because of the very small margin for error, I don't like frontal shots; it's better to wait for the buck to turn unless, again, you are fairly close and very steady. The angle is dictated to some extent by the caliber you're using and the penetrating properties of your bullet. I don't like the so-called "Texas heart shot" on unwounded deer, but, especially if you're trophy hunting, I think it's wise to use enough gun and enough bullet that you can take any reasonable shot in terms of both range and presentation.

THE RIGHT BUCK

Trophies are in the eye of the beholder, and this is perhaps truest with whitetail.

My "best ever" whitetail was this south Texas buck, taken with my David Miller 7mm Remington Magnum. A magnum is rarely required for whitetail hunting—but if you know your rifle and have confidence in it, then that's what you should use, regardless of caliber.

Fully mature, big-racked bucks do occur throughout the whitetail's range. But in many areas a combination of short seasons and intensive hunting pressure render any whitetail taken in fair chase a truly great trophy. Some areas produce bigger bucks or have greater numbers of them than other areas. There are record-class bucks roaming the East and the South, but they are so unusual—and so difficult to hunt—that seeking one is almost like hunting a unicorn. In the regions that are harder hunted, most hunters are justifiably proud of any eight- or ten-point buck, meaning a total count of eye guards and fighting tines.

In other areas it's possible to be more selective. Mind you, despite what you might read in the magazines, there are no areas that produce a lot of wild record-class whitetail! But there are areas, like the Great Plains, western Canada, and some of the well-managed ranches of Texas, where buck-to-doe ratios are high and where a fairly large percentage of the buck herd lives long enough to reach full maturity. Personally, in such areas I have never thought in terms of record-book score. Instead, I think in terms of a buck that has reached full maturity, maybe 5½ years old or, better still, 7½ and older. Such a buck may be a big eight-pointer or, more likely, a ten-pointer, or it may have more typical and some nontypical points. But it will have mass and character to its rack, and its body will be heavy and powerful, its face broad and its muzzle going gray. To me that's a trophy whitetail, regardless of how its rack scores.

WHITETAIL GUNS AND LOADS

Choosing the right gun and load is complicated by the fact that whitetail vary tremendously in body size. The average white-tailed buck taken is probably a 1½- to 2½-year-old forkhorn buck that weighs less than 150 pounds. On the other hand, big northern and northwestern bucks can weigh over 350 pounds at maturity, and, throughout most of their range, bucks exceeding 250 pounds are occasionally encountered. A wizened big-woods monster is not the same animal as an innocent adolescent, and it probably won't offer quite as simple a shot. If you're purely a meat hunter, this may not matter to you, but if you wish to be armed for the biggest buck roaming your area, you need to keep this disparity in mind.

As I have stated, millions of hunters have little choice. The law says they must use shotguns, with an option to use muzzleloaders often available. OK, no problem. The range is limited, but a well-

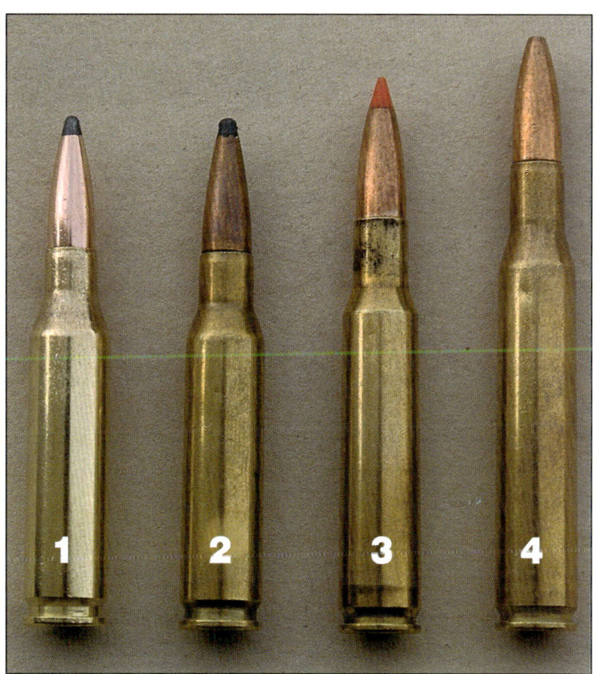

Left to right: 1) .260 Remington 2) 7mm-08 Remington 3) 7x57 Mauser 4) .270 Winchester. Efficient, light-recoiling cartridges like these are ideal for almost all whitetail hunting anywhere, the only possible exception being extremely open country—and even there shots beyond the reach of these cartridges are rare.

placed shotgun slug will handle any whitetail that walks. The real secret is to consider your slug gun the same way you would consider a rifle for sheep or pronghorn hunting. Yes, the range is more restricted, but you still want all the accuracy you can get. Modern slug guns with fully rifled barrels do extend the potential range a bit. More important, they offer pinpoint accuracy—and even though the shotgun slug is a huge piece of metal, it's still important to put it in the right place.

So take advantage of rifle-barrel technology, and make sure you have top-quality rifle sights on your deer shotgun—preferably a good, light-gathering, low-power scope. Then spend time on the range discovering exactly what slugs your shotgun groups best with. If you do your homework, the handicap posed by a modern slug gun isn't all that great, and exactly the same applies to muzzleloaders.

If you hunt whitetail with rifles, the whole world is open to you. This doesn't mean you necessarily need a flat-shooting magnum. That depends on where and how you hunt. The .30-30 Winchester has probably accounted for more deer than any other cartridge, and it remains perfectly adequate for any deer that walks. If you hunt close cover where shots much beyond one hundred yards are unlikely, then you aren't handicapped in the least with the good old lever-action carbine your grandfather carried—except that its traditional open "buckhorn" sights may be handicapping you. Good sights, either an aperture or a low-powered scope, won't extend the range of a .30-30 by much, but they will enable you to shoot faster and more accurately, especially under low-light conditions.

These days most rifle-toting hunters seem to have made the shift to scoped rifles in flatter-shooting, more versatile calibers, with the bolt-action by far the most popular. This is generally wise, because a flat-shooting rifle will work just fine up close as well as a long way out; a short-range brush gun cannot handle longer shots.

Caliber really depends a lot on where you hunt. In many states the .22 centerfires (.223 Remington, .22-250, et cetera) are legal. I have taken a lot of deer with these little cartridges, and they work, but shot placement must be extremely precise, and they do not have enough energy for longer shots. I don't think they're suitable for the largest-bodied deer, nor are they a good idea for trophy hunting anywhere; you're just too limited in the shots you can take. In Texas and much of the southeast, mild cartridges like the .243 and the .25s are extremely popular. They're just fine for the smaller-bodied deer in these regions and are excellent for "meat hunting" everywhere. But if you want to be prepared for the largest-bodied deer, and for any shot you might encounter, I think a step up is appropriate.

The good old 7x57mm is one of my favorite whitetail cartridges, which means that similar cartridges like the .260 Remington, 6.5x55mm, and 7mm-08 are also good. But for genuine all-round use under almost all conditions, old favorites like the .270 Winchester, .280 Remington, .30-06, and .308 Winchester are extremely hard to beat. I honestly believe that you do not have to have any magnum cartridge for any white-tailed deer hunting. But if a magnum gives you more confidence, then any of the magnums between, say, the new .270 Winchester Short Magnum to the .30-caliber magnums will certainly do the job on any whitetail, up close or far away.

I have often carried magnums on open-country whitetail hunts, and a couple of times I've been glad I had them. I took my best Texas buck 'way down a *sendero* with a pet 7mm

The boat-tailed bullet is damned because the jacket and core often separate. That's true, but it usually happens at the very limit of penetration. These all separated, but the jacket was lodged against the hide on the far side. On deer-sized game, what more could you want?

Remington Magnum, and I took my best plains buck in western Kansas with a .300 Weatherby Magnum. Honestly, in both cases a .270 Winchester would have done as well—but in both cases these were favorite rifles that gave me the confidence I needed to make a difficult shot. That "C" factor (for confidence) is always more important than the actual caliber.

BULLET PERFORMANCE

White-tailed deer are tough, but even the biggest whitetail isn't all that big. Under most circumstances I like to use accurate bullets that will open up fairly quickly. Depending on the rifle, I use a lot of Hornady Interlocks, Sierra Gamekings and Pro-hunters, and Nosler Ballistic Tips. I have also used a lot of factory ammo loaded with Federal Hi-Shoks, Remington Core-Lokts, and Winchester Power Points and Ballistic Silvertips. None of these are "tough" bullets, but under most circumstances all are tough enough for white-tailed deer, and all will expand fairly rapidly and do a great job.

There are exceptions. If you're using relatively light calibers, especially for large deer, then you may want to consider tougher bullets like the Nosler Partition, Trophy Bonded Bear Claw, or Barnes X-Bullet to ensure you will get the penetration you must have. On serious trophy hunts for large-bodied deer, I often use fairly tough bullets like these. I want to absolutely ensure that I will have the penetration I need even if I have to take a bad-angle shot, because if the buck of a lifetime appears, I want to be able to take any shot with confidence.

SPECIAL CIRCUMSTANCES

The little Coues whitetail is the most obvious special circumstance. This is a very small-bodied deer; even a really big buck will rarely weigh more than one hundred pounds. So, on the surface, a 6mm or .25-caliber would be a great choice—except that Coues deer live in big, rough country where shots on whitetail average a good deal longer. Some of my friends, like the famed David Miller, have made a science of shooting Coues deer at extremely long range. I have not. I have taken a couple of bucks at very long range, but most of my shots come at somewhere between 250 and 350 yards. This is still a far poke. Because of the distance, and because larger bullets resist wind better than small bullets, fast .270s and 7mms are good minimal choices. The

Millions of American whitetail hunters are obligated to use shotguns with slugs. This limits the range, but does not have to limit accuracy. It's important to spend time on the range with several different loads to learn exactly what your shotgun shoots best.

really serious guys, like David Miller and outfitter Kirk Kelso, use .30-caliber magnums and apologize to no one for being overgunned.

Although I can't imagine the situation, reader mail over the years has suggested that, in some hard-hunted woods, the only way to avoid an argument about whose tag goes on a deer is to drop it in its tracks. Under these conditions a lot of hunters use cartridges like the .35 Whelen, .444 Marlin, and .45-70. Cartridges like these are not required for any whitetail, but if you want to drop your deer in its tracks, nothing will do it as dramatically as a big, slow-moving blunt-nose or round-nose bullet. Flat-point and round-nose bullets transfer energy more quickly, which is partly the reason the .30-30 is so much more effective than its paper ballistics indicate. So if you hunt in close cover and you're not worried about a long shot, borrow a page from the brush-busters and load up your .270, .30-06, or .308 with the round-nose loads most manufacturers still offer. You will see a difference in impact with any well-placed shot.

AMERICAN ELK

Our toughest deer . . .

Few animals on earth approach the majestic bearing of a mature bull elk. Great antlers thrown back, neck outstretched, it bugles its challenge in a high Alpine meadow—and it symbolizes the high, wild country of the American West. After our various deer, the American elk is North America's most popular big-game animal. For many Westerners it represents the long winter's meat supply, but for tens of thousands of Easterners it represents the ultimate in hunting dreams. For most North American hunters it is the first—and sometimes the only—truly large game they will encounter.

Technically speaking, our elk is neither a western game animal nor a creature of the high country. Just two hundred years ago it was well distributed in the forests and foothills of the eastern United States, and little more than a century ago it was plentiful throughout much of the Great Plains. But it was forced to retreat before the onslaught of settlers, and by the beginning of the twentieth century, all that remained was remnant populations in the western mountains and forests. We think of the elk as a high-country animal, but in a natural sense this is not true, and it is becoming less true today.

One of the best remaining herds was located in what is now Yellowstone National Park, and during the last century captured Yellowstone elk were released into suitable habitat all over the continent. The bulk of the nation's elk population and most of the hunting opportunity occurs in the Rocky Mountain West and the Pacific Northwest, but there are viable herds in Michigan, Pennsylvania, Kentucky, Oklahoma, Kansas, Nebraska, Texas, and the Dakotas. This is far from a complete list, and it suggests just how adaptable the creature we call elk really is.

Our elk is a member of the Cervidae family, the round-antlered deer, with numerous species in the Old World. The American elk is species *Cervus elaphus*, but this is not an exclusively North American species. In fact, *Cervus elaphus* could be the most widespread big-game animal in the entire world. In Europe its range starts in Portugal and the British Isles and extends all the way across Europe and Asia and down into North Africa and Asia Minor. There are many subspecies with significant physical differences across this huge range. In Europe we call them red deer; they are smaller and indeed are reddish. The antlers are similar to those of American elk, but the mature bulls typically have a cluster of points at the horn tips. Farther east they grow larger and become paler; in central Asia most people call them maral stags. By the time you get to Mongolia, they are big animals with tan bodies and typical six-point antlers; in other words, they are absolutely indistinguishable from North American elk!

The tule elk is the smallest of the elk (which is a relative thing), and also the subspecies that typically occurs in the most open country. I used my 8mm Remington Magnum with 220-grain Sierra boattails, an exceptionally deadly setup for elk.

American Elk

The ancestors of our elk crossed what was once a land bridge from Siberia to Alaska during the late Pleistocene Epoch, and for eons they spread across much of North America, developing into several distinct North American subspecies. Most plentiful and widespread is the Rocky Mountain elk, *Cervus elaphus nelsoni*. The Rocky Mountain elk is a big elk with dark neck and legs and pale body, growing long-beamed antlers that, typically, will have six or, rarely, seven points at full maturity. Body size varies tremendously depending on genetics and food conditions, but a good average for a mature Rocky Mountain bull would be seven hundred pounds. Usually forgotten is the Manitoba elk, *Cervus elaphus manitobensis*, now restricted to isolated habitat in Manitoba and Saskatchewan. The Manitoba elk is somewhat larger than the Rocky Mountain elk, with similar antlers. The current population is believed to be no more than ten thousand, with some limited resident hunting currently available.

In the Pacific Northwest the elk are of the Roosevelt subspecies (*Cervus elaphus roosevelti*), a giant of an animal with bulls often approaching a half-ton. The Roosevelt elk is darker and blockier in build, and tends to have shorter, thicker antlers. Interestingly, the "crown points" so common in European red deer are often seen on the best Roosevelt bulls. In the valleys and foothills of central and southern California, the elk are tule elk, *Cervus elaphus nannodes*, also called dwarf or valley elk. The tule elk is the smallest and palest subspecies, with mature bulls running around 550 pounds. Tule elk antlers are usually short-beamed, but seven, eight, and even nine points per side is common, the upper points often coming in a cluster or "crown" similar to that of red deer.

There are two additional subspecies that became extinct during our pioneering era. The eastern elk, *Cervus elaphus canadensis*, disappeared during the mid-nineteenth century. The Merriam's elk (*Cervus elaphus merriami*) was the southwestern elk of Arizona and New Mexico. Already scarce by the end of the Civil War, the last Merriam's elk vanished at the beginning of the twentieth century. Merriam's elk had existed within living memory during the introduction of Yellowstone elk into the Southwest. Today, Arizona and New Mexico boast burgeoning elk herds that produce superb trophy quality, but they all stem from introduced Rocky Mountain elk, as do all of the elk herds now breeding in the East and Midwest.

Most American hunters will always refer to this big, pale-bodied deer as elk, but it is really a poor name for this grand animal. Elk stems from the word *elg* or *elch*, which, in several European languages, denotes a large deer; in Scandinavia, it is the proper name for the European moose. Moose also occurred in the eastern United States when the Americanized word elk was applied to *Cervus elaphus*, so exactly why it stuck is unknown. A better name, not only more befitting such a noble creature but also less confusing to Europeans, is the often-used wapiti, which comes from the Shawnee and means "white deer."

By any name our wapiti or elk is a wonderful creature. It is not only big but very strong. It can fight the deep snows in the high country with ease, and it can be twenty miles away by morning. In the fall its lilting three-note challenge echoes through the hills and valleys, and its mating battles are truly clashes of titans. The elk is also exceptionally adaptable and has prospered under modern management.

The Perfect Shot, North America

When I was a kid, there was a lot of elk hunting available, but the opportunity to actually take an elk was very limited. Put another way, in the 1960s and 1970s I knew a lot of people who went elk hunting, but I didn't know many people who had actually shot an elk. Things are different today. Elk hunting is not and never will be a "sure thing," especially on public land—but today's elk hunting is far better than it was at any time during the twentieth century. During the past fifteen or twenty years, after decades of fairly stable populations, the elk herds in much of the West have literally exploded. Wildlife biologists don't altogether understand exactly why this has occurred.

On a shot like this, much of the heart/lungs area is covered by shoulder bones. If you have a well-constructed bullet and a steady rest, there is no problem. However, on a large, tough animal like an elk, the hunter with a regular softpoint would be wise to wait till a 90-degree angle presents itself. (Photo courtesy of Leonard Lee Rue III)

This isn't altogether good news, because the increased number of elk is believed to be a major factor in the long-term decline of mule deer in some areas. It also doesn't mean there are lots of big bulls. It takes about ten years for a bull elk to reach its full antler development, so even though herds double and triple in size, it takes years of management for trophy quality before you can expect to see numbers of big bulls. In addition, hunting in the West has become a supply-and-demand business. Although there are more elk than ever before, there are also more hunters than ever before, so most tags, especially tags in good trophy areas, are obtained through drawings. Still, there is tremendous opportunity.

Almost across the board, hunter success is much higher than it ever has been, and this is good, but it must be understood in perspective. Spike and "raghorn" bulls, youngsters with three or four points per side, have always made up the largest part of the bull harvest. With elk herds at an all-time high, cow permits are also at an all-time high. There is nothing wrong with shooting a cow elk, because the meat is wonderful and, with many herds overpopulated, the management is essential. There is also nothing wrong with shooting a young bull, depending on the local management goals. But it's a great deal easier to go out and fill a cow tag or to happily take "any bull" than it is to find a big-racked, mature elk. Too many new elk hunters head to the high country each fall with their heads full of magazine stories and their hearts set on huge six-point bulls.

In special places there are numbers of big bulls. These conditions exist on well-managed private land, Indian reservations, and limited-entry trophy units on public land. But high bull-to-cow ratios and large populations of older bulls are rare. Elk are big animals that can wander over great distances, and they need a lot of room. Even where they are plentiful you won't find them everywhere. The hunting is usually weather-sensitive, and most of us are obligated to hunt elk for short periods in relatively small areas.

If conditions are right, a big bull may be in the offing, but in much of the West really big bulls are extremely scarce, and there aren't enough of them for every hunter to bring one home. You'll have a better experience if you set a reasonable goal, especially if you've never hunted elk before. Even though there are more elk than ever before, under many circumstances any elk taken in fair chase is a fine trophy.

SHOTS AT ELK

These days most rifle seasons are held after the bugling is over, but there are some opportunities to hunt during bugling. If you're fortunate enough to hunt with a rifle when the elk are really bugling, then you can expect relatively close shots. The classic situation, of course, is for a bull to answer your challenge and come charging in, offering a shot at point-blank range. It usually doesn't work that way, especially with the best bulls. The bulls that come charging in tend to be the younger, satellite bulls, which you don't want if you're looking for the best bull you can find. The old boys often have cows, and they have some experience; they may answer you, but they aren't likely to run over you. Generally, if they're bugling, you can locate them, and that gives you a tremendous advantage.

The Perfect Shot, North America

I took my first bull elk in 1972 and my most recent about two weeks ago, as I write these lines. I haven't hunted elk every single year, but I have hunted them a great deal. I've been fortunate to have hunted elk with a rifle during the bugling season eight or ten times, and I don't think I have ever taken a bull that actually came to a bugle. I have taken a bunch of bulls by stalking the bugle. This doesn't mean point-blank shooting, but it usually means you can get reasonably close.

Twice I've stalked elk that had already faded into the timber and were bugling from their beds. The first time was on the Mescalero Reservation, around 1981. The elk were bugling like crazy that morning, and we'd seen a lot of bulls but nothing really good. It was already late when we started shadowing several bulls, eventually realizing they were stationary in a patch of thick junipers. We crawled in carefully and could see nothing but bits and pieces of bedded bulls. We waited for a long time,

Elk are notoriously tough animals and should ideally be shot when standing broadside, such as seen in the stance of this bull. However, before the shot is taken, wait for the animal to move its head straight forward. (Photo courtesy of Leonard Lee Rue III)

stalemated. Eventually, a very fine six-pointer stood up at about forty yards, and I shot it, my first really nice bull elk.

Just a couple of years ago, on Arizona's White Mountain Apache Reservation, we had bugled our way through a canyon system until it got hot. We lay down to rest for a while, essentially declaring an end to the morning hunt. Then we heard a particularly deep-throated bull bugling just a short distance away. We listened for a while, then slowly still-hunted our way toward it. We actually overshot it, then turned around when it bugled once more. It got up from behind a tiny patch of cover, and I shot it as soon as it stepped clear. Several other times it seemed obvious that a bugling bull was taking its cows away from our bugling. So we shut up and hustled, trying to circle ahead. This won't work all the time but is worth trying.

Even during the bugling season, and especially when it's over, terrain and vegetation will dictate the kind of shot

The heart and lung shots are marked here. Do not shoot until the bull elk moves its head straight forward. (Photo courtesy of Leonard Lee Rue III)

Classic elk country during the bugling season, a great place to be. During bugling hunts, shots will usually be fairly close—but rifle seasons that occur during the rut are rare today. In any case it's probably best to be prepared for any reasonable shot that might be presented.

you're most likely to get. In the Pacific Northwest the cover is incredibly thick, and almost all shots are at extremely close range. In high Alpine country, and in the big sagebrush meadows where elk love to feed, there are opportunities for fairly long shooting; but in the timber and oakbrush hillsides on the lower slopes things close in. With few exceptions, shooting can vary from quite close to quite far, with the average somewhere in the middle. I have taken a number of elk at less than 50 yards and a few from 350 to 400, but most have been between 100 and 200 yards, about the same as big game throughout the world.

One of the problems with elk is that they are very large animals, and their pale coats show up well at incredible distances. There is great temptation to whale away at long range, but it is usually not necessary. Elk have wonderful noses and extremely keen ears, but I am personally convinced that they don't see as well as whitetail or mule deer. If you have enough time and a wee bit of cover, you can usually advance within sensible rifle range. Bowhunting is a different story.

If undisturbed, elk are also relatively habitual, until there is a change in something like weather or food supplies. For instance, if you see elk feeding in a distant meadow at daybreak, but they fade into the timber before you can get to them, there's no reason to panic or blunder into the thick stuff after them.

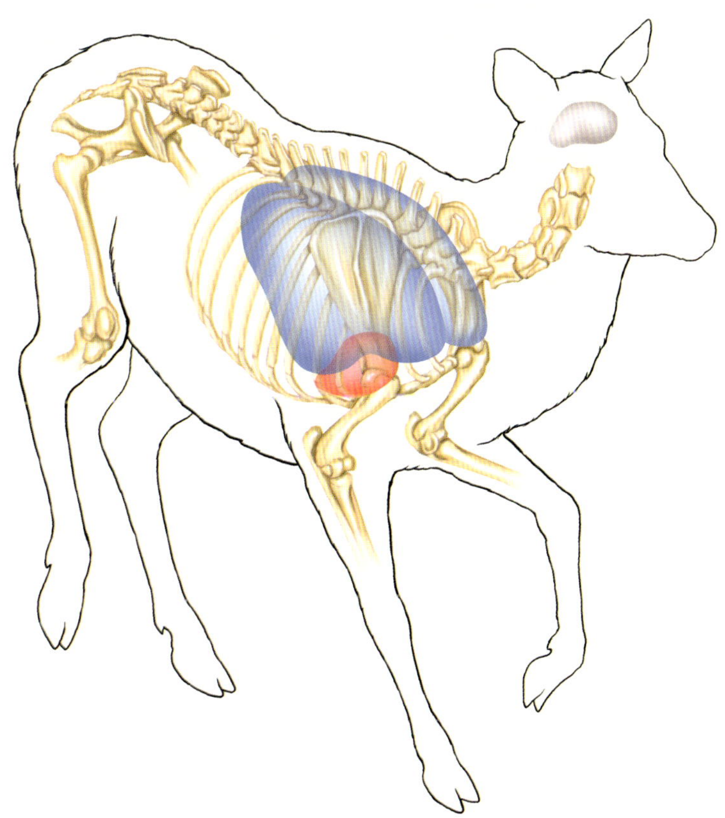

This illustrates an angled shot at an elk. Note how much bone covers the heart/lung area. These are not the bones of a small whitetail. Elk are tough, so it is necessary to use an adequate caliber with well-constructed bullets.

There's a very good chance that they'll come back into the same meadow just before dark. If you see them in a given meadow at dusk, chances are they'll be reasonably close at first light.

Elk are extremely hardy creatures that can pack a bad hit for miles. It's usually better to accept a bit of risk in trying to get closer than to attempt a long shot. Long shot means different things to different people, and it also depends on your rifle and cartridge. With an adequate cartridge and a steady position, I don't consider 350 to 400 yards a long shot on elk, but I'm not one of those guys who brags about (or even attempts) 600-yard shots on elk. Over the course of around thirty elk hunts over thirty years—not all successful—I have attempted just one seriously long shot at a bull elk. It was in Arizona, on a tag I'd beaten tough odds to draw. The bull was the biggest bull elk I have ever seen while hunting, and it was 'way up on a slide on a timbered slope. I knew the range and I knew the rifle, and I just plain shot right over its back! I've lived with that faux pas for several years, and every time it comes to mind, I remind myself that I should have gotten a bit closer.

TAKING THE SHOT

I think elk rank among this world's really tough game. I hear all this poppycock

I took this nice bull in heavy timber with a 7.82 (.308) Lazzeroni, firing 180-grain Nosler Partitions. The bull stood from his bed and gave me a shot from about 70 yards. There was absolutely no reaction to a perfect shoulder/heart shot, but he folded up about 60 yards down the ridge.

about how tough African game is, but I've hunted all of Africa's major species, and there's nothing over there that's any tougher than elk. This doesn't mean that elk are bulletproof—not at all. You simply must hit them well, because they will often travel fast, far, and hard when poorly hit, and in the rough country where they live you may never catch up.

There are no secrets and no mysteries to shot placement. The brain shot is very difficult, with high risk of wounding if you hit low and a risk of wounding and ruining the trophy if you hit high. Lower down in the thick neck it is extremely difficult to visualize exactly where the spine lies; if you absolutely insist on a neck shot, make it in the upper third of the neck. The target area is not large here, but if you place your shot right in the center, you will get your elk.

That kind of shot is the serious meat hunter's pride and joy, but I generally don't go in for that fancy stuff. To my thinking there are really just two sensible options, the lung shot and the shoulder/heart shot. Both are extremely effective, and each has its fans. At closer ranges I tend to go for the shoulder/heart shot. It isn't difficult to visualize. Just divide the body into horizontal thirds. With a broadside presentation, come up the centerline of the foreleg into the center of the bottom third. On longer shots I tend to use the lung shot because it offers considerably greater margin for error in all directions—except that, on an animal as big and strong as an elk, you must be very careful not to shoot too far back. For the lung shot, again divide the body into horizontal thirds. Come up the rear line of the foreleg into the bottom half of the center third. This shot will take down an elk—or any other game animal—very quickly.

On angling shots you must visualize where the heart and lungs lie and adjust your hold accordingly. But you must also remember that an elk is not a deer; it is at least two or three times larger and much tougher. You can make angling shots, but only if you have enough gun and enough bullet to absolutely ensure penetration.

THE RIGHT ELK

The classic configuration of a mature bull elk is six fighting tines per side. Once in a while a seven-by-seven Rocky Mountain elk is encountered, and the best Roosevelt and tule elk are far more likely to have more than six points. In record-book terms a six-point bull isn't necessarily a big elk. In Boone and Crockett's scoring system, the inside spread, beam length, point length, and four circumferences on each antler are measured. The size of a Boone and Crockett bull must be seen to be believed; beam length approaching five feet and points nearly two feet long are the hallmarks of a "book bull!" Very few hunters will ever see this kind of elk, and fewer still will take one. By the way, I'm pretty sure that the Arizona bull on which I took that long poke represented the only chance I'm ever likely to get.

Very few people hunt elk for the record book, but everybody wants a big "six-by-six." As stated earlier, there aren't enough for everybody to have one, and such a bull is unlikely or even impossible in many areas. The elk you can get is dictated largely by what is available in the area you're hunting. Remember, too, that the number of points is just one dimension. A five-by-five is usually a younger bull on its second or third set of antlers, but there are a couple of truly monstrous five-point elk in the record books. Given a choice, I'd take a big five-point over a small six-point. But you need to do a bit of homework and try to understand exactly what sort of bulls the area you're hunting normally produces. Even in hard-hunted areas there is always the chance for a monster, but in my mind there's little point in searching for a needle in a haystack—especially if you've come a long distance and you want to go home with an elk.

In an open meadow it's fairly easy to count points and judge the size of a rack, but in the timber it isn't so easy. If you have time, look for a long brow point just over the nose, and also take a quick look at the fourth point. Called the "dagger" or "sword" point, the fourth point is usually the longest point on a normal elk. If there isn't much time, ignore the bottom of the rack and look for the tip of the main beam. If it forks into a Y with the rearmost point—the actual tip of the main beam—and seems to slant down toward the rump, you are almost certainly looking at a six-point bull; if the main beam tip is straight, you're probably looking at a five-point.

GUNS AND LOADS

Since elk are extremely popular game animals, and they are also the largest game most North American hunters pursue, there is much controversy surrounding what constitutes the ideal elk rifle. One school of thought is that the standard western deer

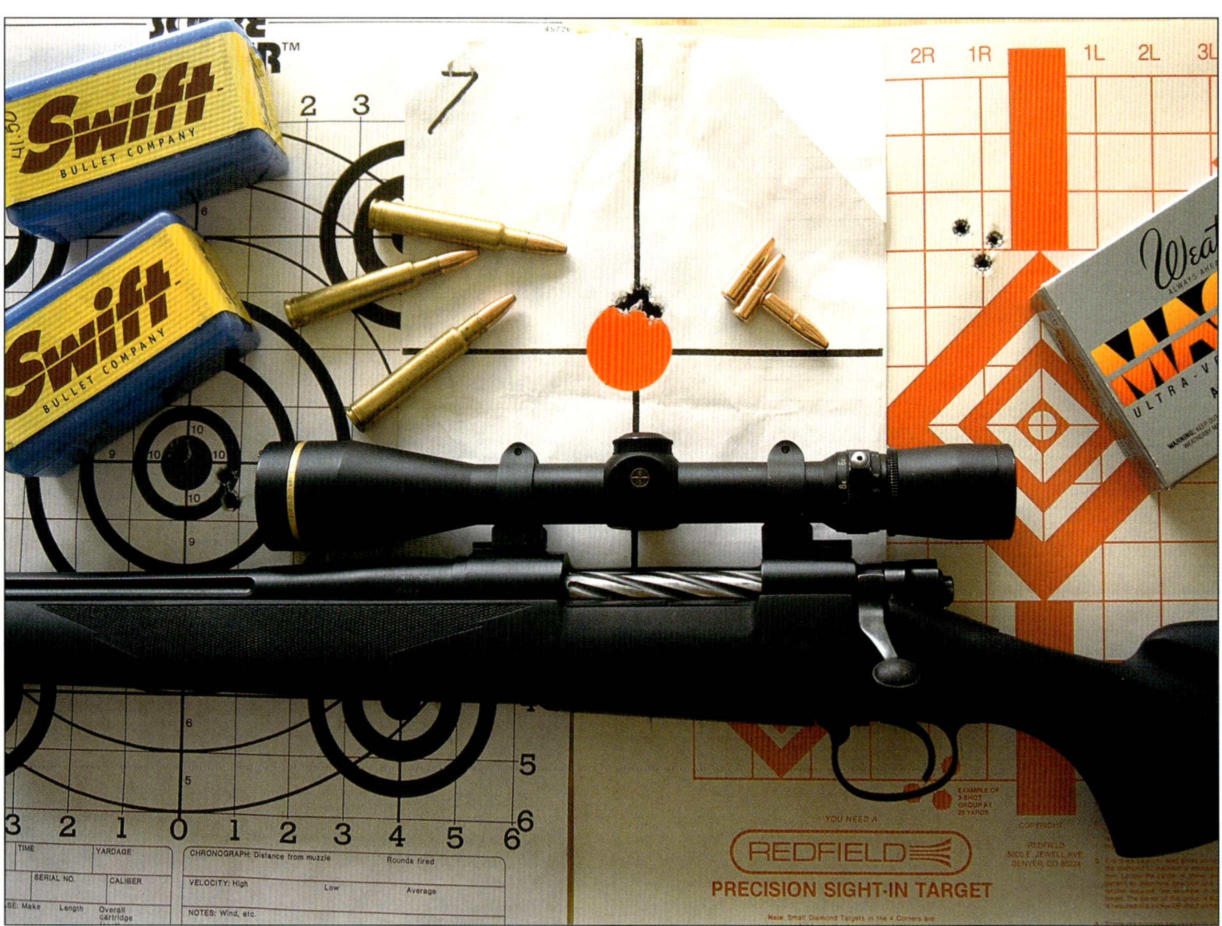

Here's my idea of a perfect elk rifle: an accurate, relatively light rifle chambered to a fast-stepping, hard-hitting cartridge. This .340 Weatherby Magnum was made by Rich Reilly at High-Tech.

MOOSE

A giant of a deer . . .

In order to really appreciate a moose, the world's largest deer, you need to see it up close. Its bulbous nose and dangling dewlap give it a comical appearance—but at its largest it stands taller than a horse, weighs as much as a Cape buffalo, and carries the biggest and heaviest headgear of any animal on earth. The best time to appreciate this animal is when it's standing on the edge of the bogs and willow thickets that moose love. The worst place is just after you've walked up on your first moose and you suddenly realize you don't have a clue how you're going to get it back to camp.

The moose is North America's second-largest game animal after the bison and the largest game animal that is commonly hunted. It is generally a creature of wilderness, northern forests, and willow-lined lakes and streams. It is rarely hunted where there are roads, and in much of its typically boggy habitat hunters can use horses. Some animals, like sheep, can be characterized as extremely difficult to find; others, like bears, can be characterized as extremely tough. Under the right circumstances the moose is neither—but it offers several hundred pounds of excellent meat, and one of the great challenges is how to recover its excellent venison without spoilage and without having a heart attack.

This doesn't imply that the moose isn't a grand game animal. Indeed, it is. Its palmated antlers can spread to spectacular dimensions. During the rut it is known to charge freight trains. That's not a contest it can win, but when it's love-crazed it might charge you—and that's a battle it can win! As big as the moose is, its forests and mountains are bigger. A moose can be almost impossible to find when it doesn't want to be found. And yet, when it's feeding on a hillside in the sunlight, you can see the shine of its black hide and the glint of its horns five or six miles away.

Like many North American game animals, including elk, grizzly, and caribou, the moose has its roots in the Old World. Its species is *Alces alces*, but the "type" race, *Alces alces alces*, is not a North American moose but the moose of northern Europe. Moose are widely distributed in Scandinavia; Finland and Sweden boast somewhat denser populations than any place known in North America. Moose extend eastward across Siberia and down into the forests of northern China and Mongolia, and, in eons gone by, they almost certainly crossed what was once a land bridge across the Bering Strait to set up shop in North America.

Our American moose are generally found in the northern forests and forest fringes from Newfoundland to Alaska, and four subspecies are identified across this huge range.

From east to west they are: *Alces alces americana*, from Newfoundland to central Canada; *Alces alces andersoni*, the moose of central and western Canada; *Alces alces shirasi*, the Shiras or Wyoming moose of the western United States; and the largest of all moose, *Alces alces gigas*, the Alaska-Yukon moose. For record-keeping the Boone and Crockett Club recognizes Alaska-Yukon moose, Canada moose (including both *andersoni* and *americana*), and Shiras moose. Safari Club International separates Canadian moose into eastern Canada moose and western Canada moose, recognizing the smaller *americana* race with a straight line across Ontario.

This is actually a bold and controversial move; everyone recognizes that Canada's eastern moose are smaller than the moose of western Canada and simply cannot compete in the record books with the moose of northern British Columbia, which obviously bump up against the Alaska-Yukon giants. The issue is where to draw the line—and this plagues all the record keepers with all of our moose. The differences among the subspecies are subtle,

With a slightly going-away angle, the shoulder shot becomes impractical. The heart and lung shots are marked. (Photo courtesy of Leonard Lee Rue III)

and there are broad intergrade areas that defy exact classification. We know that the eastern Canada moose are generally smaller in both body and antler than the western Canada moose. We know that the Shiras moose are generally smaller and darker than either, and that the Alaska-Yukon moose is the biggest of all—but where do you draw the line?

Today, the moose of the Mackenzie district of Northwest Territories—huge animals—are classified as Alaska-Yukon, along with all the moose of Yukon and Alaska. The small, dark Shiras moose almost certainly extend up along the spine of the Rockies in western Alberta and the Kootenay District of British Columbia, but it's hard to say exactly how far. Safari Club recognizes these moose as Shiras, while Boone and Crockett, generally more conservative, draw the line at the United States/Canada border.

Differences in body size are significant, and the record-book listings suggest that antler growth also varies. Alaskan bulls probably weigh from thirteen hundred pounds upward, but very few wild moose

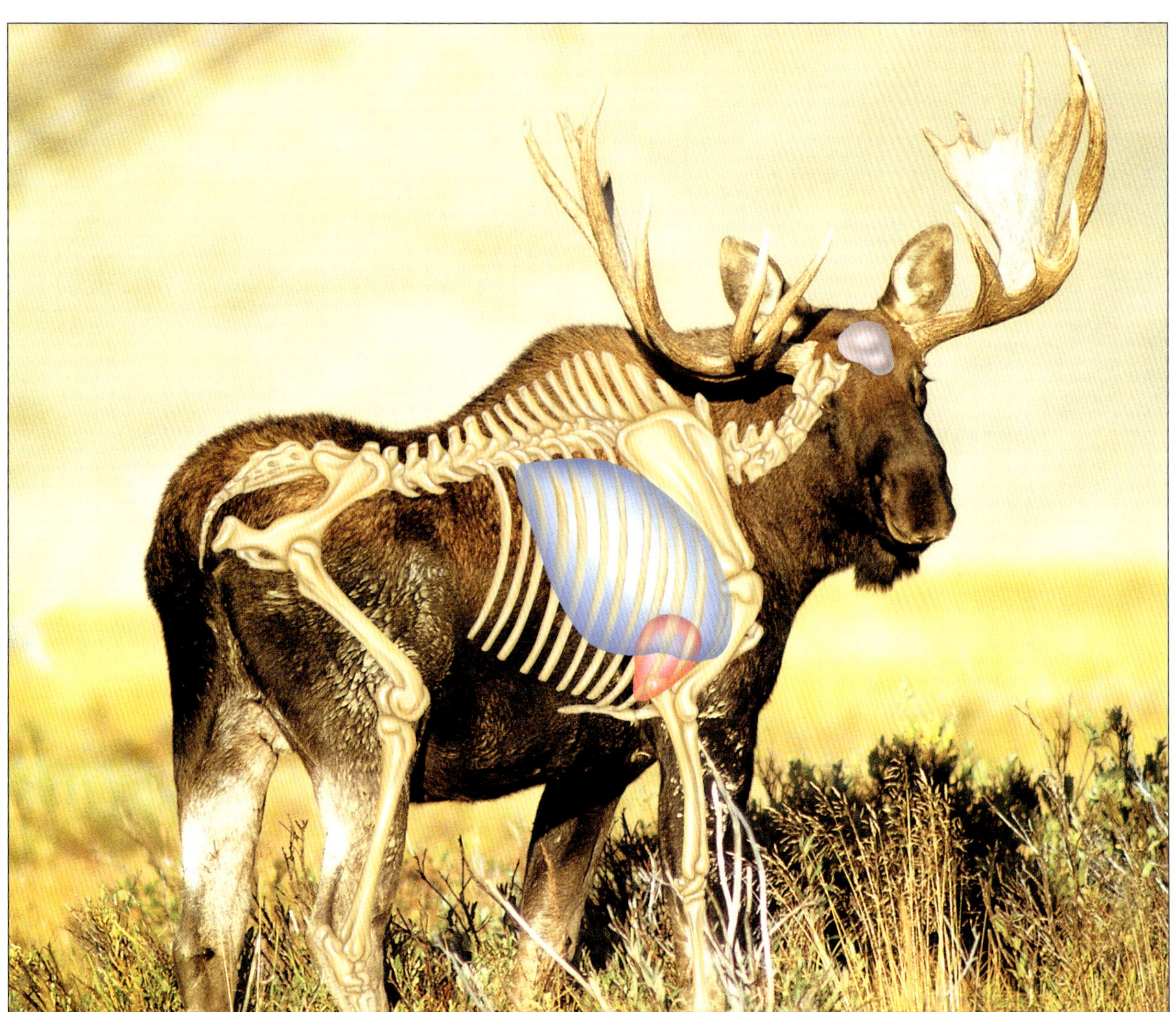

Notice how far forward at an angle the heart lies when the animal is pointing away from the hunter. On the other hand, it is easy to shoot at this angle in front of the heart, so a lung shot is preferable here since the lungs offer a much larger target. (Photo courtesy of Leonard Lee Rue III)

have ever been weighed, so it's hard to say how much they can weigh. Canada moose average a couple of hundred pounds lighter; Shiras moose are considerably smaller, with big bulls weighing around nine hundred pounds.

All of our moose, at maturity, grow palmated antlers with widely varying numbers of points coming off the edges of the palm. The best moose have smaller palms (the "brow palm") at the bottom of the rack, with long points jutting forward. Record-book measurements are attained by a mixture of palm height and width, points, and circumference. The most commonly used measurement—outside spread of the total rack—is the measurement best understood, but it may not be the most important. With Shiras moose, antlers with a spread of 40 inches should be considered very good. In the east a 50-inch moose is superb, but in northern British Columbia you can seek 60-inchers. The latter figure is a darned good moose anywhere, but spreads of 70 inches or more are quite possible with Alaska-Yukon moose.

SHOTS AT MOOSE

As is the case with so many North American animals, the shot you get at a moose depends not only on where you're

Much moose country is boggy and heavily forested. Unless there are some ridges and hills that offer vantage points, shots are likely to be close, so there's no premium on flat-shooting capabilities.

hunting but also on your hunting techniques. In mountainous or hilly country, whether in Newfoundland, Alaska, or Colorado, most moose are taken by spot-and-stalk hunting. Moose are huge creatures that can be seen at vast distances, provided they step out of the heavy cover and offer a view. As with any stalking situation, once you start you never know exactly what's going to happen. The animal might be gone by the time you get there, you might stalk in very close, or you might get hung up by obstacles and need to take a longer shot.

I'm not convinced that moose see as well as most other antlered animals, but that huge nose is sensitive, and so are those monstrous ears. If you're careful with the noise and keep the wind in your favor, you can often get fairly close to moose. Some years ago, on the Alaskan Peninsula, my guide and I were glassing from a low, open ridge down into a valley of thick willows, and we spotted a giant of a bull. The distance was about three hundred yards, which is certainly a practical shot on moose if you have the right conditions and the right equipment. On this day we had neither; I was carrying the then-new .416 Remington Magnum and had no idea exactly what the drop would be at that distance. Even if I'd known we had a crosswind blowing at thirty miles per hour,

A huge Alaskan bull taken with a .416 Remington Magnum. Obviously the big calibers work, and in terms of body size are appropriate—but this is really being overgunned for moose.

that kind of a shot would have been tricky. We watched the moose bed in the thick stuff, marked its position as carefully as we could, and attempted an approach.

We foundered in the dense willows, absolutely certain that we were right on top of the bull, but found no sign of it. After a half-hour or so we concluded that it had moved off, so we retreated to our ridge to try to relocate it. It wasn't difficult; the moose was still sleeping peacefully in the exact same place where we'd left it. We had been close, but not close enough, and the wind in the leaves had obviously covered our approach. This time we took even more careful bearings, and I shot the moose when it got out of its bed at about ten yards.

Another time, in British Columbia's Kootenay region, we were plagued by a late, dry, and extremely warm fall. The moose just weren't moving, but from a distance we finally found a couple of bulls holed up in a huge aspen patch. Lloyd Harvey and I crept in there early in the morning, finding a slight rise that would give us a bit of visibility.

I used a lever action Model 88 in .358 Winchester to take this excellent Shiras moose in Wyoming. He was bedded, so I crawled up close and took a neck shot. He never moved from his bed.

Shortly after daylight a bull fed along a low ridge far out across the aspens. There was absolutely no way to approach it; once it stepped off the ridge it would be completely hidden, and in the tall and noisy quakies we'd have to be right on top of it to get a shot. So I set up over a log and, in those pre-rangefinder days, shot it at something over 350 yards. On that particular morning I was using a .340 Weatherby Magnum, I had a good rest, and the wind was calm—ideal circumstances for a long shot.

Longer shots may be necessary almost anywhere, but, in much of the country where moose are hunted, extremely close shots are actually the norm. In the heavy forests of Maine and eastern Canada, shots tend to be very close, and, anywhere moose are hunted, calling is a primary tactic during the rut. Like most animals, moose get extremely silly during the rut. Imitating a moose's low, resonant bellow is an extremely effective way to lure moose out of the thick stuff. Like all other types of calling, it will not work all the time, nor on all moose, but it does work. When a bull moose comes to the call, the game changes just a bit. As always, the shooting distance depends on terrain and vegetation, but a lovesick bull moose comes in charged with adrenaline and full of aggression. Under certain circumstances moose can be extremely dangerous. It would be unwise to ignore this fact.

TAKING THE SHOT

The moose is a huge animal, but I have never thought of it as particularly tough. Moose seem to have a slow nervous system that doesn't respond well to bullet shock, but they don't seem to travel very far after receiving a good hit. I've seen moose show absolutely no reaction to well-placed hits with powerful rifles. Instead of heading to the far horizon, however, they have generally walked or trotted a few more yards and then toppled over without additional fanfare. I don't think it's particularly hard to kill a moose, but it's extremely hard to drop one.

It can be extremely important to drop a moose. You know the adage: "The best place is between the ruts. Wheel ruts, that is." There are very few roads or tracks in moose country, but there are streams, ponds, bogs, lakes, and patches of extremely dense willow. The first rule in moose hunting is never to shoot a moose when it's in the water. It's better not to shoot it when it's chest-deep in heavy cover, but at least you can clear away the underbrush. If you have moose down in cold water, you have a nightmarish experience ahead of you. The obvious corollary to this is that no matter where your moose is standing, water and heavy cover are almost certainly nearby. In my entire life I have seen very few animals take a bullet and run to a place where recovery was made easier!

If you're a thinking hunter—and moose recovery is such a huge job that you'd better be thinking about it—you will shoot your moose while it's in an area that won't hinder field-dressing and recovery. And you'll try to keep it there.

At extremely close range a head or neck shot might be a good option. Both are extremely tricky shots, but moose are so large that a brain shot is unlikely to ruin the trophy. Either shot will certainly drop a moose in its tracks. Just remember that these are difficult shots; the brain is small, lying somewhere between the ears, and there is a great risk of hitting nothing but nasal passages, of which the moose has plenty.

The neck shot is easier to visualize; there's a lot of neck, but the spine stays pretty much in the middle for roughly the upper half of the neck. After that it gets trickier, with the spine dropping down and coming into the body cavity a bit lower than you might think.

When I had a Shiras moose tag in Wyoming in 2000, I crawled up within about sixty yards of a bedded bull. All I could see was the head and part of the neck, and I have such an ingrained distrust of the neck shot that I didn't really want to take the shot. I thought about it. The obvious alternative was to wait for the bull to stand, but we were in tight quarters, and I thought if the wind shifted slightly it might leap out of its bed and head for the nearby timber. I would have a shot, but it might be a going-away shot at a running moose. These are things you always have to weigh. I weighed them and took the neck shot, hitting the bull centrally in the neck about a foot behind the ear. It never got up.

Left to right: 1) 7mm Remington Magnum 2) .30-06 3) .300 Winchester Magnum. Although moose are huge animals, they aren't particularly tough. Versatile, all-round cartridges like these, when mated with heavy-for-caliber bullets that will penetrate, will do just fine if you place your shot with care.

The biggest target zone by far is the lung area, not much smaller than the average Dutch door. This is also the easiest shot to visualize. On a broadside presentation, just go up the rear line of the foreleg and shoot your moose right in the middle. It might be a bit better to shoot it slightly below the middle, but either way you have a dead moose. The problem is that this shot will not seem to impress your moose very much. Come to think of it, I've shot moose three or four times in the lungs with very powerful rifles before anything seemed to happen. All shots after the first were unnecessary—but how do you know?

Other than using brain or spine shots, which are tricky, it is very difficult to anchor a moose. The shoulder/heart shot, although it damages more good meat than a lung shot, will do a better job of dropping a moose quickly. Use the centerline of the foreleg, and come up into the bottom third of the body. That shot will break the shoulder and penetrate the heart or the major vessels leading to the heart—if you have enough gun and enough bullet. If you have a bit more, the bullet will keep going and will damage the opposite shoulder as well.

THE RIGHT MOOSE

Really good moose are scarce these days. There are more wolves than ever before. There is also more resident hunting pressure in many parts of both Alaska and Canada. Resident hunters think of the moose as an extremely important meat source, so the "right moose"

These are Winchester Fail Safe and Barnes X-Bullets recovered from game. Although not especially tough, moose are huge animals, so it's essential that the bullet be tough and designed to penetrate. This is the kind of performance you want on really large game.

is a legal animal that will provide tender meat and won't be too much of a nightmare to recover. Some nonresident hunters are also in search of good venison, God bless 'em; but most are looking for antlers.

Relying too heavily on spread alone is dangerous, but that measured is the best recognized. With Shiras moose and eastern moose, a "40-inch bull" is probably pretty good. In western Canada a bull from 50 to 55 inches is almost certainly shootable, and with Alaska-Yukon moose you need to look very hard at any bull from 55 inches upward. Just remember that, as is the case with all other antlered game, spread is just one criterion. Look at the presence or absence of brow palms, the width of the upper palms or "paddles," and the number of points. Then make your decision based on the appearance of the entire rack, not just some preset spread criterion that you feel you must achieve.

GUNS AND LOADS

Moose are not hard to kill, but they're incredibly hard to put down quickly, and within broad limits I'm not sure really big guns make a difference. I've seen moose taken cleanly, but not quickly, with .270s and .280s. I've personally taken moose very cleanly but no more quickly with .375s and .416s. This is probably the range of cartridges that will work. To my thinking the sheer size of the animal suggests that our common deer cartridges from .270- to .30-caliber are on the light side. Although a moose can weigh as much as a Cape buffalo, I'm also quite certain that you don't need dangerous-game cartridges like .375s and .416s. They certainly work, but the moose is so casual about bullet shock that the big guns won't impress it as much as you think.

My own best results have come with medium-bores. The proper choice depends on whether you expect to take a longer shot. I have used the little .358 Winchester with excellent results, and I absolutely upended a very big Alaskan bull with a .35 Whelen in one of the most spectacular one-shot kills of my entire career. In more open country, faster, flatter-shooting cartridges like the 8mm Remington Magnum and the fast .33s are probably better choices. Mind you, moose are moose, and the immediate results of your perfect shot may not be spectacular. That relatively small Shiras moose I shot on the aspen ridge in British Columbia was typical. I was sure of the hold, and I shot it three times. Each time I could hear the bullet hit, but I never saw a reaction to the shot, and the bull simply walked off the ridge. That's where we found it, stone dead with the three bullet holes grouped within about six inches on its shoulder. No matter what you are shooting, this is not unusual with moose.

BULLET PERFORMANCE

Choice of bullet is actually much more important than choice of cartridge. You simply must get the bullet into the vitals, and this means you have a lot of moose to penetrate to get there. I like heavy-for-caliber bullets, and I almost always use 220-grain bullets in my 8mm and 250-grain bullets in my .33s and .35s. With heavy-for-caliber bullets like these, the construction of the bullet isn't quite as critical. My 8mm likes Sierra bullets, and with 220 grains to play with they are tough enough. My .358 likes 250-grain Speers, and with that weight and the cartridge's mild velocity the Speer is plenty tough enough. But in general you should choose bullets no less tough than a Nosler Partition. If you are hunting moose with lighter calibers, then choice of bullet becomes even more important. If you're using cartridges from .270- to .30-caliber, it's especially important to think about heavy-for-caliber, controlled-expansion bullets like the Nosler Partition, Swift A-Frame, Barnes X-Bullet, and Winchester Fail Safe. No matter what you're shooting, you must have penetration, and ultimately it is the bullet, never the cartridge, that will give it to you.

CARIBOU

Take him when you see him!

Caribou hunting is a bit different from hunting most other North American big game. Our caribou, *Rangifer tarandus*, are primarily creatures of the northern tundra. They exist, primarily in regional herds, from the northern edges of the forests all the way up to barren islands well north of the Arctic Circle. Come to think of it, their range extends to Greenland, then across northern Europe all the way to Siberia, because our caribou and the reindeer of northern Europe and Asia are slightly different varieties of the same species. All told, there are millions of caribou. Some famous herds like Quebec's Leaf River herd and Alaska's Mulchatna herd number hundreds of thousands.

With this many caribou it might seem that this is an easy animal to hunt. Indeed, caribou hunting can be an extremely simple matter—if the caribou are where you are looking for them. Even though the animals are numerous, the northern lands where they live are incredibly vast. Caribou are strongly migratory, constantly moving from summer range to winter range and back again in an endless cycle as they literally vacuum the lichen from the tundra. Although we know the general migration routes of the major herds, it's an imperfect cycle.

Either cold weather or warm weather can accelerate or retard migration. Human activity, such as mineral or energy development, can cause major shifts in the migration route. A classic example is the Trans-Alaska Pipeline, which cut across the traditional migration route of Alaska's porcupine herd. Also, the migration route naturally shifts over time, as do herd dynamics. The lichen that provides the caribou's primary food is, like almost all Arctic perennials, an extremely slow-growing plant, requiring as long as twenty-five years to mature. The tundra is vast—but so is a herd of several hundred thousand caribou. As the lichen is depleted along a given "axis of advance," to use the military term, the migration route shifts. Sometimes, over a surprisingly short period, the herd numbers plummet, as smaller groupings break off and establish fresh herds in new country.

This boom-and-bust cycle is the natural order of things for many species, but with modern management, agriculture, and developed water sources, we have stopped or at least altered the cycle of many southern species. Caribou still live in wild country that is largely unaltered by the hand of man, so in many northern regions their cycle continues unbroken. For instance, Quebec's well-known George River herd has decreased dramatically during the past decade, and it is believed that the burgeoning Leaf River herd to the west is essentially an offshoot. The new world-record Alaska-Yukon barren ground caribou, taken recently by West Virginian Dan Dobbs, came not from the Mulchatna herd but from a smaller, breakaway group a bit farther south.

The good news is that, except for extremely unusual weather conditions, caribou patterns and dynamics change relatively slowly, and those patterns are known. Also, the caribou migration isn't a single mad rush but a slow and steady advance across a broad front. When the migration is at its peak, a major herd may take several weeks to pass through, and there will be a slower trickle of caribou in the lead, in the rear, and on the flanks. So, with proper planning, there should be at least some caribou, even if you don't quite catch the migration. If you really miss it, whether due to poor planning, a sudden shift, or unusual weather conditions, there isn't much you can do about it except enjoy the scenery and maybe get in some good fishing!

This is not about gloom and doom. Caribou hunting is extremely successful—on average, more successful than almost any other North American hunting—because of the number of animals, the fact that caribou are extremely visible in their wide-open country, and the general knowledge of their movement patterns. Just being in good country and hunting hard may not be enough, however. If there are caribou around, you will probably be successful, but if they just aren't present, there isn't much you can do about it!

Caribou hunting is a game of endless glassing, either while moving from one vantage point to another or while waiting at a known crossing. Even though the country is huge, once caribou are spotted, a stalk within reasonable range is usually possible.

Fortunately, this hasn't happened to me very often, and it shouldn't happen if you do your homework carefully and plan your trip around recent movement. Clear back in the mid-'70s, when the pipeline was going through, I was briefly stationed in Alaska. A buddy and I tried to hunt caribou, and, on the rumor of animals coming through, we drove up through Tok Junction and took the gravel road toward Eagle, on the Yukon River. We knew the location of the caribou, but they were still fifty miles out in the middle of nowhere, and we had no way to reach them. Another time, on my first hunt to Quebec around 1984, the George River herd executed a major shift in its migration route. For several days we hunted mostly empty tundra—but, as is often the case, even where there are no caribou, there are still a few around. By covering lots of ground, those of us who hunted hard eventually took bulls. Those of us who chose to stay in camp and play cards didn't. You have to try even if the odds seem slim, but it's an entirely different experience if you have the good fortune to be there when the caribou are really coming through.

I haven't hit it exactly right very often, but there are degrees of "being right." A number of years ago, when Northwest Territories first opened hunting on the barrens for what became the central Canada barren ground caribou, I hit it exactly right. Groups of caribou marched across the horizon all day long. It was one of nature's great spectacles, and I will never forget it.

A perfect situation! The herd is feeding past, and it's just a matter of picking the right bull. The trick is to know him when you see him, because once a caribou herd has moved through, it can be almost impossible to catch up with them.

Another time, hunting the Leaf River herd in northern Quebec, Randy Brooks of Barnes Bullets and I hunted the last week in the season. By now the big numbers of caribou had already passed through, and we didn't see many. Often some of the bigger bulls trail a caribou herd, and by being persistent and watching crossings that were usually empty we both took very good bulls.

At the beginning of September 2001, I hunted Quebec's Leaf River herd yet again. At the beginning of the hunt there were a few caribou around, not really migrating but sort of percolating through the area. I know this because we saw the same bulls on different days and at different points of the compass from camp. There were enough caribou to hunt; I took a reasonable bull, and some of the guys filled both tags. This proved a mistake, because on the fourth night the wind changed, and in the morning we awoke to a full migration, with literally hundreds of "new" caribou appearing on the far horizon. During our last couple of days, those of us with tags remaining had our pick of very good bulls.

The caribou generally weighs as much as a mid-sized deer. A bull's body weight ranges from 275 pounds—about the size of an average mature mule deer—up to as much as 600 pounds (though this is rare) in areas where feed is exceptionally good. For record-keeping purposes we have divided our caribou into regional groupings, loosely based on average antler size. Biologically, the woodland caribou (*Rangifer tarandus caribou*) extends along the forest fringes from Newfoundland all the way to British Columbia and southern Yukon. All the record-keeping organizations have subdivided this caribou into three categories: the woodland caribou of Newfoundland and south-central Canada; the larger-antlered Quebec-Labrador caribou of northern Quebec and Labrador; and the mountain caribou of northern British Columbia, southern Yukon, and the Mackenzie district of Northwest Territories.

The Alaska-Yukon barren ground caribou of Northwest Territories' barrens are actually a unique, slightly smaller subspecies (*Rangifer tarandus groenlandicus*), and they are separated as central Canada barren ground caribou. To the west, the largest-antlered caribou of Alaska and northern Yukon are also a distinct subspecies, *Rangifer tarandus granti*, what we hunters call "barren ground caribou." To the north, on the Arctic Islands, there are a few small herds of the pure, very pale Peary caribou, but most Arctic Island herds are a genetic mixture of Peary caribou and caribou from the mainland. Recognizing this, Safari Club International now recognizes these small-bodied, small-antlered caribou as Arctic Islands caribou.

SHOTS AT CARIBOU

The hunting of all of these caribou is actually very similar. This business of hunting "resident caribou" is generally a misnomer. All caribou migrate from summer to winter range; it's just a matter of degree. The northern herds may migrate hundreds of miles, while mountain and woodland caribou may migrate just a few miles, from summer range in high valleys and plateaus to winter range in lower country. Given that caribou country is almost always roadless and is usually some combination of boggy, soggy, steep, and rough, if the caribou you wish to hunt are "hung up" just ten miles away, in many cases it may as well be a thousand miles! So you have to hunt caribou where they are, in the hope that your location and their location coincide.

It's a glassing hunt, requiring good optics and generally fast decisions. When you see the right caribou, you must move on it, make sure of it, and then take the shot as quickly as you are able. Caribou are usually on the move, and they move much better in their country than you possibly can.

This is not universal; a bull or group of bulls may hang up in a certain area for a day or two, or they may pass through an area, then reverse and come right back through if the wind changes. Like most ungulates, they often bed through the warmer part of the day, and if you find a bedded bull, you may have several hours to stalk it. But most caribou that you glass will be moving, and if they're really on the move a human cannot stay with them. So you hunt caribou from the front, not from the rear. You must make your decision before caribou pass your location, and if you see one that looks good, you'd better hustle.

A couple of years ago in the Yukon, my guide and I were watching a known crossing from several miles away. Several bulls came through, and one of them looked too good to pass. They seemed headed toward a valley about a mile to our right, and I thought we had all day to work toward them. My guide knew better, and he hustled. Though we were on horseback, the caribou were already past us by the time we came in range! I got the bull with a two-hundred-yard shot, but in another two

I took this caribou with a single 140-grain Hornady from a .260 Remington. The power is adequate, but the wind-bucking ability of such light cartridges is a handicap. At just 200 yards, I had to hold ten inches into the strong crosswind!

minutes they would have gone into some rough country where the horses couldn't go, and we wouldn't have caught them.

Despite the extremely open country, it usually isn't that difficult to get within reasonable shooting range of caribou. Caribou are not particularly wary of man, so an approach within two hundred yards is generally practical. Long shooting is possible but rarely essential. Exceptions might include really great bulls that have already passed you or that you can't approach directly because there are obstacles in the terrain or other caribou are in the way. I have hunted caribou in Newfoundland, Quebec, Northwest Territories, Yukon, British Columbia, and Alaska. I don't recall ever shooting at a caribou at genuinely long range, and I'm not even sure I've shot at one past three hundred yards. I have taken most of my caribou between one hundred and two hundred yards.

TAKING THE SHOT

The average caribou is not much larger than the average deer. Woodland caribou and mountain caribou tend to be bigger and blockier in the body, and there are a few special cases, such as the caribou introduced on Adak Island in the Aleutian chain. In the absence of predators and parasites, these caribou are giants, sometimes weighing more than seven hundred pounds.

The angle for a shot is perfect, and a heart or lung shot is ideal in this case as either would minimize meat damage. (Photo courtesy of Leonard Lee Rue III)

Caribou

Regardless of size, the caribou is not a particularly hardy animal. Hit reasonably well, a caribou will generally not travel very far. However, this animal doesn't respond well to "bullet shock." I have seen many caribou exhibit absolutely no reaction to a well-placed and obviously fatal shot. For this reason one-shot kills are relatively uncommon.

American hunters have a bad habit of concentrating on placing that first shot, then waiting for it to take effect. An African professional hunter I know calls this "admiring the shot." On dangerous game it can be a fatal error, but on any game it's a bad idea because you're banking heavily on your first shot going where you think it did, and on your bullet performing as you think it should. Although we all like to brag about spectacular one-shot kills, I believe strongly in backing up the first shot if it doesn't immediately take effect. A well-hit caribou will not travel very far, but a poorly hit caribou can travel far and fast. You can't keep up with it, and the chances are slim that it will move into an area where you can recover it more easily and pack it a lesser distance.

I believe in hitting a caribou very hard, and if the effects aren't immediate, hit it again until it goes down. Because of its resistance to bullet shock, and because the recovery of caribou is generally a matter of packing the meat by hand, I also much prefer a shoulder shot that will break heavy bone

A picture-perfect shot. Any decent bullet from a medium-sized caliber will do for a caribou bull in this position. A shot at the top of the heart will do minimum meat damage and ensure a quick death. (Photo courtesy of Leonard Lee Rue III)

and anchor the animal as quickly as possible. The target isn't as large as it is on the behind-the-shoulder lung shot, but it's plenty large enough. On a broadside presentation, just follow the centerline of the foreleg one-third of the way up the body.

THE RIGHT CARIBOU

Caribou grow the largest antlers in relation to body size of any antlered game in the world. Unlike most deer, females also grow small, rudimentary racks. The problem for most beginning caribou hunters is that all caribou look big. This is especially true for hunters accustomed to much smaller-antlered game such as whitetails. It takes a bit of knowledge and extremely good optics to sort them out, because the caribou also has the most complex rack of any antlered game.

Most of us start by judging the overall size of the rack. In profile, the total rack should appear almost as tall as the animal is from ground to shoulder. Width varies a lot, but the rack should also appear well outside the body from both front and rear. After you've got such a caribou, you look at the various features. Most caribou have a big brow tine that we call a shovel. Optimally, the shovel should reach toward the end of the nose and should be fairly broad. Everybody wants a "double shovel," but two brow tines are fairly uncommon in many areas. A double shovel really isn't that important, and in most cases the second shovel, if present, will be weaker than the first. If you're serious about a record-book bull, however, note that it's very difficult to get a single-shovel bull into Boone and Crockett, regardless of the caribou's other attributes.

Then move up to the bez, a secondary point or palmated cluster of points about a quarter of the way up from the shovel. You want the bez to be long and, hopefully, multi-pointed, something like an outstretched hand. About halfway up the main beam, facing rearward, there may be back points. These are not present in all caribou, even in really good ones, so they are almost like bonus points. Really good, matching back points add a lot to the record-book score. Now take a look at the top points. These are important to the impressive appearance of a rack. Note, however, that most scoring systems (Boone and Crockett and Pope and Young) only measure the length of the two longest top points.

Beam length, mass, and inside spread are also important. In other words, there's a lot to look at on a caribou, and if the animals are moving, you must look quickly and make up your mind. It isn't easy, and it takes practice. No caribou, even the very best heads, "have it all" in equal proportion, so you must make trade-offs while you're looking. And of course we all like different things; I like top points, while others prefer double shovels. No two racks are alike,

The new Swift Scirocco bullet combines a bonded core (for weight retention) with a polymer tip (for better aerodynamics and to promote expansion). This kind of a bullet is absolutely ideal for caribou-sized game.

which is part of the fun in hunting any antlered game.

There are numerous record-book categories for caribou, but the differences among them are not that great. Woodland caribou have the smallest, most compact rack, usually with many points, but the tops tend to be weak and the beams are relatively short. Quebec-Labrador caribou are known for strong bez formations, and mountain caribou, at their best, have spectacular top points. Alaskan caribou are known for long beams that, typically, form a big C. If you took a record-class caribou from each category and put them on the wall side by side, very few people could correctly identify each of them. So pay attention to what constitutes a good caribou for the area you're hunting, and look carefully at each feature of the complex rack. When there are lots of caribou moving, sorting through them to find the bull that pleases you most is the real fun of caribou hunting!

GUNS AND LOADS

Caribou are neither particularly large nor particularly tough. The Inuit hunt them for meat with the rifles they have; the most popular calibers are .222 Remington, .30-30, and .303 British. This suggests that a .243 or .25-caliber would be perfectly adequate. It might be, if everything goes right, but trophy hunting is different from meat hunting. You want to take the best caribou you can find, and when you find it you want to be able to take it.

Two factors suggest that somewhat more power or flatter-shooting cartridges, or both, are appropriate. First, although long shots are usually not necessary, there is certainly the potential for them on the open tundra. Second, wind is almost always a factor. Fast cartridges from about .270 to .30-caliber buck the wind a whole lot better than slower cartridges, or even very fast cartridges of lesser caliber. Not too long ago I took a caribou with a .260 Remington, a very nice cartridge that is perfectly adequate for caribou-sized game. The shot was at two hundred yards, and the bullet entered just behind the on-shoulder, transited the chest, broke the off-shoulder, and exited. You can't ask for more, and the caribou went nowhere. The reason is that there was a very strong crosswind, and to place that relatively slow (2,750 fps muzzle velocity), 140-grain bullet in the right place, I held fully ten inches into the wind, even at a mere two hundred yards. Had I not properly estimated the wind drift, I would have hit the bull much too far back and might have had a very long day!

I think ideal caribou cartridges start with the .270 Winchester or a very fast 6.5mm (like the old .264 Winchester Magnum) and go up through the 7mms to the fast .30s. There is no reason to hunt caribou with a cartridge larger in caliber than .30. But if you're combining caribou with moose, grizzly bear, or brown bear, you might consider a flat-shooting medium-magnum like one of the .33s, from .338 Winchester Magnum up through the .338 and .348 Remington Ultra Mags and the .340 Weatherby Magnum.

BULLET PERFORMANCE

To my thinking, the caribou is just a bit on the large side for the really quick-opening bullets. On the other hand, you really don't need the deepest-penetrating designs like Barnes X-Bullet, Swift A-Frame, or Winchester Fail Safe. If these bullets give you the greatest confidence, there is nothing wrong with using them—they are certainly a good idea if you're combining caribou with tougher, larger game, such as bear or moose. But for pure caribou hunting, I like bullets that offer a combination of expansion and penetration. This means that the good old Nosler Partition is extremely hard to beat.

On my most recent caribou hunt, I used the new Swift Scirocco bullet, a polymer-tipped bullet that has a lead core chemically bonded to a relatively thick jacket. The polymer tip ensures expansion, while the bonded core and heavy jacket ensure weight retention—and the design has a high ballistic coefficient, ideal for longer shooting in windy country. The Scirocco is useful in a lot of hunting applications, but it's especially ideal for hunting open-country game that is a bit bigger than deer but not especially large or tough.

PRONGHORN ANTELOPE

The classic open-country game animal . . .

America's pronghorn antelope is a truly magnificent creature, perfectly adapted to the wide-open plains it calls home. It has fabulous eyesight—certainly the best among all North American game—and the eyes are its first line of defense, though not its most important asset. It is built for speed, with outsized lungs, feet cushioned to take the pounding, and seemingly spindly legs that have the tensile strength of a cow's legs.

The pronghorn is not actually an antelope, and in fact it has no particularly close relatives anywhere in the world. Its Latin name, *Antilocapra americana*, describes it as the "American antelope-goat," which is a pretty fair description. It looks like an antelope, but it has many characteristics common to the goat family. It also has features that belong to no other animal. Unlike antelope and goat, which have true horns that form around a bony core and continue to grow throughout the animal's life, the pronghorn sheds its headgear annually, leaving a daggerlike core around which the new horns form. These horns aren't of the same material as most horns. They are more like solidified hair, a pure protein material that is probably closer to rhinoceros horn than anything else now living on the planet. The coat is unusual, too. Its relatively thick, stiff, hollow hairs give pronghorn great insulation against the bitter prairie winters.

The pronghorn is a relatively small, dainty animal, with mature bucks rarely weighing much more than 120 pounds and standing about thirty-six inches at the shoulder. Most authorities identify five regional subspecies: *Antilocapra americana americanca*, the pronghorn found throughout most of the West; *Antilocapra americana oregona*, the pronghorn of southeastern Oregon; *Antilocapra americana mexicana*, from southeastern Arizona eastward to Texas and down into central Mexico; *Antilocapra americana sonoriensis*, west of mexicana; and *Antilocapra americana peninsularis*, originally from Southern California down into the Baja Peninsula. The latter two are considered endangered, but the differences between the subspecies are very subtle, and biologists have never fully agreed on where one subspecies stops and another starts. No record-keeping organization has ever attempted to differentiate the pronghorn subspecies.

Pronghorn occur naturally in the plains, valleys, and foothills from the Great Plains west to California, and from northern Mexico to southern Canada. At one time they existed in untold millions, almost certainly more numerous than even the bison, but by the early years of the twentieth century, some naturalists predicted total extinction. Fortunately, this didn't happen. Last-minute protection saved remnant herds, and the prolific pronghorn has come back strong.

The pronghorn needs relatively undisturbed prairie, so it doesn't do particularly well in areas with intensive agriculture. It is once again quite plentiful in ranch country and badlands throughout the West. Today all pronghorn hunting is by limited permit, mostly by drawing, but there are lots of opportunities. Wyoming probably has the most habitat and certainly has the largest population, but pronghorn are also plentiful in suitable habitat in Montana, Colorado, and New Mexico. There are also considerable populations, though much more localized, in Arizona, California, Oregon, Nevada, and Utah. Pronghorn are much less plentiful on the eastern and northern edges of their domain—west Texas; the high plains of western Kansas, Nebraska, and the Dakotas; and the prairies of southern Canada—but, depending on current game counts, all of these areas have open seasons and offer some permits.

The areas that produce the very best pronghorn trophies are extremely difficult to draw, which is the case with most animals that are hunted by permit draw. Arizona, for instance, is legendary for big pronghorn—and drawing a tag is almost as difficult as drawing a sheep tag. Though you may not always draw the tag you want, pronghorn tags aren't that hard to come by. Most areas in eastern Wyoming, eastern Montana, and eastern Colorado are fairly easy to draw to, and although they are more expensive, private

Pronghorn hunting is a classic game of glassing, preferably with good optics and from as far away as possible. The trick is to properly size up an undisturbed buck before starting an approach, and that usually means from at least a half-mile away.

land tags are available in New Mexico and a few other places.

The pronghorn was my first big-game animal, so I have a special fondness for hunting it—but I also find pronghorn uniquely democratic. You may not get a tag in a great area, but if you want to go pronghorn hunting, you can go. And if you go, you should be successful. With its buff-and-white body, black nose, and unique horns, the pronghorn is a striking animal—and it also stands out in its wide-open terrain. Despite its legendary eyesight and great speed, it is relatively easy to hunt. One factor is that it is visible at great distances; another is simply that, in most areas where pronghorn are hunted, the animals are quite common.

Unless a "guaranteed" private land tag in a good area is part of the deal, most outfitted hunts are fairly inexpensive—especially when compared with other western hunts. But it's also quite possible to hunt pronghorn just as successfully unguided. The latter is a practical option. It takes a bit more research to make absolutely certain you have a good place to hunt; some areas have plenty of public land, but a lot of the best pronghorn habitat is tied up in private ranches. In the West's big country, this doesn't mean you can't find a place to hunt, but it does mean you need to do your homework.

SHOTS AT PRONGHORN

There are several misconceptions about pronghorn hunting. One is that it requires long-range shooting. An even bigger misconception is this business about racing across the prairie in a vehicle, trying to get close enough to throw lead at these speedsters. I'll dispense with the latter first. Chasing pronghorn in a vehicle is not only unsporting, unethical, and usually illegal, it's also a terrible way to get a shot. The pronghorn antelope is thought to be the second-fastest creature in the animal kingdom. Only the cheetah is believed to be capable of greater speed—but the cheetah is short-winded, while the pronghorn can sustain speeds of more than forty miles per hour for extended distances. Yes, you can get close to them in a vehicle, provided you don't destroy your rig in the process, but then you have a running shot at an animal that's going like hell. Shot placement is impossible, judging horns almost equally so. All you do is spook a lot of pronghorn and waste a lot of shells.

It isn't necessary to try to run them down, and it usually isn't necessary to shoot at extreme range. Mind you, at first glance pronghorn country looks like a billiard table, and it's only natural for beginning pronghorn hunters to believe they must reach clear across its broad expanse. Sometimes you must; there are sagebrush flats that offer almost no cover—and with a bit of pressure, pronghorn tend to know they are safe in such places. But if you study the country carefully, it usually isn't all that flat and featureless. There are usually almost imperceptible little gullies and coulees and folds, and if you read the ground correctly and put in a bit of effort, it is usually possible to get pretty darned close.

Of course, "close" is a relative term that means different things with different game animals. Shots at pronghorn probably do average somewhat longer than shots at most game animals. Pronghorn hunting is a short, inexpensive, and extremely enjoyable hunt, conducted in pretty country at a time of year when the weather is usually glorious. Pronghorn is also my absolute favorite wild meat. So I have hunted them a great deal, almost every year since the mid-1960s, and sometimes in more than one state in a given fall. When I was a kid I used to think it was necessary to try the long shots. I missed quite a few, also thinking that was par for the course. In the past twenty years or so, I doubt that my average shot at a pronghorn has exceeded two hundred yards. For hunters accustomed to close shots at whitetail in thick cover, a two-hundred-yard shot at a smaller animal in unfamiliar, wide-open country can seem like a very long poke. Though much current literature suggests that quarter-mile shots are necessary, the two-hundred-yard shot is a whole lot different and much more practical.

You can readily see pronghorn way out there at the very edge of practical shooting distance—and if they haven't been disturbed, they probably won't spook. So the first principle is to recognize that you really need to get a bit closer in order to be sure. The second principle lies in recognizing that you usually can get closer; it's just a matter of figuring out how.

Most of the time the ground isn't quite as flat as it looks. Most of the prairie is cut by shallow drainages and low ridges, and much sagebrush is tall enough to offer some cover. It doesn't take much relief to hide a pronghorn—nor does it take much to hide you from their sharp eyes. With pronghorn hunting, the whole idea is to use good optics to judge the horns from as

Although pronghorn country appears very open, there are usually hidden folds and cuts that will allow an approach to a reasonable range. With pronghorn, this means something like 200 to 350 yards, not close but not genuinely long range.

far away as possible. Once you find one that looks good enough or is worth a closer look, you need to find a way to drop out of sight—and not reappear until you're within good, sure shooting range, whatever that means to you. You should try to keep the wind in your favor, but this is small change compared to the need to stay out of sight.

Sometimes you can use hills and ridges to make a circle, but most likely you will eventually have to start crawling. This is backbreaking work, and the stuff is prickly. In warm weather you need to keep an eye out for rattlesnakes, and in any weather little prairie cacti will bedevil your hands and knees. Thick leather gloves are a must, and a lot of serious pronghorn hunters use knee and elbow pads. Maybe I have a masochistic streak, but crawling within certain range of a chosen buck is, to me, the real fun of pronghorn hunting! It means beating these sharp-eyed creatures at their own game in their own country, and it's a wonderfully satisfying experience.

Sometimes you can get very close. Dwight van Brunt (then of Burris) and I were hunting on the Gros Ventres Indian Reservation in Montana a few years ago, a place where, at that time, two pronghorns were allowed. For my second buck I borrowed Dwight's XP-100 pistol, chambered to 7mm-08 Remington. I shoot the specialty pistols a bit, and I knew a long shot was out, but I figured I was OK out to two hundred yards or so. We glassed a nice buck working its way from an open flat toward

Guide Fred Lamphere and I are entirely happy with this very good Montana pronghorn, one of my best. We simply couldn't get close to this buck, and he was taken at a bit more than 450 yards. The rifle is a Rifles, Inc., .300 Weatherby, so I was ready for such a shot.

My very best pronghorn was taken in west Texas with my David Miller 7mm Remington Magnum at something less than 250 yards. You don't really need quite this much power, but the fast 7mms are always good choices in open country.

a system of ridges, so we got ourselves in front of the buck, thinking it would walk through a little saddle maybe 150 yards away. The pronghorn thought differently. We hadn't seen it for quite a while, and then it materialized out of a little cut less than forty yards away, heading straight toward us. I shot it at about twenty-five yards, little more than a blur of white and tan through the pistol scope's narrow field.

Not all stalks work. Sometimes you wind up spooking the animal, or you can easily misread the situation and run out of cover before you get as close as you need to get. That doesn't necessarily mean the game is over, although it might be over for that particular day. Pronghorn country looks much the same to you and to me, but it doesn't look the same to the animals. They are surprisingly territorial, which offers two opportunities. Unless spooked quite badly, a pronghorn buck will usually be reluctant to leave its home ground. It probably won't run that far, which means that you can let it run out of sight and then follow.

My very best pronghorn, a west Texas head, came up out of a draw and crossed a ranch road in front of our vehicle. It was obviously big and obviously spooked—but it had slowed down quite a bit by the time it crossed a ridge about six hundred yards away. As soon as it was out of sight, I jumped out of the truck and headed for the ridge at a jog, fully expecting to find it feeding somewhere in the valley beyond.

I slowed down when I got to the top of the ridge, crossed the top carefully some distance away from where I'd last seen the buck, and got below the skyline on the far side. I almost blew it, because this buck was doing the unexpected: It was coming back my way, working back up the valley, almost certainly intending to get back to its own country. I was badly pinned down behind a tall yucca, so I let it come, got into position when it was behind some brush, and shot it from a sitting position at just over two hundred yards.

When you've spooked a pronghorn, it isn't always practical or smart to follow it up; this depends on the terrain it's gone into. But that doesn't mean the hunt is over. If you leave the pronghorn alone, there is a very good chance it will come right back to the place where you first saw it—if not later the same day, then almost certainly by the next day. This doesn't necessarily mean exactly the same place, but it does mean the same general area. That's why scouting for pronghorn a day or two before the season is so effective, especially in areas that have very short seasons and/or a lot of hunting pressure. Pronghorn are as habitual as they are territorial; unless they are seriously disturbed, usually you will find them not only in the same general areas, but also doing the same things in the same places at the same time of day. If you find a good buck watering at one o'clock on the day before opening day, chances are it will be at that watering hole between twelve and two unless another hunter waylays it. Pronghorn also tend to cross fences in exactly the same place. By the way, it is not true that pronghorn can't jump fences. I've seen them do it. It is true they prefer to go under or through a fence, and their crossings are usually well marked with trails and scraped hair.

Sometimes a long shot is the only option you've got. A couple of years ago, hunting with Leica's Terry Moore, gunmaker Lex Webernick, and guide Fred Lamphere, we found a really good pronghorn way out on a sagebrush flat. That darned flat was almost in perfect position. On the west side was a range of low hills that offered perfect cover right to the edge. On the east side was a winding, cottonwood-lined streambed, so getting to that side of the flat was a simple matter of a pleasant stroll along the cottonwoods. The problem was that the flat was about twelve hundred yards wide, and the buck and its herd tended to stay right in the middle, too long a shot from either side.

We stalked them from the hills, and we stalked them along the creek; either way, they just drifted out into the middle. We tried to surround them, but that didn't work either. Somebody—I can't remember who—tried a fairly long shot and failed, and for reasons I also can't remember that made it my turn. The next day they were right back on the flat, but they seemed to be quite close to a fence line not far from the creek.

Fred and I strolled to the cottonwoods, crossed the creek, and then crawled out to the fence line without spooking the herd. At this point "close" became a relative matter; through my Leica rangefinder the buck was 454 yards away. I was using an extremely accurate .300 Weatherby Magnum that day, so I had plenty of gun, and I knew the range and the hold. I got the buck—and I'm pretty sure that's the longest shot I've attempted on a pronghorn in at least thirty-five years!

TAKING THE SHOT

The pronghorn is not a large animal. In fact, when you walk up on your first buck, you'll probably be surprised at its actual size; its thick hair combines with its bright color to make it look much bigger than it really is. That said, pronghorn must not be underestimated. They are extremely tough for their size, and if they're hit poorly—taking a leg wound or a paunch shot, for example—they seem to be inclined to just keep going for as long as they are able.

This doesn't suggest that you need lots of power. That isn't the issue at all. On an animal the size of a pronghorn, I doubt if there's much difference between a bad hit with a .243 and a bad hit with a .300 magnum. The point is that a bad hit on a pronghorn can result in an extremely long day and, very likely, a lost animal. So pronghorn must be hit well, regardless of your choice of caliber.

The skin of a pronghorn is paper thin and extremely fragile. Also, you have the problem associated with all light-colored animals—the cape is easily stained and hard to fix. So, if you're thinking of saving a buck to have it mounted, a head or neck shot is out of the question.

Many disagree, but to me pronghorn is among the very best wild meat, provided you take proper care of it. This means skinning and cooling it as quickly as possible, and boning the meat to get it away from the strong marrow. If you handle it promptly and well, it's wonderful stuff.

For all these reasons I prefer lung shots on pronghorn. The pronghorn has outsized lungs, so the target area (or, rather, the margin for error) is proportionately larger than on most animals. The shot is absolutely deadly—but, at least from a broadside angle, it damages the skin behind the part needed for a shoulder mount. Finally, the lung shot damages very little edible meat. Placement is standard: On a broadside presentation, follow the back line of the rear leg up into the body, and shoot just a bit below the horizontal midpoint.

THE RIGHT BUCK

Pronghorn aren't particularly easy to judge. Their jet-black horns tend to look bigger than they really are, especially when the animal is running and most of all from a going-away angle. The best way to view pronghorn is from a distance with good optics, so you can evaluate them dispassionately and unhurriedly. Pronghorn enter the record books based on a combination of horn length (on the outer curve), prong length (from the back of the horn to tip of prong), and circumference (four circumferences—at the base and at the three-quarters). A long prong is fairly obvious, as are exceptionally long horns, but circumference is very hard to judge unless it's really dramatic (as is the case with all game).

The ears are about six inches long, and a normal pronghorn buck will have horns about twelve inches long, or double the length of the ears. The hard part is that much of the actual length measurement comes from the downward hook at the tip of the horns, not from the height. So any pronghorn that appears to rise up double the ears (or more) is worth a second look—but if it doesn't have tips that hook around and back down, it's probably not as long as you think it is. People talk about 16- and 17-inch pronghorn, and they exist, but I have never shot one; and since I've never put a tape on

When the front leg of any animal is fully extended backward as in this picture, it is easy to make the mistake of shooting a little too far back. Mentally keep the whole picture of the chest cavity in mind, and remember that the entire heart and much of the lungs lie in front of the leg bone in this position. (Photo courtesy of Leonard Lee Rue III)

one, I can't say for sure I've ever seen one. In most areas a genuine 14-inch pronghorn is pretty darned good, and a 15-inch pronghorn is exceptional. Then the other factors come into play: A 15-inch pronghorn with good mass and long prongs will make Boone and Crockett; a spindly 17-incher with short prongs may not.

Keep in mind that pronghorn populations are extremely subject to the vagaries of winter, and, since they grow new horns each year, springtime weather also matters. Not all areas are capable of producing really big pronghorn, even under the best of conditions. The best areas will be better in some years and not so good in others. The best course is to look around and consider what kind of bucks you're seeing. In my experience there will usually be lots of bucks of average size—sometimes twelve inches, sometimes thirteen inches, rarely fourteen inches. Whatever that "house number" happens to be, there will usually be a few bucks a bit bigger than the average, and those are the ones you're looking for.

GUNS AND LOADS

The primary consideration in a pronghorn rifle is accuracy. Your rifle should be well scoped, it should group well, and you should have absolute confidence in it. Flat-shooting capability is secondary, but you do need it. From the standpoint of the size of the animal, a .243 or fast .25 (.25-06, .257 Weatherby Magnum, et cetera) would be ideal, if you

The heart shot may also break the shoulder bone when the leg is extended back like this. The lower dot indicates the heart shot, while the upper dot indicates the lung shot. (Photo courtesy of Leonard Lee Rue III)

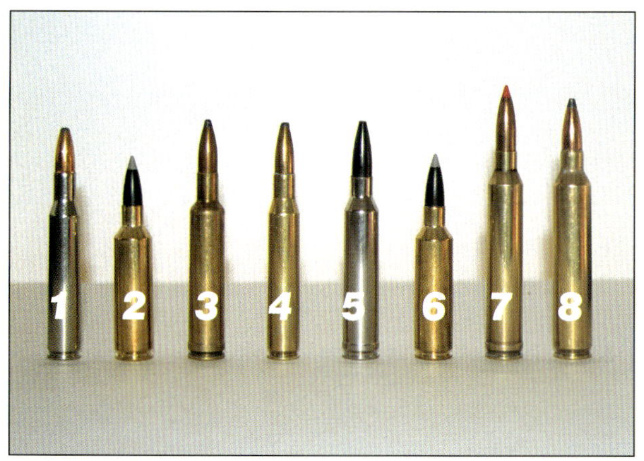

Left to right: 1) .270 Winchester 2) .270 Winchester Short Magnum 3) .270 Weatherby Magnum 4) .280 Remington 5) 7mm Remington Magnum 6) 7mm Winchester Short Magnum 7) 7mm STW 8) 7mm Remington Ultra Mag. With cartridges like these you are ready for any reasonable shot at a pronghorn. The larger magnums aren't really required, but you never know when the buck of a lifetime may be standing at long range on a wide-open flat.

aren't especially concerned about trophy dimensions and you have no interest in attempting genuinely long shots. The problem with the smaller calibers is that, regardless of how fast, wind impacts light bullets more than it does heavier bullets. Pronghorn country is always windy! In years gone by I have rated the .25-06 as the most perfect pronghorn cartridge. I no longer think it is, because I recently saw two very good riflemen wound pronghorns between three hundred and four hundred yards, one with a .25-06, the other with a wildcat .257 STW—and then have trouble finishing the job because the wind was blowing the bullets too much.

Based on these experiences, I think the very best pronghorn cartridges—for all ranges and all conditions—are the fast 6.5mm, .270, and 7mm cartridges. This includes cartridges ranging from the almost-obsolete .264 Winchester Magnum through the .270 Winchester, new .270 Winchester Short Magnum, and .270 Weatherby Magnum, and on up to the many magnum 7mms, including the red-hot 7mm Remington Ultra Mag. Obviously, the .30-calibers will work, and no lesser-caliber bucks the wind better than an aerodynamic .30-caliber. But I can't bring myself to say that you really need a .30-caliber for a 120-pound pronghorn, so I won't!

BULLET PERFORMANCE

Pronghorn are small and fairly fragile animals, provided you hit them in the right place. I prefer bullets that will open up fairly quickly, but let's not overdo it. Extremely frangible bullets can really make a mess of a pronghorn, and that is absolutely unnecessary. The point is to hit pronghorn in the right place, and if you do that with any big-game weight bullet from 6mm on up, you should have your pronghorn!

THE BLACK BEAR

Don't underestimate him!

The black bear, *Ursus americanus*, is one of America's most widespread big-game animals. It is found discontinuously from Southern California to Newfoundland and from Florida to Alaska. Although the black bear is primarily a creature of the forests, it is an extremely adaptable creature, as its huge range suggests. The black bear is found in the southern swamps, the northern hardwood forests, well out into the tundra of Canada and Alaska, the rain forests of the Pacific Northwest, and throughout virtually every mountain range from Mexico to Canada. This last includes the arid mountains of the Southwest.

The excesses of our pioneering era greatly depleted our American game, especially in the more developed regions, and so it was with the black bear. Many populations are still rebuilding, particularly in the eastern United States. It's hard to say exactly where black bear cannot survive, but at this writing the only habitat types that black bear don't inhabit are open plains and true deserts. In most cases they're nearby. In the Great Plains you don't find black bear in the open grasslands, but you find them in appropriate habitat nearby, such as the Black Hills. You also don't find black bear on the sunbaked floor of any desert—but look around in the surrounding mountains, and if there's sufficient water, there will probably be bear.

Biologists have attempted to identify numerous races, subspecies, and regional groupings of black bear. These are generally based on such subtle differences that hunters seldom find them useful. Coast to coast, and in all record-keeping systems, there is just one black bear. Not all black bear are black, however. There are many color phases; the most common variations are some shade of brown. The "brown black bear" ranges from blond to very red, but dark brown is the most common. Color phases do follow regional patterns. Most of the bear in the East are black, often with a white patch on the brisket. Bear in the Pacific Northwest are usually black, but along the Rocky Mountains brown bear are quite common—in some areas more common than black bear.

There are also a couple of localized rarities. The "glacier bear" or "blue bear" is an extremely unusual color phase of the black bear, with varying degrees of white hair in the coat. At a distance this gives the bear a very blue appearance. The glacier bear is known to occur only in southeast Alaska, generally in the Yakutat area. Once considered a separate bear, it is now known to be just a color phase, but it is an especially beautiful, rare, and highly sought trophy. Rarer still is the Kermode bear, the "white black bear." Known to occur only in British Columbia's Queen Charlotte Islands, the Kermode bear is ghostly white, but it has black eyes and dark claws, so is not an albino. This color phase is completely protected; the only one taken in recent years was shot on a museum permit by my uncle, Art Popham, about forty years ago. It is on view in a diorama at the Kansas City Museum of Natural History.

On one hunt in the Yakutat area with Jim Keeline, I saw three glacier bears, a huge number. One was a smallish bear, maybe 2½ years old, and except for dark legs and head it looked blue all over. Another was a gorgeous silver-streaked sow. The third was a very big and very old bear. In shadows it appeared black, but when it walked into the sunlight it turned a strange midnight blue.

These three unusual bear demonstrate several principles that generally hold true with all the color phases. First, the lighter-colored bear are generally small and young, so very big blond bear are rare. The beautiful light reddish-brown "cinnamon bear" are usually not the biggest bear, and the really silvery glacier bear are also usually small. Second, brown sows can have black cubs, and vice versa. The glacier bear sow I saw had two small cubs that were coal black. The color of the cubs depends on the genes carried by the sow and boar. The colors must be in the local gene pool in order to occur at all, and black is probably dominant in most areas. Finally, bear do change color as they mature. Usually the shift is from light to dark.

The average black bear isn't a large animal, but a really big bear is a different matter—and you can run into a monster almost anywhere. This North Carolina bear weighed 480 pounds on good scales. The rifle is an 8mm Remington Magnum, enough gun for any bear, at any sensible range.

I shot that big midnight-blue bear, certain I had found a monstrous glacier bear. It died in a thick patch of cover, and when guide Jack Ringus and I approached it, I was crestfallen. It was big, but it looked like—well, like a black bear. Then the sun came out and it turned blue. We looked carefully, and its generally black fur had an underlayer of white hairs on shoulders, flank, and hips. In sunlight it appeared blue, but in shadow the black completely overpowered the white underlayer. This was an old bear, and one might theorize that, in its younger days, it was very gray. A glacier bear in the Anchorage Zoo was much the same; it started out gray-blue but was very dark as an old bear.

Color phases don't vary in all areas; body size does. Body size depends largely on food, genetics, and the opportunity to mature and reach maximum size. Remote areas like Newfoundland and Vancouver Island are known to produce numbers of very large black bear—but so are strange places like Arizona's San Carlos Reservation, western Pennsylvania, and North Carolina's Lake Mattamuskeet area. In the latter three areas it is almost certainly a combination of good food and limited hunting pressure that allows bear to reach maximum size. This suggests that a really big black bear could occur almost anywhere bear are found, and I believe this to be true.

And that's one of the big problems with hunting black bear. The average black bear

Hound hunting is different from other techniques; you know going in that you'll have to scramble over rough ground to get to the tree. The shot will be at very close range, but it must *be almost immediately fatal in order to avoid danger to the hounds.*

is not a large animal. Body weight of about two hundred pounds is normal for a grown-up black bear almost anywhere, especially in the spring when the bear have just come out of hibernation and body fat is depleted. This doesn't mean the black bear should be taken lightly; I know three experienced black bear guides who were severely mauled by "small" black bear in this class. However, black bear do get bigger—a lot bigger.

I am extremely excited by all bear hunting. Black bear hunting is extremely available and affordable, and I've done a lot of it. In the field I have had few opportunities to weigh the bear I've taken, but I have taken several bear that I'm sure had honest weights over four hundred pounds and a couple that were considerably larger.

In North Carolina I hunted with some friends who have a large farm in prime bear country. They went to extreme lengths to recover all the bear taken and bring them to the local biologist, who was all set up to weigh the bear and take blood and tissue samples. My own bear was a dandy, with actual weight of 460 pounds—possibly the largest black bear I have ever taken, but I don't think so. While I was there, David Blalock shot a monster that, on official scales, weighed well over six hundred pounds—bigger and heavier in all ways than most grizzlies. That is clearly an exceptional black bear—but even that isn't as big as they get. Weights over eight hundred pounds have been recorded. I submit that such a creature is an altogether different animal from the average two-hundred-pound bear—certainly in terms of the care with which you must shoot it and what you should shoot it with!

Bear have especially keen ears and noses but limited visibility. If a bear gets your scent, the hunt is over, but if the wind is right and you are quiet, bear are extremely "stalkable," even if you don't have a completely covered approach. Mind you, they are not blind. It's always better to stay out of sight, but if you stay off the skyline and move slowly, you can approach a bear within fairly short rifle range. Bow range is more difficult, but even that is much more possible than with any horned or antlered game.

SHOTS AT BLACK BEAR

The kind of shot you get depends on the hunting technique you are using. There are three primary options, and they vary depending on the country and also on the local tradition. Perhaps the oldest technique is bear hunting with hounds. This was the way Daniel Boone and Davy Crockett hunted their bear, but hound hunting has come under heavy fire from anti-hunters who call it "unsporting" and has been outlawed in many areas. This is not the forum for discussion of hunting politics, but I should mention that hound hunting is the most selective of all bear-hunting techniques. Bear are very hard to judge, but in hound hunting you have two exceptional opportunities. The first occurs when you find the track. If it isn't a big track, or if tracks of cubs are in evidence, go look for another track. The second occurs at the tree. You will almost always get a close-range look at your bear, and there is absolutely no reason to make a mistake or to shoot a bear you aren't happy with.

In hound hunting the range will be very short, sometimes a matter of feet but rarely more than a few yards. Hound hunting is a business of following the music of the pack, keeping up with the chase no matter how rough or thick the country, and then getting to the tree before the bear gets a second wind and starts the chase all over again. The shooting will be very simple and somewhat anticlimactic . . . provided you do it right. If you don't, then you have a wounded and enraged bear on the ground at close range, an immediately dangerous situation for your canine hunting companions and potentially hazardous for yourself as well.

Baiting is another traditional hunting method, generally practiced in thickly forested areas where visibility is limited. Baiting has also been outlawed in some areas, but doesn't seem to be as politically incorrect as hound hunting. It is extremely effective: The key to a bear's heart is usually through its stomach. In the spring, after a long winter's nap, bear are ravenous and will bait readily. The fall is less reliable, but as the bear try to pick up body fat in preparation for winter they can definitely be baited. It isn't quite as easy as it sounds; consistently baiting trophy-class bears is almost an art form. Every old bear hunter has his favorite bait. Some use meat, some use fish, and some use sweets like stale donuts or a homemade molasses brew. I'm not sure the actual bait matters so much, but exactly where the bait is sited and how the blind is set up matter a great deal. Over a bait the location of the blind absolutely controls the shot. Bow hunters usually site a tree stand no more than thirty yards away. This is really too close, not only because of scent but because any movement at all is likely to spoil the show. Most rifle hunters

I used a Winchester M70 in the brand-new .300 Winchester Short Magnum to take this big Vancouver Island bear. A fast .30-caliber with a good 180-grain bullet will handle any black bear, any place, anytime—but I believe somewhat slower cartridges with heavier, flatter-nose bullets will put them down more quickly.

The Black Bear

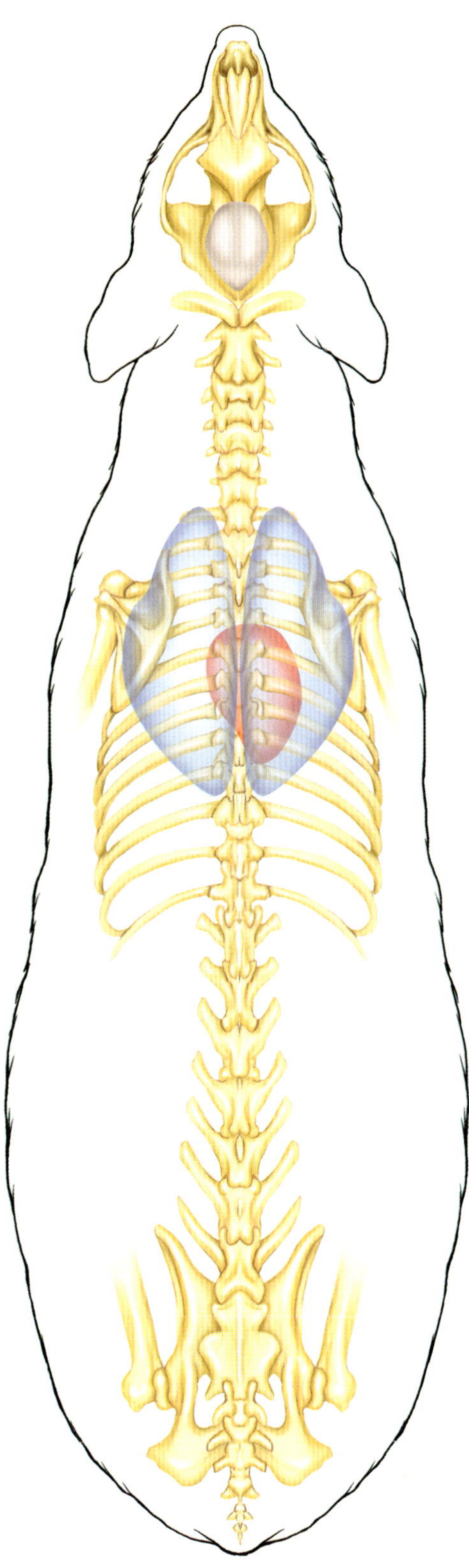

Notice how the lungs of a black bear are in a more forward position than those of a deer. Also keep in mind that if a bullet or arrow hits the spine from a top-angle shot like this one, a lot of tough material needs to be penetrated before the projectile will reach the heart/lung area.

place blinds seventy to eighty yards from the bait. This still results in a good, close shot—but allows at least a little movement during the long waiting hours.

Though distance is no problem when hunting bear over a bait, a primary challenge is that bear, especially bigger bear, almost always come at last light. To complicate the problem, a good bait is set close to heavy cover so the bear will feel secure in its approach. The hunter must take a black animal in black shadow—and he must take it cleanly, because nobody wants to stumble around in dark woods looking for a wounded bear!

Hunters take a lot of bear through chance encounter, by wandering around in the woods looking for something else while bear season is open and there's a tag in the pocket. Under such conditions the shots can vary infinitely, from a close encounter to a shot at considerable range. The same is true of spot-and-stalk bear hunting, but the technique is different. Spot-and-stalk, or glassing, is a common bear-hunting technique in the western United States, Canada, and Alaska. For this method the terrain must have scattered openings where bear might be moving and feeding—and you also need enough relief so you can gain vantage points and see some of these likely spots. Then you need a bear population that is dense enough so that you aren't looking for a needle in a haystack. When conditions meet these criteria, and when you use good

Most black bears are similar in size to a large deer; however, the construction of the bullet needs to be more robust than that for a deer. (Photo courtesy of Len Rue Jr.)

optics intelligently, its amazing how many bear you can see.

Feeding areas are key to spotting bear. In spring, bear come out to feed on new grass, so hunters glass bear slides, sedge-grass beaches, and recent clear-cuts in logged areas. Winterkilled carcasses are also an obvious draw. In fall, berry patches are prime places to glass. Sometimes you'll look all day and never see a bear, and sometimes you'll see a half-dozen. On a recent hunt on Vancouver Island, guide Guy Shockey, Kevin Howard, and I glassed twenty-six bear in one day, a truly incredible number. Bear are actually easy to spot and are visible at great distances. At first you glass every burnt stump, but after you've seen a bear, you recognize the difference: Even a brown black bear is darker and shinier than any stump! It's fun to see lots of bear, but you only need to see one good bear. Sometimes they'll get away from you, but if a bear is feeding and if you get the wind and the location right, the chances for a successful stalk are very high.

The stalk concludes when you're close enough to make an absolutely certain fatal shot. Optimally, that means within a hundred yards, but sometimes wind or intervening terrain and vegetation won't allow it. I don't approve of genuinely long shots at any tough or potentially dangerous animal, but in spot-and-stalk hunting you should be armed and prepared for at least a two-hundred-yard shot, perhaps a bit

An ideal shot on a mature, good-sized black bear. For a shot like this, a premium, well-constructed bullet is not needed. Then again, in another ten seconds an entirely different picture may present itself; therefore, well-constructed bullets are good to have. (Photo courtesy of Len Rue Jr.)

more if you have the confidence, the skill, and the right equipment.

TAKING THE SHOT

The average black bear is no heavier and probably not much tougher than the average white-tailed buck. Bear do have heavy shoulder and leg bones and incredibly solid musculature, but they are not bulletproof, and certainly the average two-hundred-pound bear is no tougher than a three-hundred-pound northern white-tailed buck. As discussed, however, you might encounter a bear weighing four hundred pounds (or twice that much!), which is a whole different beast. Either way, black bear can be dangerous. Even a small black bear can be incredibly fast and ferocious. The three men I know who were mauled by small black bear were literally torn from end to end. All spent some serious hospital time, and all have some interesting scars to show. I'm not sure they'd be alive to show them had they encountered really big bear!

Making the perfect shot is always desirable, and it becomes particularly important when you encounter any animal that just might turn the tables if you mess up. Head shots are especially bad on bear and cat because only skull measurements are used; though a brain shot will surely work, it will also ruin an interesting trophy and, if the bear is big enough, will preclude entry into the records. Even if you don't

The point of aim for the heart, lung, and shoulder shots is indicated. Although the black bear is, on average, not any heavier than a whitetail, its bones and muscle mass are certainly a lot tougher. (Photo courtesy of Len Rue Jr.)

care about that, the head shot is just too dicey; the target is very small, and shot placement must be absolutely perfect. Neck and spine shots are just as tricky. Bear have thick necks and broad backs, and it isn't easy to visualize exactly where the spine lies. It's far better to forget the fancy stuff and go for the surest shot. In this regard bear are the same as all other game: Heart shots and well-placed lung shots are absolutely fatal.

Both shots are just a wee bit tricky with bear. The lungs sit a bit farther forward, tucked in a bit closer behind the shoulder than is the case with ungulates. The heart sits very low, perfectly guarded by the massive shoulders. The lung shot is much the same as with other game: On a broadside presentation, follow the rear line of the foreleg one-third of the way up the body. The difference is that you don't have much leeway; with antlered game, a shot just a couple inches too far back will still be immediately fatal, but on bear you'll be just on the edge.

The shoulder/heart shot is also similar to that used on most other game: Follow the centerline of the foreleg into the center of the first third of the body. I prefer this shot, but not because it's easier; it really isn't. You've got plenty of leeway if you're a bit high or a couple of inches too far back, because you'll be well into the lungs—but if you're low, all you'll do is break a leg, and if you're a bit forward, you'll get brisket and, probably, a lost bear. However, the shoulder/heart shot is particularly good for bear because they show

Especially with heavy-bullet loads like Garrett's 310-grain hard cast flat-points, a .44 Magnum is a good black bear gun at short range. A scoped T/C is a good choice over bait, while an open-sighted revolver is probably a better choice for hunting with hounds.

very little reaction to "bullet shock." A bear might drop to a shot that isn't immediately fatal, but it won't stay down very long. To get a bear down on the spot you need to hit it hard, preferably breaking heavy bone as well as wrecking the heart and lungs.

Obviously, you need a broadside presentation and a heavy bullet to get both shoulders. If at all possible, that's what you should wait for. Quartering shots that take either the on or off shoulder as well as the heart and/or lungs are almost as good, but I really don't like facing shots on bears, and I won't take a going-away shot on an unwounded bear.

THE RIGHT BEAR

Bear go into the record books based on skull measurements, but skull size is almost impossible to judge. On Vancouver Island Jim Shockey and his guides—who see a lot of bear and take a lot of big bear—are amazingly adept at "calling" skull size, but I've never seen anyone else who could do it. It's better to concentrate on body size on the generally correct theory that a big bear will have a big skull. Even this is hard to judge, and it takes a lot of experience. On a bait you can judge body size by reference points, but in most situations you must look for subtle indicators. A big bear swaggers or waddles as it walks, with feet that seem to be wide apart. The ears appear small and set well apart on the skull. With bear, the adage that "the big ones look big" generally holds true.

With black bear any bear that "squares" six feet is a nice bear, anywhere. (Lay out the hide with no stretching, measure across the front paws, then measure from nose to tail. Divide by two for the "square of the bear.") There are some areas where "seven-foot bear" are relatively common, and you may encounter eight-footers. However, there are two other considerations, and, depending on how you feel about it, they may be even more important than size. First and foremost is a well-furred hide. Always look for rubbed spots, making sure your bear has a thick, silky, uniform hide. Then there's color. In areas that have bear of different color phases, you can hunt for color or you can hunt for size—but you can't always find both in the same bear.

GUNS AND LOADS

You can take black bear effectively with any good deer cartridge from .270 upward. The various .30-calibers from .308 Winchester on up are excellent choices. However, there's

Left to right: 1) .358 Winchester 2) .350 Remington Magnum 3) .35 Whelen. Of these three only the .35 Whelen remains commercially viable, but I really like all three of these "medium-velocity" .35s for general-purpose black bear hunting. They will work well for any sensible shot, regardless of your hunting technique.

a difference between just killing a bear and stopping it—not necessarily in a charge, but before it gets into the heavy cover and you have to go dig it out.

I have taken a lot of bear with .270s, 7mms, and .30-calibers, and I've never had any serious problems—but with one of these I've never had a bear go down in its tracks and stay there. I like cartridges that aren't necessarily more powerful, in terms of energy, but that carry heavier bullets of larger caliber. Exactly what you choose depends on how you hunt. For hound hunting you need a light, fast, easy-to-carry rifle that will produce a lot of punch at nearly point-blank range. A .44 Magnum in either a carbine or a handgun, firing heavy-for-caliber bullets (for instance, 300-grain bullets rather than the standard pistol bullets) works well. So do old-timers like the .35 Remington. In North America, hound hunting is one of the few types of hunting where open sights are superior to scopes. If the bear bays on the ground or gets out of the tree, you must take your shot at very close range and be cognizant of the dogs darting in and out while you're doing it.

In bait hunting you certainly don't need a flat-shooting rifle, but you do need a low-powered scope that will gather lots of light. This is the ideal place for a "brush cartridge" like a .356 or .358 Winchester, a .375 Winchester, a .444 Marlin, or a good old .45-70.

Spot-and-stalk hunting is different from bait hunting and hound hunting; the hunter shoots most of the cartridges just mentioned at not much more than a hundred yards. You probably shouldn't consider a shot much past 250 yards on any bear, but you do need a bit of reach because you can't always get close to bear. To my thinking the perfect cartridges for stalking black bear are the faster .35s—the old .350 Remington Magnum and the .35 Whelen. A .30-06 will do the job, as always—but I don't believe there's such a thing as too much gun for bear. Far better are the .33-calibers, the .338 Winchester Magnum, and all the rest. For the record, I have taken many black bear with a .375 H&H, and I have never, ever felt overgunned—especially when a really big bear comes along!

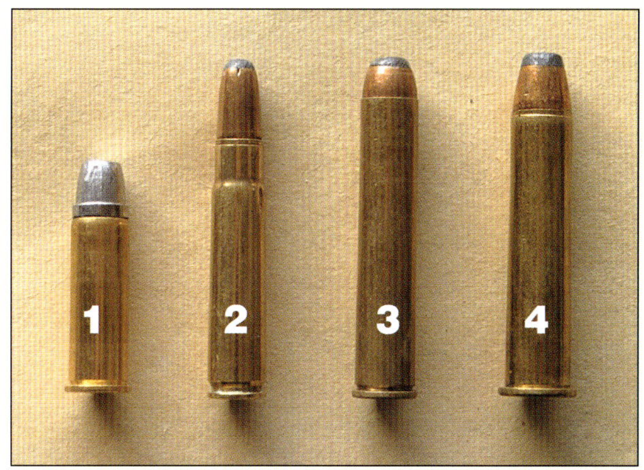

Left to right: 1) .44 Magnum 2) .35 Remington 3) .444 Marlin 4) .45-70. For close-range work, either over bait or with hounds, I like the traditional brush cartridges with heavy, large-caliber bullets—but none of these rounds are good choices for shots past 100 yards.

For this kind of hunting you should have a scoped rifle, but you don't need a whole lot of magnification, and you should be prepared for the very close shot as well as the longer shot. A scope in the 1.75–5X range is adequate, but the newer 1.75–6X scopes or a 2–7X are probably ideal.

BULLET PERFORMANCE

With bear this should be an easy decision. You want tough, heavy-for-caliber bullets, period. The only black bear I have ever seen lost was shot squarely on the shoulder—perfect shot placement—with a 150-grain

.270. The loss occurred because the bullet, although heavy-for-caliber, was a quick-opening conventional softpoint, and it just didn't penetrate. With bear you want bullets in the medium-for-caliber or, better, heavy-for-caliber range: 180- to 200-grain in .30-caliber; 225- to 250-grain in .33-caliber; 250-grain in .35-caliber. And you want them to be of strong design, like Nosler Partition, Swift A-Frame, Winchester Fail Safe, Trophy Bonded Bear Claw, and Barnes X-Bullet. Shot placement is always critical, but with bear you must also penetrate those heavy bones and corded muscles.

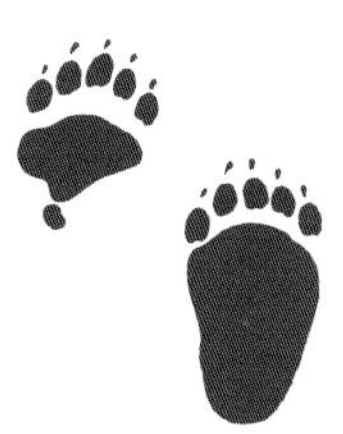

GRIZZLY AND ALASKAN BROWN BEAR

Hunting the humpbacked bears is deadly serious business!

The grizzly bear's scientific name used to be *Ursus horribilis*, the horrible bear. This was unfair. While one is being mauled, one might well consider it quite horrible—but the grizzly is far more magnificent than it is horrible. It is the true symbol of wilderness, and that does not mean just American wilderness.

The grizzly bear and the Alaskan brown bear are really the same species, now designated *Ursus arctos*. There are many races, not only in North America but in the Old World as well. The "brown bear" of Europe and Asia are also dish-faced, humpbacked bears. Even today they can be found in remote areas from Spain to Siberia. Millions of years ago some of their ancestors crossed what was then a land bridge across the Bering Strait, and over the eons they spread east and south, eventually occupying most of western North America.

Lewis and Clark found plenty of bears on the Great Plains, and most of California was superb grizzly country. But men and grizzly didn't agree, and during the nineteenth century the grizzly was either eradicated or pushed into the remotest areas. Today, there is no such thing as a plains grizzly or a California grizzly—but thank God there are still grizzly, and they are even staging a slight comeback.

There have always been remnant grizzly in Montana's remotest country. Today the populations in both Yellowstone Park and Glacier Park are spilling over, so grizzly sightings are relatively common throughout the region. The occasional wanderer turns up in Washington, and a grizzly was killed in an encounter with a man in Colorado some years ago. It is still rumored—but not confirmed—that a small population of Mexican grizzly may be hanging on in central Chihuahua's Sierra del Nido. But the Yellowstone-Glacier ecosystem represents the only viable grizzly population left in the continental United States, with no current hunting.

This is sad. Though relatively few of us will ever hunt grizzly bear, such a hunt must surely be the dream of most American hunters. To take the "horrible bear" in fair chase truly is an ultimate sporting experience, and little opportunity remains. Today, despite

The method for almost all hunting of grizzlies and brown bears is by painstaking glassing and stalking. It can mean days of sitting on a vantage point, glassing the same good ground—but when things happen, they happen fast.

the many identified (and often hotly disputed) races and subspecies, we know that the Alaskan brown bear and the grizzly bear are the same animal. However, it is also absolutely proper for us hunters to consider them differently, not only in our record books but also in our hunting plans and dreams.

The grizzly bear is the interior bear, the bear of the high mountains and timbered valleys. Today it remains fairly plentiful from the Alberta Rockies west through British Columbia; and from western Northwest Territories west through interior Alaska. Hunting opportunities are shrinking; it is now protected in Alberta, and, somewhat inexplicably, it is not hunted in the Mackenzie district of Northwest Territories, although this area holds good numbers of bear. Even British Columbia, with a large and healthy population, was briefly closed in 2000-2001 due to political pressure from anti-hunters. At this writing the grizzly is hunted in British Columbia, Yukon, the barrens of Northwest Territories, and Alaska. Although in total there are plenty of grizzly, hunting them is extremely difficult because they are widely scattered across big and rugged country. A grizzly hunt is a quest, usually lengthy and difficult—and not always successful.

The size of grizzly depends largely on climate and available food, but genetics also play a role. As with black bear, almost any area can produce a huge bear—but in the northern mountains most grizzly are not that large. The record books only record skull measurements for bears; skull size is almost impossible to judge, but it is the only irrefutable, unchangeable measure of a bear's size. Most hunters speak in terms of "squared hides." Properly, the fresh hide is laid out flat but not stretched. For the square, measure from nose to tip of tail, then from front claw to front claw. Add these measurements and divide by two. The problem is that it's very tempting, extremely easy, and quite common to stretch the hide just a wee bit while taking these measurements.

One might assume that eight-foot grizzly are normal. This is not the case. Especially in the harsh climate of the interior mountains, a grizzly that squares six and a half to seven feet and weighs 350 to 400 pounds is a pretty good bear. Eight-foot grizzly, and occasionally the genuine nine-footer, do occur. But they are rare, and they are most likely found where climatic conditions allow a longer growing season and where the diet is especially good. British Columbia's Bella Coola region is famous for big grizzly—and these are fish-fed bear. Alaska's Seward Peninsula, although very far north, also has salmon streams and plentiful moose, and the bear grow big. Just a short distance farther north and east, in the Brooks Range, the bear are beautifully furred but rarely large.

This illustrates the real difference between Alaskan brown bear and inland grizzly. They are really the same bear, but Alaska's southeast coast, Kenai Peninsula, Alaskan Peninsula, and her southern islands are warmed by Japanese currents and cut with salmon streams. The bear eat better and hibernate for shorter periods—and they grow much larger. The line between the two is man-made and indistinct, and the bear care little about it. On the boundary a bear might be a very large grizzly one day and a medium-sized Alaskan brown bear the next. Generally, the Alaskan brown bear is considerably larger than the grizzly. At its best it is huge.

Everyone talks about the ten-foot brown bear. It exists, but brown bear that actually reach these dimensions without stretching are very rare. An eight-foot brown bear is a good trophy, and such a bear will probably weigh seven hundred pounds. A genuine nine-foot bear is a very good trophy, and might weigh as much as half a ton. The ten-footers, for those who are fortunate to find them, are genuine monsters, with weights that might exceed fifteen hundred pounds. Brown bear hunting is, on average, considerably more successful than grizzly hunting because the bear are much more concentrated by the salmon streams.

SHOTS AT THE BIG BEAR

Whether you're hunting grizzly or Alaskan brown bear, you'll almost certainly hunt them by spot-and-stalk techniques. The only alternatives are tracking, if there's snow, or still-hunting slowly along a salmon stream. Because of the mountainous country in which they are hunted, shots at grizzly probably average a bit longer; close encounters are more common in the alder thickets of good brown bear country.

Either way, shots can vary from extremely close to not much more than two hundred yards. You can see bear from much greater distances—the humpbacked bear are huge animals, and it isn't uncommon to glass them at distances of several miles. But you usually won't shoot them where you first see them. The game is stalking, not necessarily to get as close as you can but to get close enough that your shot is

It was more than 20 years ago when I took this giant Alaskan brown bear, but it was a great day, and I remember it as though it were yesterday. The rifle is a Sako Safari Grade in .375 H&H, still the classic choice for Alaskan brown bear.

absolutely sure. This should be the goal with all game, but it means something different with an animal as large, tough, and potentially dangerous as a big bear. With a good centerfire rifle, the goal should be to keep your shots within a hundred yards or so, and if you do it right you should be able to get that close—sometimes.

The big bear aren't gifted with particularly good eyesight. If you move slowly and quietly, keeping off the skyline and using a bit of cover, you can usually get close enough for a good shot—if the wind holds. Bear have an extremely keen sense of smell, and this forms their first line of defense, as well as their primary means of locating food. Never underestimate the power of a bear's nose! Once, up in the Skeena Mountains of northern British Columbia, I was stalking a really good grizzly, feeding busily in a choice berry patch. The breeze was crossing, and everything was going just fine, until it shifted. I had barely felt the breeze kiss the back of my neck when the bear, still more than three hundred yards away, suddenly froze. It raised its snout, then stood on its hind legs and sniffed. Then it was gone, bounding away into thick cover.

Even if the wind holds perfectly, it isn't always possible to get as close as you would like. On that particular bear I wasn't close enough to shoot, even if I'd felt the wind shifting in time, but had it happened a couple of minutes later, I might have been. There are many other reasons

This grizzly bear from British Columbia was shot with a .300 Remington Ultra Magnum. A .30-caliber should be considered minimum for any grizzly. (Safari Press photo library)

why you can't always get as close as you really should get. The bear might be moving into heavy cover, or it might be in cover so thick that you can see it from where you are but wouldn't be able to see it from over there.

On that same hunt in the Skeenas, on the evening of the last day, we had a bear on the far side of a deep cut. It might have been possible to drop down and climb back up before it got dark, but there wasn't time to go around, and it seemed almost certain that we would spook the bear if we tried to clamber up after it. So I elected to shoot across, a distance of about 250 yards. I would never try to tell anyone else how far he or she should take a shot; that's a personal thing depending on skill, confidence, and the power of the rifle in relation to the game. This was a very long shot on a grizzly, probably pushing the sensible maximum. But here's the point: It was the last day of a long, hard, frustrating hunt, and it was the shot I had. I took it and came home with a nice bear. With the big bear, you try hard for the close shot, but you must be prepared to take the shot you get.

TAKING THE SHOT

Grizzly bear are incredibly powerful creatures. They live long, hard lives in tough country, and I have watched them excavate Volkswagen-sized boulders in search of a bite-sized marmot. They are not much impressed by bullet energy. They

Once a hunter decides to hunt a grizzly, he needs to start thinking about larger calibers and heavier, well-constructed bullets. (Photo courtesy of Dusan Smetana)

must be hit very hard in the right place. Even then, the clean, one-shot kills we all prefer are unusual. They absolutely will not happen unless you place that first shot almost perfectly.

You should generally avoid brain and spine shots, primarily because they're just too tricky. There's almost no margin for error, and if there is error, the only possible results are a lost bear or a dangerous encounter with a wounded animal. Also, since bear enter the record books based on skull measurements, a head shot will ruin an important trophy. As on all game, the lung-shot bear is deadly, but on big bear you need to add the modifier "eventually." A lung-shot grizzly can cover a lot of ground. If you have stalked it well, it probably won't know where you are when the shot goes off, but it does have its choice of points on the compass, and it might well come your way. It's far better to break heavy bone, shooting through the heavy shoulder bone into the heart.

A bear's heart is very low in the chest and almost perfectly centered between the forelegs. On a broadside presentation, follow the centerline of the foreleg a bit less than a third of the way up. This is the shoulder/heart shot, by far the best option for a really big bear. You can't always get the perfect presentation, and this presents a dilemma. On these animals you really need a good shot angle, or you don't have a shot at all. On the other hand, the hunts are very expensive, and there aren't many opportunities. Waiting for that perfect

To anchor a bear, smash the shoulder bone with a good bullet. A brain shot is not recommended unless the bear is charging and must be stopped on the spot. Shown here is the triad of heart, lung, and shoulder shots. (Photo courtesy of Len Rue Jr.)

broadside presentation isn't always the wisest course.

Just remember that you simply must get your bullet into the heart/lung area. Angled shots will work if the angle isn't too steep and you have plenty of gun and bullet—but you must be able to visualize exactly where the vitals lie and adjust your aim accordingly.

THE RIGHT BEAR

Sometimes a decent-sized brown or grizzly bear can be almost impossible to find, and sometimes it comes easily. There isn't much you can do about this, other than to try hard to put yourself in a good area and then hunt hard when you get there. In the better areas most coastal brown bear hunts will be successful, but even in the best areas few grizzly hunts offer more than 50 percent success. Supposing you do spot a bear, the next challenges are figuring out how big it is and then deciding if it meets your expectations. Neither is simple.

Bear are extremely hard to judge. If you're working from tracks, you will have a pretty good idea of the size of the bear, but judging a bear on a distant hillside is difficult. On my first brown bear hunt, my guide, Slim Gale, told me to look for a bear with a small head. This sounded odd, because it takes a huge skull to make the record book. He told me: "They've all got big heads, so if the head looks small, the body is huge."

Even with premium bullets, a brown bear can be shot only when at a 90-degree angle. Almost all guides advise the hunter to keep shooting till the animal no longer moves. Good advice! (Photo courtesy of Len Rue Jr.)

Most interior grizzlies aren't much larger than good-sized black bears—but grizzlies are very hard to come by, and there won't be many opportunities. This bear was taken in northern B.C. from about 250 yards, a long shot on a big bear. The rifle is a .340 Weatherby Magnum, ideal for such hunting.

Maybe. One morning, from more than a mile away, Slim got a quick glance at a bear and said that we had to go after it. It was early in the hunt, so I wasn't sure. Slim was sure. "Man, that's a ten-foot bear. Let's go!"

The bear measured eleven feet, two inches, across the front paws and ten feet, eight inches, nose to tail—a giant of a bear. But how did Slim know? Simply because he has seen a lot of bear.

That was more than twenty years ago, and I've seen a lot of bear since then, but to this day I can never be that sure. Indicators of size are a swaying, swaggering walk and ears that look tiny and set far apart on a huge skull. It isn't easy to be sure, unless your guide is very experienced.

Another problem is unreasonable expectations. This problem is far more severe with Alaskan brown bear than it is with grizzly bear. Most hunters accept that grizzly are extremely hard to come by. A huge bear would be nice, but any well-furred, mature grizzly taken in fair chase is a great trophy—especially after a week or ten days of extremely hard hunting. Brown bear are different, and it's partly the fault of people like me, whose writings seem to suggest that ten-foot bear grow on trees. Everybody wants a ten-foot bear, but very few people will ever see one. They exist, and sometimes they seem to come out of the woodwork. In the best Peninsula or Kodiak areas, an outfitter might take two or three such bear in a single season and then not see another for a couple of years.

The sad part is that, armed with unrealistic expectations, too many hunters turn down perfectly good trophy bear in the search for a monster. Then they either go home empty or, in the closing days, take a bear smaller than others they have passed up. The average of bear taken on the Peninsula and on Kodiak Island, by both residents and nonresidents, is less than eight feet. So, unless you're prepared to return year after year, a well-furred, eight-foot bear (by honest measurements) is a good brown bear and a fine trophy.

GUNS AND LOADS

As I said, shot placement is extremely important on the big bear. There is no substitute; anything less than a good shot is no shot. I am a firm believer in powerful rifles firing heavy-for-caliber, well-constructed bullets. Make no mistake, you can take any bear that walks—especially the smaller grizzly—with a .270, 7mm, or .30 caliber loaded with a good bullet. Many brown bear are taken every year with popular deer cartridges like these, but that's not the issue. The smaller calibers will surely kill big bear, but only if both shot presentation and shot placement are perfect. This severely limits

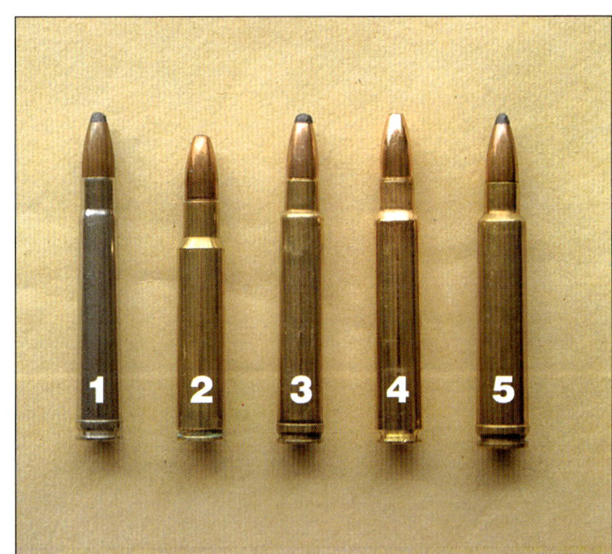

Left to right: 1) .375 H&H 2) .375 Dakota Magnum 3) .375 Weatherby Magnum 4) .375 Remington Ultra Mag 5) .378 Weatherby Magnum. To my thinking, the various .375s are the best choices for the largest of bears. They have enough reach for any sane shot . . . plus plenty of power to put a bear down and keep him down.

the shot angles that you can practically take, which means that you may not be able to take advantage of the only opportunity you get. Perhaps more important, the smaller calibers may not have enough steam to get you out of trouble if something goes wrong. Shot placement isn't always perfect, so it's important to be able to stop the bear, which is different from just killing it.

The classic broadside presentation is always most desirable if you can get it, but that may not be the shot you have. There are plenty of other options if you have enough gun and enough bullet to do the job. That bear in the Skeenas was feeding on a slanting hogback, head downhill, facing directly toward us. I waited a little while, but the light was going and the presentation didn't change. I had a very steady position and plenty of gun, although at 250 yards the range was pushing it. I was shooting a .340 Weatherby Magnum with a 250-grain Nosler Partition, and I had plenty of confidence in that gun and that load. So I put the cross hairs right behind the head and just in front of the hump, expecting the big bullet to break the spine and penetrate down into the chest cavity. It did more than that, exiting between the bear's front legs, but I doubt the bear was aware of that. It was already dead, driven down into the hillside.

Grizzly bear are smaller than brown bear, and they may also be taken at somewhat greater range because of their mountainous habitat. You could get by just fine with a .300 magnum firing heavy bullets, and the .375s

Here's an excellent rifle for the big bears: stainless steel metal, stable and durable laminated stock, 1¾–6X scope, and chambered to the powerful .338 Remington Ultra Mag cartridge.

(.375 H&H, .375 Remington Ultra Mag, .375 Weatherby Magnum, et cetera) pose no handicap. But I believe the 8mm Remington Magnum and the fast .33s, from .338 Winchester Magnum upward, are just perfect.

These cartridges also work well on brown bear. A few years ago I shot a very big Siberian brown bear, essentially identical to the Alaskan variety, with the same .340 Weatherby Magnum. The bear was striding toward me through deep snow, and I let it come. At sixty yards it paused and quartered slightly to me. I put the cross hairs just inside the on-shoulder. This is a tough shot, because with any frontal presentation you have to be just right or you'll catch just one lung or, worse, skin just inside the shoulder, and you'll do little damage. This time I got it right. The bullet centered the heart, then penetrated through the rest of the bear, coming to rest against the hide on the far hip.

The bear's reaction was a tribute to this animal's stamina. It was clearly dead, but it showed no reaction other than to charge to the right in a cloud of snow, disappearing behind some trees. It was dead when I reached it a few seconds later—but even a cartridge as powerful as the .340 didn't stop it! I bow to the consensus of Alaska's professional brown-bear guides, who, on average, reckon the good old .375 H&H is the best of all brown-bear cartridges.

Mind you, many of them carry .338s, which will certainly do the job. Others carry open-sighted big-bores; a smattering of big-lever actions in .450 Marlin or .45-70 with hopped-up handloads; a lot of .458s; and even the occasional double-barreled Nitro Express. But the brown bear guide's primary concern is stopping an enraged bear if the need arises.

As hunters, our primary concern is killing it with a perfect shot. For our purpose we want a rifle topped with a low-powered scope, chambered to a cartridge that will cleanly take the biggest of bear, not only in a close encounter but also at two hundred yards if necessary. The .375s—the old H&H as well as the faster .375s, like the .375 Remington Ultra Mag and .375 Weatherby Magnum—are easily the best choices.

BULLET PERFORMANCE

Penetration, penetration, penetration. The big bear are massive creatures with dense muscles and extremely heavy bones. No matter what cartridge you choose, you must mate it with tough, well-constructed, heavy-for-caliber bullets designed to penetrate. Note that the lighter the caliber, the more important it is to use the toughest, deepest-penetrating bullets available—but even with big cartridges like the .375 you want tough bullets. A really big brown bear is every bit as big as an African Cape buffalo and asks just as much of a bullet to ensure penetration.

Left to right: 1) .35 Whelen 2) 8mm Remington Magnum 3) .338 Winchester Magnum 4) .340 Weatherby Magnum 5) .338 Remington Ultra Mag. All these cartridges are ideal for grizzly hunting and will do fine for the larger Alaskan brown bear.

On big bears, choice of bullet probably matters more than choice of cartridge. You must get through tough bone and muscle to get into the vitals, so it's important to choose bullets designed for deep penetration. Nosler Partitions, Swift A-Frames, and Barnes X-Bullets are three good choices.

When I shot that monster Alaskan brown bear in 1981, I was carrying a .375 H&H, but I had it loaded with then-new 300-grain Sierra boattails. That's plenty of gun and plenty of bullet weight, but those early .375-caliber Sierras had thinner jackets than these bullets do today, and their penetrating qualities weren't up to the task. I shot the bear five times, all good hits, finally managing to stop it just short of some dense alders that I did not wish to follow it into. In part this happened because it was a grand old bear, big and tough and unwilling to give up. But I will always believe that, with the shot placement I had, tougher bullets like the Nosler Partition, Trophy Bonded Bear Claw, Barnes X-Bullet, Swift A-Frame, or Winchester Fail Safe would have done better. Note that, of these great, tough, penetrating bullets, only the Nosler Partition was available back then. Today we have a great choice of fine bullets, ideally suited to almost every occasion. There really is no excuse not to tailor the bullet to the game at hand, and with the biggest bear you want the toughest bullets available.

POLAR BEAR

Man is just another meal!

I don't think the argument will ever be resolved about which is the larger bear, the Alaskan brown bear or the polar bear. The polar bear, *Ursus maritimus*, grows to incredible size on its diet of seals and anything else it can find. In the record books the skull sizes of the largest representatives of both species are of similar size, and the old Alaskan polar-bear hunters tend to believe the white bear, at its best, is slightly larger. It is a rangy, streamlined bear, built for swimming in the icy waters of its Arctic world. In the old days, when hunters took big bear readily with the aid of an airplane, polar-bear hides squaring fully twelve feet weren't uncommon. The Alaskan brown bear, however, is much more heavily built, and I would guess the biggest Alaskan brown bear would outweigh the largest polar bear.

Whichever is the larger, the polar bear is unquestionably the more dangerous of the two and ranks as the most dangerous game in North America. On the world scene of dangerous game the polar bear is often overlooked in favor of African nasties such as the lion and Cape buffalo, but I think this is because few people today have experience with polar bear. A polar bear, at its biggest weighing about the same as the average Cape buffalo, outweighs a lion at least three-to-one, maybe more. But danger doesn't come from size alone; moose and eland are bigger than Cape buffalo, but neither is considered dangerous.

The polar bear is genuinely dangerous for two reasons. First, unlike almost all other animals on our planet, the polar bear has never learned fear of man. Although the Inuit have hunted polar bear along the fringes of their range for centuries, pressure from sport hunters has always been light and on the edges of the polar bear's vast, frigid domain. Most polar bear live and die without ever encountering a human being. When they find one of the strange two-legged creatures, they regard it as nothing more than another morsel of animal protein in the great bears' never-ending search for food. Upon scenting man, most black, brown, and grizzly bears will head the other way. The polar bear may run, but it's just as likely to rub its tummy and come on in for supper.

The second reason the polar bear is so dangerous has to do with its environment. As dangerous as the polar bear is, the weather and the cold it thrives in are even more dangerous. Temperatures of fifty and sixty degrees below zero are common, and deadly storms can come out of nowhere. Polar bear habitat is not man's habitat, and in that icy world a slight mishap can mean death.

A generation ago, prior to the Marine Mammal Act and Alaska's restriction concerning "same-day airborne hunting," hunters commonly employed light aircraft from which to

Modern polar bear hunts are conducted on pack ice with dogsleds, a great adventure and probably the most physically demanding hunt in the entire world. (Photo courtesy of Randy Brooks)

hunt polar bear, flying in pairs. They could cover vast areas of the pack ice north of Alaska, looking for tracks and actual bears. Once a bear was spotted, the pilot would search for a place to land across the bear's route of travel. The hunters would intercept the bear, and that was that. By today's standards it sounds unsporting, and perhaps it was. But it was also a very selective technique, because hunters could fully judge bears before making a decision, and, if the weather held, hunters had their pick of several bears in just a few days.

Ethical or unethical, this airplane hunting was also extremely dangerous. Just being out over the pack ice involves staking lives on the skill of the pilot and the reliability of the aircraft. Also, the pack ice off Alaska is unstable, subject to cracks that widen into icy rivers or "leads." These leads can open without notice, separating the hunters from the airplane or even swallowing up the airplane altogether. Actual loss of life during the period of airplane hunting was small, but the old polar-bear hunters all have hair-raising stories.

It is entirely possible that the old airplane hunting was even more dangerous than today's hunting by dogsled. Experienced Inuit hunters guide the current hunting out of numerous villages in Arctic Canada. These guides are not conversationalists or raconteurs but good men who truly understand their native land. Camps and emergency supplies are carried everywhere by dogsled. Hunters can weather the storms, and the pack ice above eastern Canada tends to be more stable than the Alaskan ice, so it is much less common to be marooned by open leads.

However, hunting polar bear by dogsled out on the pack ice is the most difficult and challenging hunt commonly available to sportsmen anywhere in the world, and certainly one of the most dangerous. A limited amount of ground—*er*, ice—can be covered by dogsled, so the hunts take a lot of time. Most hunters are actually out on the ice two to three weeks. This extreme cold is dangerous in itself, especially for us people from warmer climates. The Inuit guides work hard to take care of their hunters; they understand that this is not our world. But they can't always keep us from making mistakes, and mistakes can be costly. Frostbite is common, usually caused by forgetting to change socks, taking off a glove in the excitement of shooting a bear, or stoically (and foolishly) keeping your mouth shut and ignoring trouble when you know you're in it. I know relatively few hunters who have hunted polar bear. Among the few, I know several who have lost toes, and my old friend Richard Van Vorst nearly lost a hand.

Personally, I fear the cold. I've had frostbitten feet twice, once in the Marines and once on a Marco Polo sheep hunt. I know I'm at risk, so I fear the polar-bear hunt. But it is something I want desperately to do, and in 2004 (the earliest booking we could get) my buddy Joe Bishop and I will go do it. There is no warm-weather polar-bear hunting; you simply must be prepared to accept the cold. The good news is that wonderful Arctic clothing is available today. This is a hunt you must suffer through, and it isn't always successful—but if you pay attention there is no real reason to leave pieces of yourself in the high Arctic.

The polar bear truly is a marine mammal; most polar bear, especially the big boars, never touch dry land throughout their lives. Many do come ashore on the Arctic Islands, and in North America a lot of bear, primarily sows with cubs, come down onto the mainland. Churchill on Hudson Bay, actually quite far south, is famous for its polar bear. The polar bear is confined to the northern polar ice cap, but it is not exclusively a North American animal. It is found in the waters of Greenland, Iceland, and Norway; and it is also found above Siberia's northern coastline. It is said that the Russian polar bear are among the largest. When the old Alaskan bush pilots were flying for polar bear during the Cold War, it was almost an unwritten rule among those rogues that their bear had to be taken within Russian waters!

Here's an interesting story. A hunting partner of mine, Chris Kinsey, is quite an adventurer. He went on a voyage to Antarctica, and at one point they put in at one of the earliest explorers' camps, finding many of the supplies still intact. Among the gear was a huge quantity of century-old ammunition, including a large quantity of .50–110 ammo, a big-bore, black-powder cartridge chambered to the 1886 Winchester. Why? Because early visitors to Antarctica fully expected to run into polar bear or similar big beasties. They did not know the polar bear is confined to the ice cap in the Northern Hemisphere.

SHOTS AT WHITE BEAR

These days the polar-bear hunts by dogsled are largely a matter of simply covering ground until you either spot a bear or find fresh tracks. Nothing on earth is as open as the pack ice, so there is obvious potential for long shooting. Most of the time this isn't necessary. When the Inuit spot a bear, they typically close the distance until the bear becomes alarmed, then set free some of the sled dogs, and a spot-and-stalk hunt instantly becomes similar to a hound hunt for black bear. If everything goes right, the dogs distract the bear until the hunters can approach within range.

There are exceptions to this scenario. On the open ice a bear can simply outdistance its pursuers, and there also may be escape routes. The Canadian ice doesn't have as many open leads, but they do occur, and only bear and the other marine mammals can swim in the icy water. There are also pressure ridges, huge and jagged uplifts created by the constant shifting of the great plates of ice. Bear can negotiate them; dogsleds cannot. So there are times when a longer shot may be required to prevent a bear from going where humans cannot follow.

Then there are the occasional surprises. A polar bear will usually flee when caught on the open ice. This is a natural reaction to what is, to the bear, an unnatural disturbance—but this doesn't mean that it is afraid. During the long Arctic nights, when the camp is quiet, the polar bear is just as likely to come calling, enticed by the aromas of food cooking, tasty sled dogs, and even those strange two-legged morsels. During the hunt you may search the endless

Randy Brooks of Barnes Bullets took this superb polar bear on a dogsled hunt. Because the dogsled limits the ground you can cover, very few hunters are fortunate enough to take bears this large. Of course Randy used a Barnes X-Bullet in his .375! (Photo courtesy of Randy Brooks)

ice for days and weeks looking for sign of a bear—but the bear you're looking for is just as likely to come into camp looking for you. A significant number of polar-bear hunts end when the bear wanders into camp and the sled dogs go crazy—which means that a very close shot is every bit as likely as a long one!

TAKING THE SHOT

With an animal as big, powerful, and potentially dangerous as a polar bear, the choice for a perfect shot should be obvious. It isn't enough just to kill the bear; you simply must stop the bear, as quickly and dramatically as possible. A brain or a spine shot will do this, but both are altogether too tricky to be sensible if there are other options. Since all bear enter the record book based on skull measurements alone, a brain shot may also destroy what could be the trophy of a lifetime. The best option is to shoot for heavy bone, aiming to break one or both shoulders while penetrating the chest cavity and taking out the heart and lungs.

With a broadside presentation, simply follow the centerline of the foreleg no more than one-third up into the body. You need a tough bullet, preferably heavy-for-caliber, to break the shoulder bone and penetrate the heart—but a well-constructed bullet of appropriate caliber will do this, and if you have enough power the bullet will keep going and will smash the opposite shoulder as well. This is the kind of performance you want. On shots with less optimum presentation, you

Many people have heard how the Inuit of the North shoot polar bears with very small calibers; however, this is not advisable for the sport hunter. Note how the position of the heart is quite far back when the animal is taking long strides, as shown in this picture. (Photo courtesy of Leonard Lee Rue III)

probably have no chance to take out both shoulders, but you must visualize where the heart lies—low and well protected between the shoulders—and direct your bullet accordingly. A standard lung shot will surely kill the bear, but in my experience the big bear are so tough that they can withstand even a perfect lung shot long enough to be extremely dangerous. On this type of animal I am convinced that a shoulder/heart shot is the best approach.

THE RIGHT BEAR

Although polar bear enter the record book based on skull measurements, almost no one can accurately judge skull size. Look for the biggest bear you can find, though even this is complicated by the featureless Arctic terrain. Tracks are the most reliable indicator; a big track almost always indicates a big bear. However, on today's dogsled hunts you must be careful not to have unrealistic expectations. Hunters occasionally take the giant bear that were fairly common in the days of flying over the ice, but a lot of the big, old boars stay far out on the pack ice, beyond the reach of dogsled hunting. These hunts, too, are a test of stamina and patience. The limitations are such that few hunters will see more than a handful of bear on a two-week hunt.

A trophy bear should be a mature specimen, preferably a boar but certainly a lone traveler. Today an eight-foot bear

A polar bear hunt will likely be a once-in-a-lifetime adventure. Shoot with a large caliber and aim, if possible, to break the shoulder bone, which is the most forward shot indicated. (Photo courtesy of Leonard Lee Rue III)

you have taken by dogsled, not only in fair chase but on one of the world's most arduous hunts, is a great trophy. The nine-foot, ten-foot, and even larger bear are out there, but if you pass up an average specimen, there is a very good chance that you have just walked away from your polar bear.

GUNS AND LOADS

Throughout this book I will make few references to action type. In many cases the cartridge will dictate the action you choose, but most of the time it really doesn't matter whether you choose a lever action, slide action, semiauto, or single-shot, provided you are comfortable with your choice. In this case it does matter. Because of the potential danger, and because it can be extremely difficult to fumble for cartridges in the extreme cold, you need a repeating rifle for polar bear. You also need a rifle that will be absolutely reliable in the subzero cold. To me this means a bolt action, because the bolt action is the easiest action to degrease, and it will work best with just a bit of dry graphite lubricant. Before embarking on a polar-bear hunt, strip the bolt completely and soak all the parts in a good degreasing agent. Then reassemble with just a touch of dry graphite lubricant. A low-powered scope is absolutely necessary, but the polar-bear rifle should also have detachable mounts and auxiliary iron sights that are properly zeroed. You probably won't need

Proper clothing is an absolute must on a polar bear hunt; in fact, it can mean the difference between life and death. (Photo courtesy of Ralf Schneider)

them, but they're essential because equipment takes a tremendous pounding on the dogsled day after day.

The proper cartridge takes a bit of thought. The Inuit shoot polar bear with the rifles they have. Historically, the local hunters—not only highly skilled but incredibly brave—used what they had. Spears eventually gave way to .30-30 Winchesters and .303 Enfields. Then the accurate little .222 became extremely popular. It is ideal for hunting seal, an Inuit staple, and was widely used for polar bear as well. Privately, however, Inuit hunters have admitted that they usually had to shoot their bear a number of times. Today the 7mm Remington Magnum is extremely common in the Inuit communities.

Personally, I don't think any of these cartridges is a good choice. The possibility of needing to anchor a bear at longer range suggests that a fast .33, like a .340 Weatherby or .338 Remington Ultra Mag, would be good. That is true, and with a well-constructed 250-grain bullet it would also stop a charge at close range. However, I know the good old .375 is better medicine for Alaskan brown bear than the .33s. Polar bear are of similar size, but the wide-open ice and the possibility of a longer shot complicate the situation. For the ultimate polar-bear cartridges, I would look to the faster .375s: the .375 Remington Ultra Mag, .375 Weatherby Magnum, and .378 Weatherby Magnum. These offer the large-caliber and heavy-bullet punch of a .375, but

Paul Schneider with a large boar polar bear from the Canadian Arctic, shot with a .375 H&H. (Photo courtesy of Ralf Schneider)

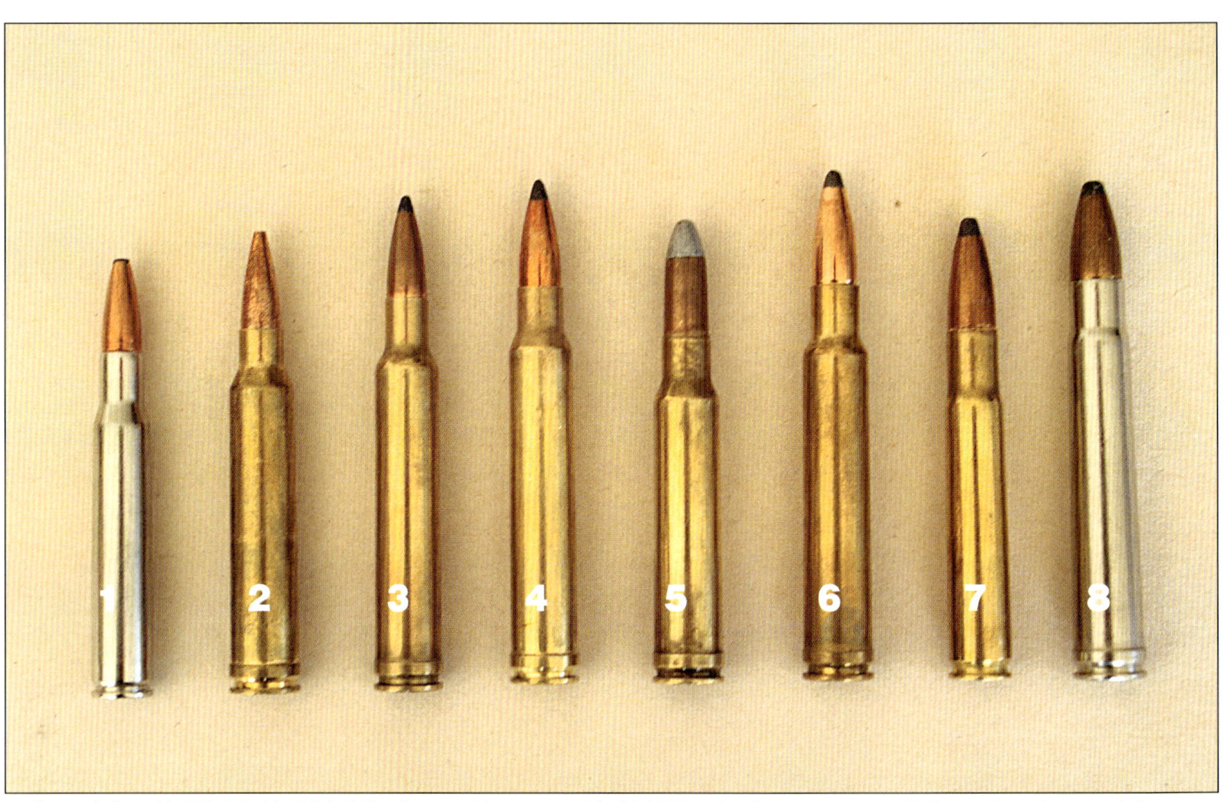

Left to right: 1) .30-06 2) .300 Winchester Magnum 3) .300 Weatherby Magnum 4) 8mm Remington Magnum 5) .338 Winchester Magnum 6) .340 Weatherby Magnum 7) .35 Whelen 8) .375 H&H. With good bullets, any cartridge from the flat-shooting .30s up to the .375 is adequate for the biggest bears, but for polar bear I'd stay right in the middle of this group—the fast .33s—combining power with the reach that you just might need.

flatten the trajectory considerably more than what the old .375 H&H can offer.

BULLET PERFORMANCE

Bullets must be heavy-for-caliber and tough. Even with a perfect broadside presentation, the bullet must get through a lot of bear—dense muscle, heavy bone, resilient hide. The opportunity to take a polar bear is indeed the chance of a lifetime. Most people who endure the cold don't want to make a regular thing of it, so you want enough gun and enough bullet to take advantage of any reasonable shot, even if the presentation falls short of perfect. Shooting a fairly stout cartridge helps, but bullet performance is even more important than choice of cartridge. On this hunt you want the toughest, deepest-penetrating bullets made! Depending on your cartridge and choice of ammo, think about Barnes X-Bullet, Swift A-Frame, Winchester Fail Safe, and Nosler Partition.

COUGAR

The mountain lion may be
North America's most elusive animal . . .

Variously called cougar, mountain lion, catamount, panther, and painter, our long-tailed tawny cat is just one animal, *Felis concolor*. The cougar is one of nature's most efficient predators. Almost always a solitary hunter, it is able to bring down creatures many times its size—elk and even moose—with little difficulty. Deer are its natural and preferred prey, however. An adult cougar averages one deer per week, year in and year out.

Although cougar don't run in packs, herds, or prides, and they are so secretive as to be almost impossible to count, they are relatively common throughout much of their range. That range, by the way, is huge. Historically, cougar have existed from the Atlantic to the Pacific and from Canada's northernmost forests south to the Straits of Magellan in southern South America. The Latin American variety is generally small and reddish in color, and indeed numerous subspecies have been identified—but there are no dramatic differences throughout the cougar's vast domain.

Until recently the cougar had been persecuted throughout most of North America, so during most of the last century, its primary domain was the West. With either complete protection or regulated seasons, this is changing. The Florida panther hangs on in the Everglades region, and in recent years there have been fairly reliable sightings from Georgia to New Brunswick, and in most states between there and the Rocky Mountain front that begins what we think of as true cougar habitat.

The cougar is so elusive and secretive that sightings are fairly rare even where the great cat is common. Individual cats wander great distances, so a chance encounter a vast distance from known populations may not indicate a resident or breeding population. But sightings in the East, Southeast, and upper Midwest are now so common that it seems almost certain that the cougar—without any protection from man, save closed seasons—is reestablishing itself over much of its former range. Clear back in the late 1960s, while quail hunting in northern Kansas, I saw a tawny long-tailed cat cross an open field. Everyone thought I was a crazy kid, because of course there were no cougar in Kansas. But I know what I saw, and I will never forget it!

The cougar is generally an extremely shy beast when it comes to man, which may seem odd for so efficient a predator. It is probably fortunate for both cougar and the humans who encounter them that, at least historically, the cougar has rarely been aggressive and has almost never figured out that the two-legged creatures that invade its domain might be easier prey than deer. If our mountain lion had the disposition of the smaller but much more aggressive leopard, there would be many more historical accounts of cougar attacks, and the cougar would undoubtedly have been persecuted mercilessly. Though humans have always had an innate fear of hunting cats, there were very few genuine, documented cases of cougar attacking or attempting to prey upon humans—until recently.

During the past twenty years or so, the incidence of cougar preying on livestock has escalated dramatically, and there have been numerous documented attacks on humans, including several fatalities. This may suggest that the cougar is becoming more aggressive, but this probably is not the case. Humans are not the cougar's normal prey, and in many cases humans have survived attacks because the cats, although clearly able to overpower a human, have been inept at taking down bipedal prey. The increase in encounters with cougar probably comes from several factors.

In some areas, such as California, cougar have now been fully protected for several feline generations and have lost their fear of man, like bears in the national parks. This is hardly a complete answer, however, because many encounters have taken place in areas where cougar are still hunted. A better answer is that humans are now encroaching more deeply on the wilderness that cougar call home. As more people penetrate cougar habitat, there will be more encounters. Most cougar are benign, and the cougar is so secretive that, most of the time, humans will never know they have been close to a great cat. But sometimes a hiker, biker, or jogger will trigger a predatory response, and the result can be disastrous.

Simple hunger is another factor. In nature almost all animal populations go from boom to bust and back again, depending on food sources. When prey is plentiful, the predators breed up. When prey diminishes, some predators die off, and others move to better hunting grounds. Today, with roads and towns and agricultural development, better hunting grounds are not always available for cougar to move to. The cats turn to livestock and, once in a while, to human prey.

The "endangered" mountain lion has become a darling of the anti-hunters, and they have had great success in severely limiting—or, in the case of California, altogether halting—the wildlife managers' ability to manage them. Ultimately, the consequences will be disastrous. When the mountain lion was first protected in California in the early 1970s, the Golden State had one of the West's largest populations—an estimated two thousand big cats. Thirty years later there may be an estimated seven thousand cougar in California, with daylight sightings common in many areas. Do the math: Two thousand cougar could take 100,000 deer in a year. Seven thousand cougar could take 350,000—this from a herd that was long estimated at 750,000. The deer population cannot support this decimation. Many other factors are associated with the long-term decline in California's deer herd, but mountain lion predation is particularly significant.

In California the cougar is now a "nongame species," meaning that it is altogether beyond the control of the California Fish and Game Department. Fortunately, no other western states have

I took this excellent tom cougar in Arizona, dry-ground trailing at its best, with Warner Glenn and his father, the late Marvin Glenn. The pistol is a T/C Contender in .45-70, a good choice of pistol but really too much cartridge for cougar.

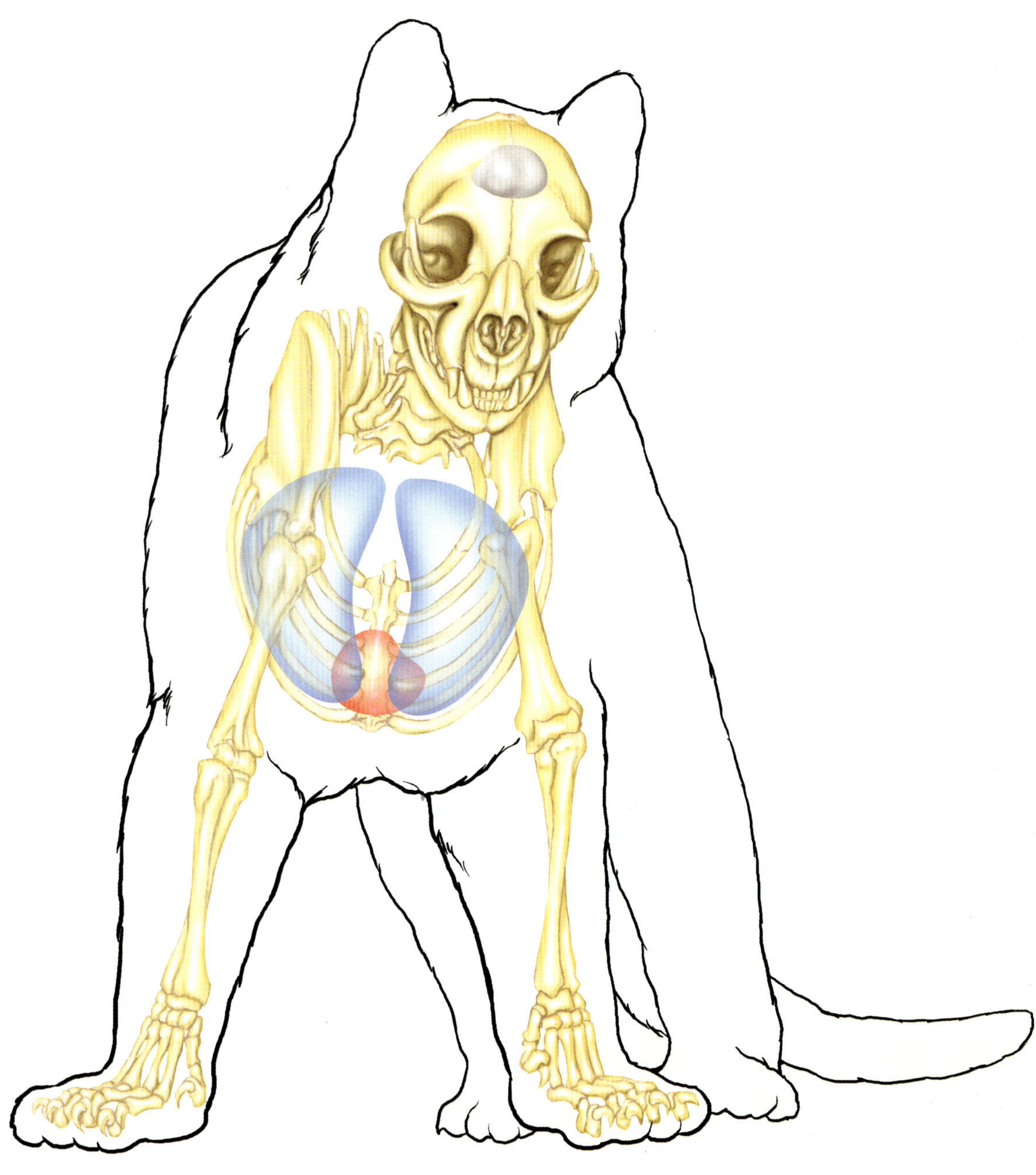

When a hunter is ready to take a shot, he will most likely find the cougar in this position. Most cougars are shot after being treed or confined to a high rocky outcrop by dogs.

followed this model, but most of the western states have shortened mountain lion seasons and enacted license quotas. Oregon has retained a liberal season but has outlawed the use of dogs. For those who wish to hunt a cougar, all this is unfortunate because the opportunity is shrinking. For everyone who loves wildlife, this is serious stuff, because wildlife's only hope for survival is through man's management.

SHOTS AT COUGAR

The unfortunate encounters where humans have fallen victim to mountain lions have been widely publicized, but they should be considered extremely rare. The cougar is almost invariably timid before man—especially in hunting country. There have been a few instances in which cougar, habituated to humans and unafraid, have become aggressive. They have deliberately stalked people in Southern California parks and have ventured into back yards and onto porches to prey on livestock and pets, despite human efforts to drive them away. This is rare. Most of the recent attacks, and especially the fatal attacks, have apparently resulted when an unaware human passed by a hunting cougar and sparked a charge. If you pay close attention to your surroundings, there is really nothing to fear in cougar country. Even where there are lots of cougar, the likelihood of an armed human encountering one and getting a shot is almost nil.

Like other large cats of the world, cougars tend to have their hearts rather far back in the rib cage. (Photo courtesy of Len Rue Jr.)

The Perfect Shot, North America

Historically, and to this day, the only truly reliable way to hunt a cougar is with a well-trained pack of hounds. The most difficult part of the hunt is finding a fresh trail for the dogs to follow. Good houndsmen usually know their country and have a good idea where to look, but most of the time it takes several days of scouring rugged canyons before a hunter can locate the track of a mature cat. Then the chase is on, and houndsmen live for this time. Like all cats, the cougar is relatively short-winded, but it will lead the dogs over the roughest country around. The length of the chase also depends on the exact age of the tracks, and this is usually impossible to determine.

The primary opportunities to hunt cougar are in the western Rocky Mountains and western Canada. In the southern areas such as Arizona and Nevada, hunting cougar is usually a matter of dry land trailing without snow. This is generally considered difficult, and certainly it's more difficult to find and evaluate tracks—but the dogs are used to this. In northern areas cougar are generally hunted in snow, where it is much easier to size and age tracks but not necessarily to follow the hounds.

No matter where you hunt, the real key is a serious houndsman with a pack of well-trained dogs. Even with the best outfitter and the best pack, it is always possible you won't find the fresh tracks of a big cat, but this is unusual. Cougar

Note how far back behind the leg the point of aim is for the heart shot. (Photo courtesy of Len Rue Jr.)

Many guides and houndsmen prefer a hunter to use a blunt-nosed .30-30 for a cougar with good reason because this combination has a great propensity for transmitting shock and energy. The heart shot is indicated. (Photo courtesy of Len Rue Jr.)

hunting is generally very successful, especially if you give it ten days in good country. Eventually you will find a big track; the dogs will jump the cat, and after a heart-pounding chase the cat will either tree or bay up in rocky outcroppings. The shot, when it comes, will usually be very close and anticlimactic; the actual hunt is the chase.

TAKING THE SHOT

Hunting cougar is primarily the houndsman's game. He has trained the dogs, and he derives the greatest pleasure in seeing them work. Unfortunately, the hunter who accompanies the houndsman in search of a cougar rug is little more than an observer—until it is time to take the shot. When that moment comes, the shot will probably be simple, but it must be done right. A wounded cat can wreak havoc on valuable dogs that deserve a better end to the chase, so the shot must be extremely well placed.

Head shots are out, not only because cats enter the record book based on skull measurements but because cats are thin-skinned and fragile. A head shot will not only ruin the skull but may also ruin the trophy. The only genuine options are lung shots or heart shots. Either is effective; the choice depends somewhat on the angle and presentation that is available. You don't always have a lot of choice; the cat may be partly hidden and protected by branches in a stout tree, or it may be backed up a rocky crevice. In any case, it is absolutely essential that you hold your fire until you are certain of a killing shot.

The actual placement differs not at all from placement for most other four-footed game. For the heart shot, shoot into the bottom third of the chest between the forelegs; for the lung shot, shoot into the bottom half of the center third of the chest along the rear line of the foreleg.

THE RIGHT CAT

Northern cats average a bit larger than cats from southern climes, but anywhere cougar are hunted, a male tom will average around 150 pounds. Weights over 200 pounds are possible but rare. Females are considerably smaller, usually running around 100 to 110 pounds. In most areas females without young are perfectly legal game, but a trophy cougar is a tom, and any mature tom is a great trophy. Although cougar enter the record books

Left to right: 1) .25-20 WCF 2) .30-30 Winchester 3) .44 Magnum. Cougars aren't particularly hardy creatures, and the shot will be close. Choice of cartridge isn't nearly so important as shot placement—and avoiding undue damage to the pelt. These three cartridges—including the pipsqueak .25-20—have been favored by houndsmen I have known.

purely on skull size, this is almost impossible to judge. Serious houndsmen look for a large track, generally a reliable indicator of a big-bodied male. A big cougar will probably have a large skull, but it will certainly have a tawny hide that stretches eight feet or more from nose to tail—which is the real trophy of a cougar hunt.

GUNS AND LOADS

Cougar are generally considered "soft" animals, and you can obtain clean kills without extremely powerful cartridges. Shooting is quite close, and there is usually no excuse at all for anything other than perfect shot placement. The skins are fragile, however. A cougar is essentially the size of a small deer, and you can take it cleanly with any deer-sized cartridge. In hound hunting a scoped, high-velocity rifle is really not necessary, and the exit wound from such cartridges can be messy.

To this day the favorite among houndsmen remains a good old lever-action carbine in .30-30. The rifles are light and easy to carry, and the relatively low-velocity bullet will dispatch any cat cleanly without doing a great deal of damage. Some prefer much lighter guns; an outfitter I hunted with in southern British Columbia carried an old slide-action Colt Lightning in .25-20, and insisted that his hunters use it to avoid pelt damage. Handguns are also extremely popular and effective. My old buddy Bob

Hunting cougar with hounds is an ideal game for handguns because a holstered pistol leaves the hands free while scrambling to the tree. If a rifle is to be used, a good old carbine in .30-30 is ideal—short, light, and with more than enough accuracy and power.

Milek took his cougar very efficiently with one bullet from a .22 magnum revolver, but I personally would prefer a .41 or .44 Magnum.

BULLET PERFORMANCE

The difficult part isn't killing the cat cleanly. The range is close, and when the cat is treed or bayed, there is usually no reason to rush the shot; you simply don't shoot until you are absolutely certain of a perfect shot. The difficulty is to kill the cat cleanly without damaging the pelt, even though most shots are at more or less point-blank range. Caliber isn't terribly important, but avoid extremely frangible bullets, unless the cartridge is so light that complete penetration is unlikely—like the .22 WMR or .25-20. Expect that the bullet will exit, and understand that a large exit wound is not needed. In rifles, use fairly tough bullets that will exit without a great deal of expansion; in handguns, avoid hollowpoints and use hard-cast, flat-point slugs.

SPECIAL CIRCUMSTANCES

If you're hunting cougar by any other method except hounds, things change dramatically. There aren't many successful alternatives, but there are possibilities. A chance encounter is extremely unlikely, but a hunter in cougar country, during open season with a tag in his pocket, can always bump into a cat, and a few do each year. It is almost impossible to bait a cougar, but, rarely, a cougar will come to a varmint call. And it is possible, though extremely difficult, to track a cougar without dogs.

It is often said, though widely disregarded, that a good man can walk down a cougar in tracking snow. I don't know any good man who has done it, but I do know one good woman who has. Debra Bradbury, publisher of *Blackpowder Hunter* magazine, had a crazy idea that she could track down a cougar without dogs. Over the course of several Wyoming winters, she followed a number of tracks, and she finally pulled it off. So it can be done, but it isn't easy.

Whether you're tracking or calling or you simply run into a cougar while hunting something else, any shot you can get is a great and rare opportunity. Forget the close-range guns you might use for hound hunting, and carry an accurate, flat-shooting, scoped rifle you can handle well and in which you have absolute confidence.

WOLF

Like it or not,
the wolf is coming back!

The wolf engenders a deep-seated, atavistic response in many humans. The howl of a wolf in the night brings the hair up on the back of the neck—an unnamed and irrational fear rooted deeply in our prehistoric past. With the urbanization of our society, many have lost this fundamental fear of the wolf, and it is probably they who are clamoring for the wolf's total protection and reintroduction.

People of the land, especially farmers and ranchers, take the opposite approach. Many of them are in favor of continuing mankind's total war against wolves. But the wolf is coming back. With successful reintroductions of Canadian wolves in national parks, sightings are now common in much of western Wyoming and Montana, and the wolf continues to expand its range in the upper Midwest.

There are strong feelings on both sides of the wolf issue. On the one hand, the wolf looks altogether too much like the family dog; on the other hand, it is surrounded by superstition and dread. In reality it is a highly intelligent animal and an efficient predator. The wolf is a threat to wildlife and can be hard on livestock. Wolf are an important part of true wilderness, however, and I think our wild country is much the poorer without their distant howls. On the other hand, there is very little true wilderness that isn't subject to some degree of management by man. The proper position is probably a balanced one. A few wolves are wonderful, but too many wolves can be a serious problem.

Some people believe that the reintroduction of the wolf is an insidious long-term plot to end hunting. I don't subscribe to that theory. I think, in the main, the extensive and expensive efforts to return the wolf to the western mountains are well intentioned, but the law of unintended consequences does apply. Where there are wolf, there will be a smaller huntable surplus for sportsmen. Wolf will kill and eat deer and elk with relish—but they will also kill and eat high-profile species like bighorn sheep, which have been brought to their present level through extensive time, effort, and money. Wolf will also kill and eat livestock, which is the primary reason man has waged war against the wolf for centuries. I well remember a monument I saw in northern Scotland commemorating the place where Scotland's last-known wolf was killed some 250 years ago!

Unfortunately, there isn't a ready solution. The wolf is coming back, not only to the western mountains but also to the northern forests. For the foreseeable future it will undoubtedly be fully protected in the Lower 48, but perhaps someday, at least in some states, it will be considered a game animal as it is in Alaska and much of Canada. Mind you, this business about the wolf "coming back" is a very subjective term. The wolf isn't easy to count, but estimates run as high as seven thousand wolf in Alaska and more than thirty thousand in Canada. Minnesota has as many as twelve hundred, not a small number—so the wolf has never been endangered in North America. It's also questionable, at least to some of us, that it was ever truly gone from the western mountains.

Clear back in 1971, on a deer hunt in the Maroon Bell Wilderness in Colorado, just at dusk, my Dad and I heard an incredible howling that seemed straight out of a Dracula movie. It wasn't coyotes; any good Kansas boy knows what a coyote sounds like. But it couldn't have been wolf, because everyone knew there were no wolf in Colorado. Just like everyone knew there were no grizzly bear remaining—until a bow hunter killed (and was almost killed by) a grizzly bear in the Sangre de Cristo Mountains a few years later! I wasn't sure what I had heard until I heard wolf howling in Alaska many years later. Then I became certain, and am still certain, that I heard wolf in Colorado in 1971.

Undoubtedly, there have always been a few remaining wolf in the most remote areas. I saw a wolf track in Montana's Swan Valley, not far from the Bob Marshall Wilderness,

That's a white wolf 'way out across the tundra, and that's me lining up to shoot at it. This was a great opportunity, but in those pre-rangefinder days, I misjudged the range and blew it, shooting right under him.

long before the recent reintroductions. My old friends, Warner Glenn and the late Marvin Glenn, saw very few over the years on their remote ranch on the Arizona-Mexico border. I don't believe the wolves have ever been completely gone, but right now they are definitely coming back.

Our North American wolf is properly the gray wolf, *Canis lupus*, also called timber wolf and tundra wolf. Although many generally indistinct subspecies have been identified, our wolf is really the same animal as the wolf of Europe and Asia—yes, just the same as Count Dracula's "children of the night" in far-off Transylvania! *Canis lupus* is the largest wild member of the dog family and is almost certainly the ancestor of our domestic dog. Gray is the most common color, but wolf range from pure white to pure black, with innumerable shades of gray and brown in-between. Most packs have individuals of various colors. The lighter shades are common in the north, and darker wolf are common in the southern parts of their range. The wolf stands about thirty-two inches high at the shoulder, with full-grown males running about 80 to 120 pounds—but occasional outsized specimens weigh 150 pounds or more.

More than a century has passed since we began to aggressively manage our wildlife, and the bounty we now have in North America is the result. The wolf, however, didn't receive much protection through most of the twentieth century. Until quite recently its tribe has been trapped, poisoned, and shot on sight—and it survived in spite of our best (or worst) efforts. Today, in some Canadian provinces and in Alaska, it is hunted in accordance with seasons, under a big-game tag or a furbearer license. Either way, it genuinely deserves the status it has attained as a full-fledged big-game animal. In fact, by any standard and ethical fair-chase method of hunting, there are very few animals in the world as difficult to hunt as the wolf! The Boone and Crockett record book does not recognize the wolf as a big-game animal, but Safari Club International's record book does.

SHOTS AT WOLF

Today most wolf are taken incidental to big-game hunts for other species. Wolf are present throughout most hunting areas in western Canada and Alaska, so you might encounter a wolf at any time. If the season is open, it's foolish to not have a wolf tag in your pocket, because you never know. It's very difficult to plan an encounter, but under Murphy's Law, it's almost certain that if you don't have a wolf tag or if the season isn't open, you'll see them all over the place!

Wolf do respond to varmint calls, so if you see fresh tracks or hear wolf howling at night, you have a chance to bring one in. Along with a wolf tag, a good, loud varmint call is another good item to put into a daypack. Wolf will also come onto winterkilled carcasses and the remains of hunter-killed game. In areas where black bear are baited, wolf may also come onto bait piles. These encounters are hard to plan and require a whole bunch of luck—but this is probably the best way to get a good shot at a wolf. When returning to any downed game, wilderness hunters use extreme caution to avoid encounters with bear, but if you desire a wolf, the best approach is to try to view the carcass from a distance. It isn't easy to sneak up on a wolf, even if it's on a kill, but it can be done.

Chance encounters are just that; they are almost impossible to predict, and they can take any form. Typically, wolf hunt along the edges of rivers and streams, and they follow the glacial streambeds when moving from one area to another. These are the most likely areas for a meeting engagement. I know a number of hunters who, over the course of several hunts in Canada and Alaska, have taken more than one wolf. Others, like me, have never shot one and wish to desperately!

These days, when the wolf is elevated to big-game status in many hunters' minds, there is a growing market for midwinter wolf hunts. Under some circumstances Alaska's prohibition against "same-day airborne" hunting didn't apply to wolf, so until fairly recently a common hunting technique was to search for wolf from the air, then shadow the pack until the hunters reached a safe place to land on snow skis, and jump out and shoot. Hunters no longer do this, but they conduct some midwinter wolf hunts on snowmobiles here and there in the far north. This is an extremely cold and difficult endeavor. Basically, hunters cover ground until they find fresh tracks, then follow until they sight the pack, and they eventually jump off and shoot.

This means that the shot will be a difficult attempt at a fast-moving target, while the shooter is bundled in multiple layers of bulky clothing. But here's the deal: A shot at a wolf is so difficult to obtain and so rare an opportunity that any shot at a wolf is a great opportunity. If you're fortunate enough to spot a wolf on a kill and can make a covered and concealed approach, you

Wolves almost always are trophies of opportunity during a hunt in Canada or Alaska. Because of this, the hunter will be equipped with a caliber suitable for moose, sheep, bear, or caribou. What is suitable for these animals will do well for a wolf, too. (Photo courtesy of Len Rue Jr.)

might get a very simple shot, but most shots at wolf are difficult, either at long range or at a moving animal, or both. I've never taken a wolf, but I can't say that I haven't had any chances. I have had chances, and I shoot a rifle as well as most people. But I don't have a wolf to show for my efforts!

TAKING THE SHOT

The wolf is an extremely intelligent animal, with the keen eyes, excellent ears, and sensitive nose common to all canines. After centuries of attempted extermination, it is ingrained in them that humans are bad news. Whether through luck or skill, if you can get past these defenses and get a shot within reasonable range, you have done well. The idea now is not to blow it (like I have)! Wolf are extremely tough animals; on the hunt they run many miles daily, so a healthy wolf is in great physical condition. A wolf can and will travel far and fast with a bad hit, so if you get that rare opportunity to take a wolf, you must hit it well. The chest cavity is the largest vital target, so that is your aiming point—but, if at all possible, go a step further and try to break its shoulder en route to the heart.

THE RIGHT WOLF

Safari Club International accepts wolf trophies based on skull measurements, but the real trophy to most hunters is the luxurious hide. Either way, opportunities

For practically all hunters, a wolf skin is a much-sought-after trophy. Take the heart/lung shot to avoid shattering leg bones, which, in turn, tend to cause large exit holes that damage the skin. (Photo courtesy of Len Rue Jr.)

to take wolf are so rare that it's ridiculous to speak in terms of trophy quality; any legally taken wolf is a great trophy. Period. Obviously, if you get the drop on a pack, you will probably pick out the largest wolf in the group, which should be a big male. But you might choose a wolf of unique color instead, preferring a black or white wolf to a gray wolf of larger size. Don't spend a lot of time making a decision; the moment will be fleeting!

GUNS AND LOADS

Since most wolf are taken incidental to hunting other species, the right rifle is probably whatever you have in your hands, if it makes the shot possible. Sometimes it won't be possible. In Alaska, while bear hunting with a .375, I watched a group of wolf for about half an hour. I was on a little knoll, and they were resting in a little depression about five hundred yards below me. There was no point in trying such a shot with the .375, and there was no way to get closer. I'm not at all sure I could have made such a shot had I been carrying a .300 magnum, but I probably would have tried. As it was, all I could do was enjoy watching them!

Given a choice, the right rifle is probably an accurate, flat-shooting rifle chambered to anything from .243 to one of the .300 magnums. Obviously, it should be scoped, but there is one other criterion that is extremely important: The rifle should fit you well, and you should know it well,

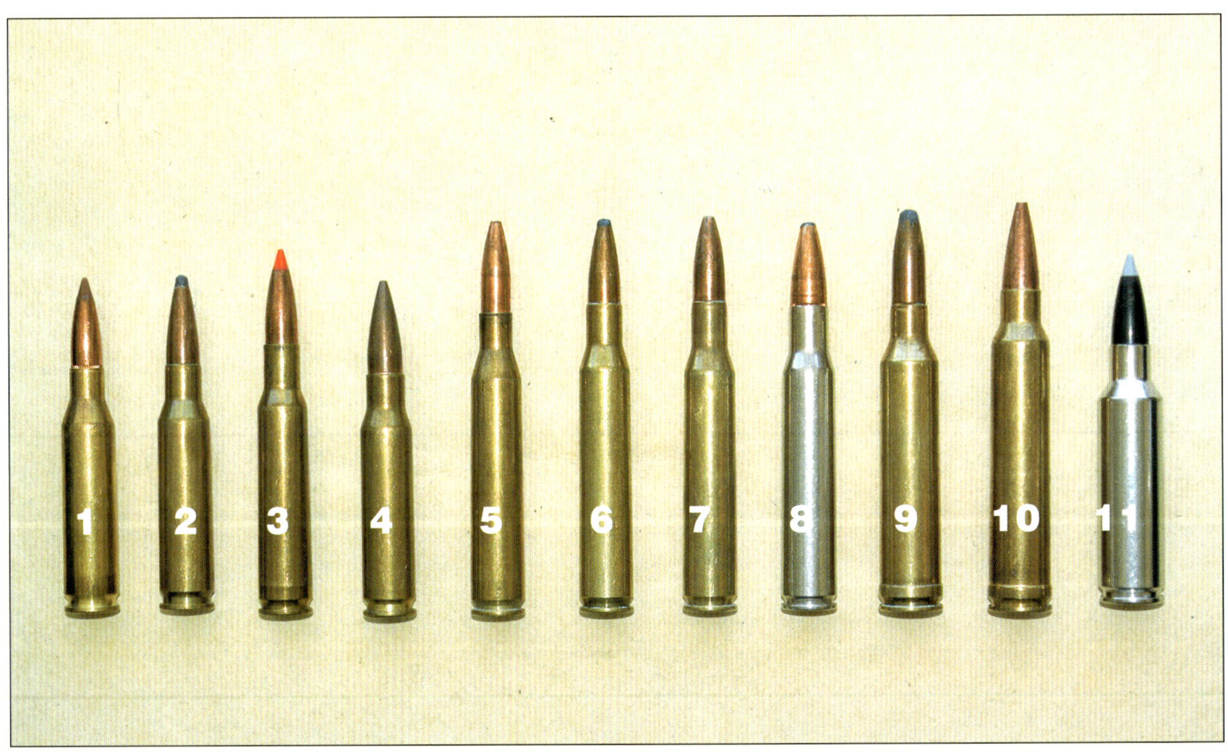

Left to right: 1) .260 Remington 2) 7mm-08 Remington 3) 7x57 4) .308 Winchester 5) .25-06 6) .270 Winchester 7) .280 Remington 8) .30-06 9) 7mm Remington Magnum 10) .300 Winchester Magnum 11) .300 Winchester Short Magnum. The Alaskan hunters often use semiautomatic .223s for wolf hunting, but I'd be more comfortable with a flat-shooting, general-purpose round—like any of these . . . and a bunch of others not pictured. A big wolf is the size of a deer but perhaps tougher, so good deer cartridges with fast-opening bullets should be ideal.

Any shot at a wolf is a rare opportunity, so you want to be able to take advantage of any chance you might get. The rifle should be accurate and should fit you well so that you can take a fast-running shot if you must. This is one of my favorite .30-06 rifles, grouping well with 150-grain Ballistic Silvertips. This is the kind of rig I would like to have in my hands next time I encounter a wolf.

because the only shot you get may well be a running shot. The snow-machine hunters generally use semiautomatic .223s, like the Ruger Mini-14, also a favored gun during the days of fly-and-shoot wolf hunting. This is somewhat opposed to my idea of the right rifle, but running shots are all you get under these circumstances, so I understand where they're coming from. Also, I'm not about to argue with someone who has shot more wolf than I will ever see.

BULLET PERFORMANCE

As is often the case, this is far more important than choice of caliber. I'll give you one of my wolf stories. Guide Jack Ringus and I were camped along a river in southeast Alaska, hunting for bear. It was late in the afternoon, and we were glassing from camp when a lone wolf came trotting along the far bank, maybe 225 yards away. I grabbed my .300 magnum and got into a sitting position, hoping it would stop. Instead, it saw us and speeded up. Still, it was the chance of a lifetime. I got the cross hairs on it and swung in front of it, and when the rifle went off, I knew I had it.

Almost. I hit it hard, somewhere in the front quarter, but it got into the thick conifers just up from the riverbank. We got into our waders and crossed the river, easily picking up the spoor. It was hands and knees in the thick stuff, but we could follow the trail. Two or three times we heard the wolf moving in front of us, but eventually it got too dark to follow. No problem; I was sure we'd find it in the morning. Except that it rained hard that night, and we never found another trace.

Now, it should be obvious that a .300 magnum is plenty of gun for this size animal. This being the case, it should be equally obvious that I didn't hit it exactly right. But the wolf was more or less broadside, and the tracks indicated that the on-side foreleg was broken high. So I wasn't very far off! When an animal is lost, you never know exactly what transpired, and it's altogether too easy to blame the bullet. But I was using a tough, deep-penetrating Barnes X-Bullet, just right for the bear I intended to shoot but perhaps a bit too tough for a slender animal the size of a wolf. Perhaps I'm wrong, but to this day I believe I would have a wolf rug in my den had I been using a bullet that had opened up more quickly and done more damage to the animal's vitals. Anyway, it was a sad chapter that still bothers me. When I go on a specific wolf hunt (and I will), I will load up with a faster-opening bullet like a Nosler Ballistic Tip or a Sierra Gameking.

WALRUS

North America's biggest game!

The walrus is not the only marine mammal that humans hunt for food, skins, and commercial products (like whale oil). It is, however, the only aquatic animal that is generally considered big game, almost certainly because of its long, gleaming ivory tusks. Those tusks are important to the hunters who pursue walrus, but they are even more important to the walrus. It uses them for fighting, digging, pulling itself onto islands and ice floes, and propelling itself across land and ice, where its flippers are of limited utility. This last characteristic is what gives this genus its Latin name, *Odobenus*, which means "one that walks with its teeth."

The walrus is of the family Pinnipedia, fin-footed carnivorous mammals that spend most of their time in the water. The group also includes hair seals, fur seals, and sea lions; but there is just one species in the walrus group, *Odobenus rosmarus*. Two subspecies are generally accepted: the Atlantic walrus (*Odobenus rosmarus rosmarus*) and the Pacific walrus (*Odobenus rosmarus divergens*). Although their habits and hunting are similar, they are considerably different. Boone and Crockett and Safari Club International have separate categories for each.

The Pacific walrus is considerably larger. Bulls can weigh up to 3,500 pounds, making the walrus indisputably the largest big-game animal in North America. In perspective, the walrus can be twice as heavy as a bull moose or a Cape buffalo bull and is about the same weight as a black rhino. The walrus is a bulky animal, yellowish-brown with no tail and with four well-developed flippers. Awkward and ungainly on land, it is a great swimmer, generally feeding at depths of up to three hundred feet on mollusks and other shellfish but occasionally killing and eating seals. Its famous mustache of thick bristles is believed to act as a sensory organ, enabling it to feel its way around in the depths.

The tusks are greatly elongated canine teeth, considerably larger on the bulls than on females. Pacific walrus bulls commonly have tusks as long as thirty inches, and lengths up to forty inches (with ten-inch circumference) have been recorded. The Atlantic walrus is considerably smaller, with bulls rarely weighing more than a ton. Tusks are proportionately smaller as well; the world record in Boone and Crockett, from Greenland, measures 30½ inches, but tusks over twenty inches are pretty good.

The Pacific walrus ranges from west of Victoria Island in Northwest Territories, around Alaska to the western edge of the Alaskan Peninsula, and on across the Bering and Chukchi Seas to western Siberia. The Atlantic walrus has a much larger range, extending from Hudson Bay north and east to Greenland, and east to Russia's northern coast.

Hunting the walrus has been on-again, off-again. For many years Inuit hunters from villages along the Alaskan coast hunted Pacific walrus. They conducted these hunts in the Bering Sea in the springtime, when walrus in the thousands were migrating to the Chukchi Sea. The walrus is an unusual trophy, but hunting it in small boats among the ice floes is even more unusual. According to the reports of the hunters I know, it was a truly wonderful experience. Unfortunately, those days seem to be over. The last legal walrus hunting in Alaska took place in 1979. The closure has nothing to do with a shortage of walrus; most authorities agree that there are so many Pacific walrus that they are eating themselves out of house and home. Unfortunately, the issue isn't management but politics. The closure is the result of a dispute between the United States government and the state of Alaska over jurisdiction; the dispute stems from the passage of the Marine Mammal Protection Act in 1972.

Native hunters continue to hunt walrus in both Alaskan and Canadian waters. Though sport hunting for Pacific walrus was once a common thing, historically there have been very few opportunities for outsiders to hunt Atlantic walrus. Boone and Crockett's records list just eight Atlantic walrus, all

Traditionally, the Inuit people go out among the ice floes in small, frail craft in search of walrus and seals. Today modern hunting is usually done from somewhat sturdier boats—but it's still a daunting adventure.

from 1955 and earlier, and six of the eight are of uncertain origin. Only two Atlantic walrus in the Boone and Crockett book were taken by a hunter, D. B. MacMillan, who took both in Greenland for the American Museum of Natural History clear back in 1916. This situation is going to change.

Atlantic walrus are not nearly so plentiful as the Pacific variety, but the Canadian government believes there are enough to sustain limited hunting. Inuit villages in the right areas have walrus quotas, and today they are allowed to sell permits from that quota to nonnative hunters. So it is possible to hunt walrus once more, and for the foreseeable future the smaller Atlantic walrus is probably the only opportunity there will be.

The bad news is that, thanks to the Marine Mammal Protection Act, once again the U.S. Fish and Wildlife Service will not issue permits for the importation of walrus trophies, even when they are legally taken in other countries. This regrettable policy greatly restricts the demand for these hunts, which bring tremendous economic benefit to the Inuit communities. Perhaps in time the policy will change, as it has with the polar bear. For now, most Americans who hunt walrus take the measurements of their tusks and have an artificial trophy made.

SHOTS AT WALRUS

The walrus hunts and plays in the ocean and comes onto land primarily to rest. Using

A rare photo of a polar bear attempting to catch a mature walrus. This goes to show how tough walrus really are, because they did not attempt to flee into the water but bunched up in a defensive heap. (Photo courtesy of Ralf Schneider)

all four flippers and its teeth, it can get around on ice or land but is awkward and slow. It apparently has reasonable vision, but neither its sense of smell nor its hearing is especially keen. Regardless of its sensory acuity, it is not particularly wary. In the ocean it has no enemies save the killer whale, and on land no enemies save man—and it may live its entire life without seeing a human. It isn't usually difficult to get close enough to a walrus to shoot. The difficult part of the hunt is getting to the walrus.

The current Canadian hunts, like the historic Alaskan hunts, go out in small boats from Inuit villages, on the icy ocean, choked with floating ice. Provided the weather holds—and the guides are able to read the weather—the hunts are fairly safe, but they are not for the fainthearted. In the old days hunters used sealskin boats; today small aluminum craft with outboard motors are more common. Hunters most often use flat-bottom boats so they can drag the boat across ice floes.

Typically, the Inuit hunters know when and where the walrus are moving through, so it's a matter of threading the small boats along the edges of the ice floes, looking for resting pods of walrus. When the hunters spot a suitable bull, they can make the shot from the boat, but when possible they go onto the ice and make a stalk. The shot is usually from fairly close range, but it must be perfect. If the animal isn't killed almost instantly,

This Atlantic walrus was shot with a .375 H&H, a sensible caliber for such a huge animal. (Photo courtesy of Ralf Schneider)

it will almost certainly flounder into the water, and then it is lost.

TAKING THE SHOT

Walrus hide can be as much as two inches thick at the shoulder. Getting through the hide and into the vitals of this huge animal requires a powerful cartridge and a very tough bullet. But killing the walrus isn't enough; it will never be far from the water, and the hunter must stop it before it gets there. Amid all that bulk (even in the neck), it is extremely difficult to visualize where the spine lies, and no other body shot will be certain to immobilize such a huge animal. The only sensible shot for a walrus is a head shot.

This requires power and penetration, but it also requires precision. As is always the case with a head shot, if you flub it, you've got immediate difficulty, and, though you can always back it up with body shots, you will probably get just one chance at the brain. The proper placement is essentially in the upper center of the skull, between and slightly above the eyes from the front, or just in front of the small ear hole from the rear. Even at very close range, this shot is difficult from a bobbing boat. By far the best course is to get on firm footing, take your time, and do it right.

THE RIGHT WALRUS

The trophy is obviously the tusks, and they are quite visible, though individually

Walrus are not easy targets, especially when shooting from a wobbly boat. The problem is compounded because of the necessity of hitting the brain, which is the only shot that will anchor a walrus. (Photo courtesy of Ralf Schneider)

they aren't easy to judge. One walrus looks much like another, especially if you aren't familiar with this animal. Fortunately, walrus are gregarious creatures, and you will usually find them resting in groups, the size depending primarily on how much space is available. It is relatively easy to compare one walrus to another in the group. If the weather holds and the migration is going through the area you're hunting, it is possible to see hundreds of walrus before making a decision; but in the Arctic the weather usually determines hunting time.

In any case, since the actual ivory cannot be imported, the real trophy of the hunt is the experience of seeing the great animals and hearing them barking and roaring among the ice floes. This you will carry home, and it's far more important than a couple more inches of tusk.

GUNS AND LOADS

A walrus hunt is no place for the common North American hunting cartridges. The size of the beast calls for African cartridges; the fact that you must stop the walrus before it gets into the water makes them an absolute requirement. Lighter cartridges offer enough penetration on the brain shot that you must attempt, but not all brain shots are perfect, and it takes a lot of power to clean up the mess.

The .375 H&H is a good, sensible minimum, especially for the smaller Atlantic

It is not widely known, but a full-grown male walrus will easily outweigh a mature bison bull. Almost all shots for walrus are directed to the brain because this is the only shot that will ensure an immediate kill as well as prevent the animal from entering the water, where it is easily lost. (Photo courtesy of Len Rue Jr.)

walrus. In the old days of Alaskan hunting, the .458 Winchester Magnum was by far the most popular, and it's perfect—a big, heavy bullet that makes a big hole and penetrates deeply. The various .416s are also good, but you don't need the versatility of a .375 or .416. Unlike all other North American hunting, hunting walrus requires close-range stopping power, pure and simple.

The rifle you choose should be a repeater, because one shot may not do it, and once you open the ball game, you must finish it quickly. A double rifle would be just fine—but I wouldn't be real keen about carrying a nice double out there among the ice floes! The best choice is probably what the Alaskan outfitters settled on: a dependable, inexpensive bolt-action in .458 Winchester Magnum or a similar genuine "stopping cartridge."

BULLET PERFORMANCE

Here again the walrus is different from all other North American big game. For most hunting we can discuss the merits of one bullet style versus another, some of us preferring very tough bullets and others preferring bullets that open up more quickly and create a larger wound channel. Remember that a big walrus is as big as a rhinoceros, with skin that is even thicker. Since jacketed bullets were invented, it has been clear which type of bullet is best suited for this class of game. You can call them solids, full-patch, or full-metal-jacket, but the only bullet you want for walrus

None of the three "normal" shots—heart, lung, shoulder—apply to the walrus because of the need to guarantee an anchoring shot on an animal that can weigh 3,500 pounds. Since the walrus will be mere yards from water, it's important to shoot for the brain, which is an immediately incapacitating shot. (Photo courtesy of Len Rue Jr.)

is a nonexpanding bullet designed for the largest game on earth. Again, you probably don't need such a bullet if you make a correct brain shot—but if you miss the brain, or if the circumstances are such that a body shot seems practical, then only a solid will guarantee the straight-line penetration you must have.

There is a very limited market for this type of bullet, but there is enough interest to sustain several types. Hornady's steel-jacketed solid, covered with gilding metal, is an excellent bullet available in .375, .416, and .458. Speer's African Grand Slam with tungsten core is superb, as is the Woodleigh (another steel-jacketed solid). Barnes's Super Solid is a homogeneous alloy bullet with no core, and there are some others. All perform extremely well, so it doesn't matter which solid you choose, as long as you insist on this type of bullet for walrus hunting.

Unlike all other American game, walrus hunting is a game exclusively for the most powerful rifles and the toughest bullets. The best choice is solid, nonexpanding bullets like the two .470 bullets to the left. With enough caliber and weight, good expanding bullets like the two Woodleighs (on the right) will work—but solids are better.

THE THIN-HORNED SHEEP

Harder to come by every year!

Widely regarded as two entirely different sheep, the snow-white Dall sheep and salt-and-pepper Stone sheep are actually races, or subspecies, of the same wild sheep, *Ovis dalli*. The white sheep, *Ovis dalli dalli*, inhabit the mountain ranges of Alaska, northern Yukon, and the Mackenzie district of the Northwest Territories; a band of pure-white sheep dips into extreme northwestern British Columbia. Many of us think the dark Stone sheep are named for the gray rocks they live in. Actually, *Ovis dalli stonei* is named in honor of an early naturalist named Stone.

In British Columbia, Rocky Mountain bighorns inhabit the southeastern mountains, and the smaller California bighorns are found in the southwestern part of the province. There is considerable expanse before you get into Stone sheep country in northern B.C., so there is no overlap between the two species and no natural hybridization. This is not the case with Stone and Dall sheep. In northern B.C. the Stone sheep tend to be quite dark, and some bands of very dark sheep range up into south central Yukon. But the intergrade area is quite large, and the two subspecies interbreed freely. Where white sheep and dark sheep meet, individual animals can range from pure white to fairly dark, and everything in-between. A classic hybrid is mostly white with a distinctive dark "saddle patch" on the flanks. This is the Fannin sheep, once thought to be a separate race but now recognized as an intergrade.

The horns of the Dall and Stone sheep are similar. They are generally golden, with relatively thin horns (compared to bighorns) that usually make a full curl and then flare outward as the ram matures. On average, Stone sheep are slightly bigger-bodied than Dall sheep, and the biggest Stone rams grow slightly larger horns than the biggest Dall rams—probably because Stone sheep have better nutrition and milder winters in their more southerly mountains. The record books endeavor to keep things simple: A pure white sheep is a Dall sheep, and a sheep with dark hair is a Stone sheep. We can assume this refers to the intergrade area of the Yukon, because well into Alaska it is not unusual to find Dall sheep with some dark hairs here and there!

The hunting of the two varieties is essentially the same. Hunters painstakingly glass until they locate a suitable ram and then plan a stalk that will keep them out of sight until they are within shooting range. Sheep can hear quite well, and there's nothing wrong with their noses. However, they rely mostly on their keen eyesight. Rolling rocks are part of their lives, so absolute silence is not as essential as it is when hunting other species. Human voices and the rattling of equipment are taboo, but if you can keep out of sight and keep the wind more or less favorable, it is usually possible to approach the sheep.

One of the main differences between hunting Dall and Stone sheep is that Dall sheep are much easier to spot. Their northern mountains tend to have sparser vegetation, and nothing shows up as well as a pure white sheep; you can see their brilliant white bodies at incredible distances. The darker Stone sheep are considerably more difficult to spot. Of course, after the snow flies, the white sheep are camouflaged while darker sheep stand out.

The actual hunting involves getting to a high vantage point, then letting good optics do the looking, but there are various ways of attaining those vantage points. In most Stone sheep country, horseback hunting is traditional; it is also common in the Yukon, and there are a couple of horse outfitters in Alaska. Most Dall sheep hunting is by backpack hunting on foot. This is a two-edged sword. Nowhere is it particularly common to simply ride up on a ram, jump off, and shoot. It happens, but most likely you will reach a point where you must tie the horses and climb on up into the real sheep country. You can cover a lot of country on horseback, and a packhorse can carry more and better supplies and can also pack out the game—but eventually you must go back to the horses. Backpack hunting is a fine way to hunt sheep—you can roam where you will and set up camp when you're tired—but you are limited by your physical condition and the amount of food you can carry with

To some extent the conditions of the hunt dictate the rifle that should be used. Backpack hunts are tough, and every ounce—in both rifle and ammo weight—makes a difference.

you. Overall, I have always preferred backpack hunting, but I'm reaching the age where horses look better all the time.

SHOTS AT THINHORNS

The common belief is that sheep hunting is a game for long-range shooting. Whenever you get into big country, there may be the opportunity for a long shot, but, especially in the northern mountains, extremely long shooting isn't all that common. Sheep are absolutely gorgeous animals, but they are actually not as "switched on" as any variety of North American deer. The difficult part is climbing into their country—definitely a game for physically fit hunters who really want to do it—and locating a suitable ram. If you can find a ram, you can probably find a way to get a shot.

Sometimes it will be a long poke, but usually the mountains have enough ridges and furrows to allow a reasonably close approach. Still, you should be prepared for a long shot. My best Dall ram, taken in the Yukon, was bedded on a little ridge with its buddies. We should have been able to get within a hundred yards of it, but the approach was circuitous and took so long that the sheep were up and feeding before we got to them. They had dropped down into a grassy valley, which was OK, except it appeared they were headed into some cliffy stuff where we couldn't follow them. So I got as close as I could, still well over

The end of a successful backpack hunt. In some areas guides aren't allowed to carry rifles. There is no backup, so whatever rifle you choose must be first and foremost absolutely reliable.

four hundred yards, set up a good rest, and took the only shot I seemed likely to get. I had the equipment for such a shot, and it worked perfectly.

That was actually the longest shot I have ever attempted on a wild sheep, whether in North America or Asia. Most of the time you can get closer. In the Northwest Territories we stalked a Dall ram on a series of descending benches, taking it at about sixty yards. This shooting distance is not unusual, but with a centerfire rifle there is no reason to push too close and risk spooking the ram. So, the world over, most of my shots at wild sheep have come between 150 and 300 yards—not really a tall order for a reasonably flat-shooting rifle with a good scope.

Patience is often the key. Sheep move a little bit in the early morning but bed most of the day, with their peak movement usually during the late afternoon and early evening hours. If you can bed a ram in the morning, you have all day to work in on it. Depending on the situation, you may also be able to predict with some accuracy where it will move when it starts to feed. Maybe the situation will get worse, as it did when I shot that Yukon ram—but maybe it will get better. In the evening you often have a scramble on your hands as you try to close on a ram before it gets dark. Sometimes you have a choice between a longer shot in failing light or trying again in the morning. Sheep usually don't move

Dall sheep are identical in body size to Stone sheep, and both animals can be hunted well with cartridges in the .270, 7mm, and .308 class of calibers. (Photo courtesy of Leonard Lee Rue III)

a great deal during full darkness, so if you locate a ram in late evening you have a very good chance of relocating it at daylight, when you have plenty of time to make a good approach.

TAKING THE SHOT

Wild sheep are not particularly tough or hardy creatures, and there are no tricks or special considerations in planning the perfect shot. Because almost all wild sheep are taken as trophies, you should avoid brain or neck shots, not only because of the obvious difficulty but because you could ruin the valuable and nearly irreplaceable cape. I personally prefer the behind-the-shoulder lung shot because wild sheep offer the very best of all wild meat, and a lung shot causes the least meat damage. It also places the shot far enough back to cause minimal damage to the cape. Wild sheep tend to have an obvious "pocket" just behind the shoulder; look for it just above the back line of the rear foreleg, and place your shot about one-third up the body. No wild sheep will walk away from this shot.

There is an exception. Wild sheep are properly creatures of the high basins and meadows, but they will cross through and often bed in extremely rough, rocky places. If there is any chance that your ram will drop into a crevasse or roll off a cliff, think hard before you shoot. You don't want your ram bouncing down a thousand-foot cliff,

When at a steep angle like this one, it is easy to shoot too far back. The point of aim, from top to bottom, on this Stone sheep is: lung, shoulder, heart. (Photo courtesy of Leonard Lee Rue III)

ruining the meat, horns, and cape, and possibly lodging in a spot from which you can't recover it without great risk. This is a judgment call, but if you have the opportunity for a shot and you need to anchor your ram, then forget the lung shot. Shoot it carefully on the center of the shoulder, one-third up the body, so you will break heavy bone as well as wreck the vital organs. Even better, look for a broadside presentation so you can break both shoulders—and by all means shoot again if it isn't down!

One note on the white sheep or, for that matter, any white animal: Blood stains the cape badly. Remove the cape as quickly as possible and use cold water to wash out as much of the blood as possible. There will almost always be clear, cold streams in northern sheep country.

THE RIGHT RAM

Whether you're talking Dall sheep or Stone sheep, really good rams are increasingly hard to come by. Alaska's human population has grown considerably, and there is resident hunting pressure in all but the most rugged and remote ranges. This is also true in Stone sheep country. More and more Canadians make walk-in or fly-in hunts into country the sheep outfitters formerly had all to themselves.

Historically, the magic number for both Dall and Stone sheep was a ram with horns over 40 inches around the curl. These days

A flat-shooting, medium-light caliber is adequate for Stone sheep as well as Rocky Mountain goat, which are often encountered on the same hunt. (Photo courtesy of Leonard Lee Rue III)

Stone rams over 40 inches are rare, even with very limited quotas and frightening prices for outfitted hunts. Hunters are taking big rams, both in the classic country in British Columbia and in the Yukon, where the few outfitters who have dark sheep are trying to meet the greatly increased demand for sheep hunting—but not everybody is going to get one. These days you should consider a mature ram from 34 to 39 inches a very fine Stone ram, unless you're willing to go empty and try again another year.

The chances of getting a big Dall sheep are somewhat better. Part of the reason is that Dall sheep occupy a much larger range, so there are many more options. Most of the Dall sheep country in the Yukon, and in the Mackenzie Mountains of the Northwest Territories, is still very lightly hunted. Neither is likely to be a good place to get a ram that is genuinely over the magic 40-inch mark, although such sheep surely exist. On the other hand, both areas are good places to get an old ram with mass, character, and horns in the upper thirties.

Alaska's more accessible ranges are hard hunted today. There are lots of sheep, but most full-curl rams are in the 32- to 35-inch class, and older, bigger rams are fairly scarce. This is not universally true. Sheep in the remote Brooks Range tend to be a bit smaller and thinner-horned due to the extreme climate, but there are a lot of good rams, and good trophies are possible. Perhaps the biggest Dall sheep today are

This nice Stone sheep was shot on the Turnagain River in British Columbia with a .270 Winchester and a 130-grain Nosler Ballistic Tip. Well-known Stone-sheep guide Eugen Egeler is on the right. (Safari Press photo library)

Although beautiful walnut takes a beating in sheep mountains, a rifle doesn't have to wear a synthetic stock to be light enough and reliable enough for sheep hunting. My David Miller 7mm Remington Magnum weighs a bit over seven pounds and never changes zero.

available in the rough, tough ranges of southern Alaska, especially the Chugach. A lot of this country is limited entry and requires drawing for a permit—and it's all extremely steep, rocky, and difficult. It depends on what you want. A nice full-curl Dall ram is a beautiful trophy and is not that difficult to come by, but if you want a really big ram today you'll work hard, and probably more than once.

GUNS AND LOADS

Dall and Stone sheep are good-sized animals. Fall weights of mature rams run from about 180 pounds to as much as 250 pounds, though the latter is rare. These sheep are not as large as the biggest whitetail or mule deer buck—nor, in my opinion, are they nearly as tough. Though you need to be able to take longer shots if necessary, you don't need a cannon to hunt sheep. From the standpoint of caliber alone, something on the order of a .25-06 would be just fine, and some sheep hunters prefer the fast .25s.

Left to right: 1) .270 WSM 2) 7mm WSM 3) .300 WSM. The new short magnums, typified by the growing family of Winchester Short Magnums, are ideal for sheep hunting—accurate and flat-shooting, they can also be housed in a shorter and lighter rifle based on a short bolt action.

Personally, though, I want a bit more gun. You will work very hard for any shot you get at a wild sheep, and you should be prepared to take any reasonable shot that is within your capabilities. Somewhat larger calibers not only give you more energy and bullet weight but also buck the wind a bit better. The faster 6.5mms are good choices, and there's nothing wrong with any of the .300 magnums.

When I got that long shot at my Yukon ram, I was carrying a big Lazzeroni rifle in the superfast .308 Warbird cartridge, so I was well prepared for such a shot and had confidence I could pull it off. However, when it comes to sheep rifles, there should be a balance between capability and portability. In the Warbird I had all the capability I could ever use—and then some—but I was in extremely steep and rugged mountains, and I'm not sure I will ever carry such a heavy rifle up another sheep mountain.

Jack O'Connor wasn't all wrong when he considered the .270 Winchester an ideal sheep rifle. Although the cartridge is seventy-five years old, it's still ideal for this size game and this kind of hunting. It will reach out to 350 yards and more without difficulty, and can be built into a nice, light, easy-to-carry rifle. The various 7mm rifles are also excellent. I have used both the .280 and the 7mm Remington Magnum on sheep hunts, and they're excellent—not necessarily better than the old .270, but just as good. Another great choice is the .270 Weatherby Magnum. It is one of the flattest-shooting of all cartridges, but it still has light recoil and can be housed in a reasonably light rifle.

The only thing that might be better than the cartridges I've mentioned is the new breed of short magnums that can be housed in compact, short-action rifles. These include Lazzeroni's .284 Tomahawk and .308 Patriot; Remington's 7mm and .300 Short Action Ultra Mags; and Winchester's family of the .270, 7mm, and .300 Winchester Short Magnum. All of these are fine cartridges, but my pick would be the .270 Winchester Short Magnum because the .270 really is just right for this size game.

BULLET PERFORMANCE

Our northern sheep are blocky animals but not so large as to require extra-tough bullets. Going back to O'Connor once more, one of his favorite bullets for sheep was the old Remington Bronze Point. Still available, this bullet has a sharp alloy tip that precludes battering in the magazine, improves aerodynamics, and upon impact drives back into the bullet to promote expansion. It is really a forerunner of the modern polymer-tipped bullets: Nosler Ballistic Tip, Winchester Ballistic Silvertip, Hornady SST, Swift Scirocco. These are ideal bullets for hunting our smaller-bodied northern sheep.

You don't want or need extremely tough bullets for any sheep; their body size doesn't call for it. Though you don't want to ruin any more of that tasty meat than is necessary, you definitely don't want your ram to run into the crags where recovery

A really good Yukon Dall ram taken with a Lazzeroni rifle in the big .308 Warbird cartridge. This was a long shot, and the reach of the fast Warbird was welcome—but a rifle like this is really too heavy to carry up sheep mountains . . . it punished me!

can be difficult. The bullets we have discussed tend to be extremely accurate, but, depending on what works best in your rifle, don't overlook good old conventional softpoints like Sierra Gameking, Hornady Interlock, and tried-and-true factory bullets like Winchester's Power Point, Federal's Hi-Shok, and Remington's Core-Lokt. All offer the relatively rapid expansion you want on this kind of game.

SPECIAL CIRCUMSTANCES

From British Columbia's Cassiars to the Brooks Range, hunting the northern sheep is basically the same from the standpoint of shooting, shot placement, and choice of rifles and cartridges. The wild card, however, is that northern sheep are often hunted in combination with everything from goat to moose, caribou, and even the big bears. Goat rifles and sheep rifles are indistinguishable, and caribou rifles aren't much different. But ideal moose and grizzly bear rifles are probably not ideal sheep rifles. If you are planning a combination hunt, you should choose a rifle and cartridge that are adequate for the largest game but that also have the capability, in terms of accuracy and range, to take your sheep. My first sheep hunt was a combination hunt in northern B.C., and I took my Stone ram with a .375 H&H. It did the job just fine, but it wasn't perfect. Today I would probably take a faster, flatter-shooting magnum on such a hunt, probably a fast .30 if moose were on the agenda and an 8mm Remington Magnum or fast .33 if the hunt included grizzly.

BIGHORN SHEEP

There's a lot riding on the shot!

Everybody has his or her favorite game animal, because each of our North American big-game species is magnificent in its own way. Although the mighty grizzly bear runs awfully close, the bighorn sheep gets my vote as the most magnificent game animal in North America. To me the bighorn—a dramatic creature with wondrously thick horns—symbolizes the great mountain ranges of the American West. When I see a mounted bighorn ram I think of those snowcapped peaks in the late fall, and imagine I can hear the crashing of those horns as the mountain monarchs fight.

We call them bighorns not for the length of their horns—those of our thinhorn Dall and Stone sheep are actually longer—but for the tremendous mass of the horns. The base circumference on bighorns averages a couple of inches more than on Dall and Stone sheep. Good mature rams approach 16 inches in basal circumference and occasionally exceed 17 inches. This weight carries through the quarters quite well, but length is rarely extreme. The horns of bighorns typically curl tighter to the skull, unlike those of thinhorns, which tend to curl around and out.

As with all true horned animals, the horn continues to grow outward from the base throughout the animal's life. When bighorns approach or reach full curl, the horns start to interfere with the rams' peripheral vision, and they rub or broom them against rocks. Thus, at maturity, most bighorns have tips that are thick and worn, increasing the mass at the last quarter. This is part of the character of a good trophy.

There is just one species of bighorn sheep, *Ovis canadensis*, which has several subspecies. Traditionally, hunters have divided them into two groups: the big-bodied, darker-pelaged Rocky Mountain bighorn and the smaller-bodied, lighter-colored sheep adapted to life in the arid Southwest—the desert bighorns.

The Rocky Mountain bighorn is the type specimen *Ovis canadensis canadensis*. It originally occurred in huge numbers from northern New Mexico, north along the Front Range all through the Rocky Mountain chain, and west to the Sierra Nevada. Today there are very few "low-country" bighorns, but aggressive reintroductions—by both game departments and hunters' groups like the Foundation for North American Wild Sheep (FNAWS)—have restored bighorn populations to suitable high-country habitat in all the Rocky Mountain states. Huntable populations have also been developed in the badlands of western South Dakota. These replace the extinct "badlands bighorn," *Ovis canadensis auduboni*, the bighorn that Theodore Roosevelt hunted in the 1880s.

Bighorn Sheep

The Rocky Mountain bighorn is a big-bodied sheep, and mature rams often exceed three hundred pounds. Note that some of this weight is tied up in the horns—the fresh skull and horns of a really large bighorn can weigh more than forty pounds! Pelage ranges from gray-brown to very dark, with white nose patch, white on the back of the front legs and the inside of the back legs, and a large white rump patch surrounding the short dark tail.

Traditionally, the smaller California bighorn (*Ovis canadensis californiana*) has been lumped with the Rocky Mountain sheep for record-keeping purposes. This is changing, and Safari Club now separates the California subspecies in its record book. Typically, the California bighorn is about 20 percent smaller in body. Its horns are shorter and less massive and typically grow with more outward flare, so a mature California bighorn is less likely to have broomed tips. California bighorns also tend to be paler in body. Formerly, they ranged from south central British Columbia, south along the mountain chains to northern California. In addition to native-range herds in British Columbia, Washington, Oregon, Nevada, and California, transplanting has now developed herds of California bighorn in southwestern Idaho and western North Dakota. Most of these states and provinces also have herds of either desert sheep or Rocky Mountain

Bighorn hunting is generally more difficult because there is more timber, with the sheep usually bedding in heavy cover where they are invisible. Most movement will occur in the early mornings and late evenings, which makes a long day on the mountain.

bighorn, so there are some areas where the subspecies intergrade.

There are actually four subspecies that we call desert sheep, all much smaller and paler than the northern bighorns. Body size on mature desert sheep rams runs much less than two hundred pounds. Skulls, ears, the whole works are scaled down from the Rocky Mountain sheep—except that, on the very best rams, the horns aren't actually that much smaller. The new Boone and Crockett world-record Rocky Mountain bighorn was taken in Alberta, scoring 208⅜—a huge ram. Surprisingly, the world-record desert bighorn measures 205⅛—imagine how horns like that would look on such a small sheep!

Nelson's bighorn (*Ovis canadensis nelsoni*) is the most widespread of the desert bighorns. It is found from New Mexico to California, and there is an introduced herd in southwestern Colorado that is now huntable. From southern Arizona into Sonora the subspecies is *Ovis canadensis mexicana*. Mexico's Baja Peninsula has two subspecies, *Ovis canadensis cremnobates* in the north and *Ovis canadensis weemsi* at the southern tip. At least in recent times, northern Baja has produced the largest rams, and the weemsi is believed to be the smallest—but this doesn't matter too much. Desert bighorn hunting is carefully regulated, and all tags are so hard to come by that very few hunters much care which subspecies they get to hunt!

This was my shooting position when I took my Wyoming bighorn in 1998. He was bedded in the cover on the far side of the draw, and we waited for what seemed ages before he stood and offered the perfect shot.

You might think that bighorns are harder to spot than northern sheep because their coloration offers much better camouflage. This is true to a degree, but the white rump acts almost like a signpost. The sheep aren't always facing away, but at some point one will turn its rump to you—and you can glass this white circle at incredible distances.

SHOTS AT BIGHORNS

As with all sheep hunting, hunting a bighorn is largely a matter of painstaking glassing in the right habitat. The primary difference between hunting bighorns and hunting the northern sheep is that there is much more vegetation in bighorn habitat, so it's more difficult to locate sheep unless they're up and feeding. Today most bighorns are found where there are timbered slopes or pockets of heavy timber. The sheep bed in the timber, where it's almost impossible to spot them. Even if you know they're there, it's usually unwise to go in after them because bighorns are herd animals, and usually the ram you want is in a band of rams. If you go into close cover after them, there are too many sets of eyes, and the chances of getting a shot at the right ram are slim.

Like all sheep, bighorns tend to be most active in the evening; morning movement is somewhat more limited. You need to find them while they're feeding in the meadows and sagebrush pockets above timberline, or

I shot my Wyoming bighorn from around 275 yards, not a difficult shot with a .300 magnum—but it was the eleventh day of a ten-day hunt, and it was the only shot I was going to get. When there's pressure like that, you must have great faith in yourself and your rifle.

on the open fingers between the timbered draws, and then plan an appropriate stalk. They bed in the open as well, especially later in the fall when the weather cools down. In November the bighorns rut, and all bets are off. Like all animals, bighorns lose their caution during this period, and the big rams are much more visible as they wander in search of ewes.

The vegetation is much different for desert bighorns, but the hunting is not. They live in desert mountains—very much a living desert, with tall cacti, scrub oak, and mesquite. All of this can easily hide armies of small-bodied sheep. You need to locate desert sheep while they're moving and feeding, and in their warmer climate this movement is often restricted. The bonus is that, because the vegetation is sparser and more scattered, it is much more likely that you can bed a desert bighorn and move in on it. You may not actually shoot it in its bed, but you can discover exactly where it is and get in position, then wait until it moves.

Bighorns have exceptional eyes, which are their first line of defense. They also have keen noses, and they can hear perfectly well, so you need to keep the wind in your favor and be stealthy in your approach. However, virtually throughout their range, sheep hunting is so limited and tightly controlled that, if anything, most bighorn bands are actually less wary than Dall and Stone sheep. And no wild sheep are naturally as wary as our various deer. The hard part is finding the ram you want, but if you find it, there will usually be enough cover to allow an approach within reasonable rifle range. In other words, though a long shot is always a possibility in any mountain hunting, most shots at bighorns are well within three hundred yards. If you can locate a ram that meets your standards, you should be able to get a shot at it.

The new world record was taken by Texan Guinn Crousen at just seventy yards. I haven't been quite that fortunate, either in size of ram or in shooting distance. I took my first bighorn at the head of a timber pocket in Montana, distance about 125 yards. My second—which means that I have drawn two tags, putting me well ahead of the game—was a bit trickier.

I was hunting in Wyoming with Ron Dube, and it had been a long, hard hunt. We'd seen lots of young rams but simply couldn't find a mature ram. Finally, on the tenth day, we separated, each climbing to a separate vantage point. I had just made the top when I heard Dube's whistle from far below, the "come back" signal. I slid back down the mountain, and he announced with a grin, "The hunting phase of this Ron Dube hunting adventure is now over. The harvesting phase has just begun." If you find a good ram, you can say that with some confidence (which is not the case with so much hunting), but it wasn't that easy. The ram was a long distance away, and we couldn't locate it by dark. So we slept on the mountain and we found it the next morning, bedded in a little sagebrush opening. I waited a nerve-racking hour for it to get up, then shot it at about 275 yards.

TAKING THE SHOT

A Rocky Mountain ram is big enough that you must give some consideration to its body mass when you choose cartridges and bullets. However, wild sheep are not particularly strong or tough. A solid hit into the chest cavity will drop any ram that ever lived in short order. The problem is that opportunities to hunt any breed of bighorn sheep are so scarce today that hunters experience great pressure with any shot. If you're financially challenged like me, you applied for permits for many years before drawing a tag—and you know that you may not live long enough to draw another one. State and provincial game departments make available "governor's tags," sold at auction at hunters' conventions. These are a really good thing because they bring fantastic sums of money that directly benefit wildlife, but the prices are such that even a wealthy hunter will feel the pressure when a big ram is in range and it's time to do business. There are other options: In Sonora the desert sheep are now privatized, and some Indian reservations in the United States offer sheep hunting. Again, the prices are high enough that anyone will feel special anxiety when a shot is available.

On any bighorn, forget the fancy stuff about brain, neck, or spine shots. As in most cases, I prefer the lung shot because it offers by far the largest vital target and the most room for error. On a broadside presentation, divide the body horizontally into thirds. Follow the back line of the foreleg up into the body, and shoot the ram in the bottom half of the middle third. The other option, as always, is the shoulder shot. Follow the centerline of the foreleg upward, and place your shot at the top of the bottom third. True broadside presentations are rare, so you must visualize

Rocky Mountain bighorn tend to be somewhat larger than the sheep farther north. Even so, the bighorn is not a large animal when compared to some of the other North American ungulates. A good quality, nonpremium softpoint bullet will do well on broadside shots like this one. (Photo courtesy of Len Rue Jr.)

where the vitals lie in relation to the shot angle you have.

THE RIGHT RAM

Horn size varies among the states that offer permits and even among areas within those states. As is always the case with trophy quality, horn size partly depends on genetics, feed, and minerals, but it's also a matter of the way a given herd is managed. Some states are extremely conservative in the number of permits they offer; others are more liberal. Bighorn tags are so hard to come by that, unless your budget is absolutely unlimited, you should plan on filling your tag with a ram representative of the area you are hunting. Do your research to learn what that means in the area you will be hunting. It would be a shame to shoot a mediocre ram in an area that produces really great sheep. It would be an equal shame to waste the tag by passing good rams for the area while searching for the monster that may not exist where you are hunting.

However, that doesn't mean "any legal bighorn" is a good ram in marginal areas. In most states a legal bighorn is a three-quarter-curl ram. Such a ram may be a ten-year-old monarch with heavy bases and massive, broomed tips, or it may be a 3½-year-old youngster, skinny in the bases and still carrying its sharp lamb tips. The former is a trophy ram anywhere bighorns are hunted—but in some areas you might

Bighorn sheep are not overly tough; however, it is still necessary to place the bullet properly. The point of aim for the lung shot is indicated. (Photo courtesy of Len Rue Jr.)

pass it and do better. The latter, in my view, is not yet a bighorn sheep. A trophy is in the eye of the beholder, but to me a bighorn must have mass and character.

I have hunted Montana's rough, tough "unlimited permit" areas, and I have passed barely legal rams and gone home empty. When I drew my Montana tag, I knew it was a great area, so I passed up lots of rams in all age groups in search of a really good one. We found it, lost it, then found it again, and took it. My Wyoming tag was different. I knew the area had plenty of sheep, but I also knew that big rams were scarce and record-class rams perhaps nonexistent. The goal was simply a fully mature bighorn. In the search, we passed more than a dozen legal rams and finally found a grown-up ram, no monster, but a trophy of which I am very proud.

BIGHORN GUNS AND LOADS

Even the largest Rocky Mountain bighorn isn't a particularly huge creature, and sheep aren't hard to put down, so large calibers aren't really necessary. Long shots generally aren't necessary, either, but you need to be prepared for them. Traditional sheep rifles like the .270 Winchester and .280 Remington are ideal: adequate in power, able to handle almost any potential shooting situation, and easily tailored into a light, trim package, which is important in a sheep rifle. However, there's another school of thought.

When I drew a second bighorn tag, I carried my Rifles, Inc., .300 Weatherby Magnum loaded with the 180-grain Hornady bullets, which it shoots so well. I was ready for any shot!

On my first bighorn hunt I used a .270 Winchester, and it was ideal for the shot I got. Several days earlier I had seen that same ram, and I would have taken it then, but we were pinned down on the far side of a sagebrush flat while the sheep rested quietly about four hundred yards away. I didn't feel comfortable taking that shot with a .270, so we waited, hoping the rams would move. They did, but it was too late, and we lost them in the dark. Worse, we couldn't find that ram again for four days.

When I drew my second tag, I carried a .300 Weatherby Magnum, somewhat heavier but still portable enough for me, and I felt I was prepared for any reasonable shot. Those tags are so precious that the right rifle is the most accurate, most dependable, flattest-shooting rig you own that you have confidence in and that is light enough for you to carry all day in the mountains. Of course, any sheep rifle needs to wear a good scope. A 3–9X is plenty of power, but there's no harm in stepping up to more powerful variables like the 4.5–14X.

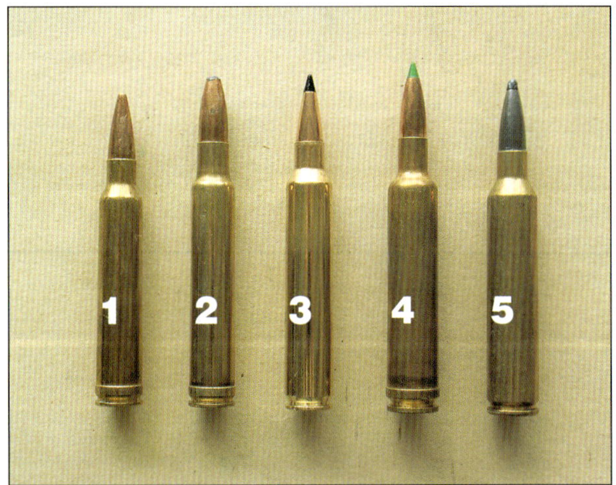

Left to right: 1) .300 Winchester Magnum 2) .300 Weatherby Magnum 3) .300 Remington Ultra Mag 4) .30-378 Weatherby Magnum 5) .308 Warbird. Bighorn sheep don't really require the power of a fast .30—but the opportunity to hunt them is so rare that you want to be able to take any sensible shot. The fast .30s are absolutely the best for true long-range shooting, but they also work well up close.

BULLET PERFORMANCE

I like a bullet that expands well so that the vital organs are wrecked and the ram goes down as quickly as possible. Some bighorn country is very steep, and you don't want your ram to run off a cliff or roll down a shale slide if you can avoid it. On the other hand, shots at bighorns are rare enough that you want to have enough bullet so that you can penetrate the vitals from almost any angle—you can't always wait for the broadside presentation we all prefer. With sheep I generally use fairly quick-opening bullets, but I ensure penetration by using relatively heavy-for-caliber slugs. I have taken most of my wild sheep with conventional softpoints from Sierra and Hornady, and with polymer-tipped bullets like the Nosler Ballistic Tip. All of these bullets open relatively fast, which is good on sheep—but I don't use light-for-caliber bullets. In my .270 I shoot 140-grain bullets rather than the traditional 130-grain slugs; in 7mm I usually shoot 160-grain bullets, and in the .30s I use 180-grain bullets. I have taken several rams with strongly angled "raking" shots, including my first bighorn and also the larger-bodied Marco Polo argali, and adequate penetration has never been an issue.

SPECIAL CIRCUMSTANCES

Almost by definition, all shots at bighorns are "special circumstances." The opportunity to hunt these creatures is extremely rare and precious. I drew for twenty years before receiving my first

Well-known desert bighorn guides, Larry Altimus (left) and Bo Morgan (right), with a ram from the Kofa range in Arizona. (Safari Press photo library)

bighorn tag, and I have now applied for desert sheep for nearly thirty years without drawing. In all hunting, the goal is to make the "perfect shot." A well-placed shot is a moral responsibility, and it equates to a home run with all bases loaded in the bottom of the ninth inning or a winning touchdown as the final buzzer sounds. With bighorns, making that perfect shot is even more important, because the opportunity to attempt that shot may never come again in your life.

ROCKY MOUNTAIN GOAT

A tough customer in tough country!

Our mountain goat takes a back seat to the four varieties of wild sheep as a desirable game animal, but for the life of me, I have never understood why. It is absolutely true that the sharp, short horns of the American mountain goat of the Rocky Mountains aren't nearly as impressive as the curling horns of a Dall ram. But against this you have the mountain goat's long, luxurious white coat, which, on a mounted trophy, makes a perfectly acceptable trade-off against headgear. It is true that the meat of a Rocky Mountain goat, especially an old billy goat, is usually strong and as tough as boot leather, while the meat of a wild sheep of similar age is mild and sweet. But, after all, sheep hunting isn't a meat hunter's game!

Those who have never hunted goat do not understand the most significant thing about goat hunting, which is that goat country starts where sheep fear to tread. Goat are generally hardier creatures than sheep; they are less picky in their diet and are able to negotiate much steeper terrain with seeming ease. Wild goat tend to inhabit country that is steeper, rougher, and less hospitable than that of wild sheep, and this is generally true of the many types of wild goat the world over. So I have never understood why the wild goat is such a neglected and underrated trophy—but I'm thankful for it because, while outfitted sheep hunts have continued to escalate, good goat hunts in some of the best areas remain quite affordable!

Our American mountain goat, *Oreamnos americanus*, is not exactly a true goat (genus *Capra*) but is most closely related to the "rock goats" of the Old World—the chamois of Europe and the goral, serow, and tahr of Asia. Over the years various biologists have tried to identify four subspecies, but most authorities believe that the differences aren't marked enough to rate such a distinction. For hunters there is only one goat, the American mountain goat. Its primary range follows the coastal mountains from Alaska's Kenai Peninsula south to Washington State, and along the spine of the Rockies from British Columbia to Utah. To the north its range thins out quickly, but it is found in diminished density across southern Yukon into the Mackenzies. Introduced herds have also done well in suitable habitat throughout the West, including Colorado, South Dakota's Black Hills, and Alaska's Kodiak Island.

Both males and females grow horns. The nannies often have slightly longer horns, but the billies' horns are much thicker and far more impressive. Males are usually up to 30 percent larger than females, with big billies weighing up to three hundred pounds, maybe a bit more. This isn't particularly helpful to know; a nanny with kids is obvious, but it is extremely difficult to judge the size and sex of a lone goat, and mature goats are often loners. Typically, the billies have a slightly yellowish cast to their coats; nannies tend to be whiter. This is not definitive, however, especially if there is no snow and the coats are generally dirty. With good optics it is not difficult to see the heavier bases of a really good male, but extremely large nannies and mid-sized billies can still fool you. The only absolutely foolproof way to tell a male mountain goat from a female is to look at the base of the horns with good optics and lots of patience. Male goats have a black, padlike gland at the rear of the horn bases; females do not have this.

Hunting season usually opens in late summer in much of goat country. This is a beautiful time to be in the high country, but it's generally a poor time to hunt goat. The animals tend to be in very high, rough country, so you have to climb a lot more to get to them. The real problem, however, is that the mountain goat's summer coat is thin and patchy and makes a poor mount. Later on, when snows come to the high country, the goat will move down—at least a little way. This doesn't necessarily make the hunting easier; you may not have to climb as high, but you'll have to deal with snowy, icy, treacherous slopes. Hunting goat as late as is safely practical is by far

The best time to hunt goats is late in the fall. There will usually be plenty of snow and the mountains will be treacherous, but the goats will have come down a bit lower. More importantly, however, they will have their luxurious winter coats.

the best, because by late fall the winter coats are in their full glory, long and soft and luxurious.

SHOTS AT GOAT

Wild goat rely heavily on their ability to negotiate the crags. They see well, and there's nothing wrong with their senses of smell and hearing—but up in the rocks they are supremely confident that they can go where no predator can follow. For this reason they are generally not particularly wary or difficult to stalk. Mind you, it is extremely difficult to stalk them from below, because their instincts tell them danger is most likely to lie there. If you can get above them and keep the wind in your favor, you are likely to get close enough for a good shot.

It is often purely a problem of terrain. You will see many goat in such rough, horrible stuff that it is either impossible or too doggoned dangerous to get close enough for a shot. You will also see goat that you can easily shoot but that you could not recover without great risk, without technical climbing gear, or both. So if you do enough goat hunting, you will find goat that you simply must walk away from. Unless badly spooked, they are quite habitual, so if you find a good billy in a bad place you can usually find it again, and it might be in a better spot. The bad news is that, if there's enough grass and a bit of water, a goat may stay

Goats tend to live in country that is rougher, steeper, and rockier than sheep, although not necessarily higher. Hunting goats is a tough game, and keeping gun weight down is an important consideration.

I took this excellent B.C. billy with a 7mm Remington Magnum. The cartridge is a good choice, but even so I put a tight group on his shoulder, and he still walked into this chute and tumbled over the edge. This is normal; goats are extremely tough for their size.

on the same unreachable ledge for days on end!

Glassing and stalking is the only way to hunt goat. Like all white animals, they can be spotted at tremendous distances before the snow flies. In snow it's a bit more difficult, but their yellowish cast shows up against snow far better than, say, the pure white of a Dall sheep. Once you spot a goat, the secret is to find a safe, sane, and hidden approach that will bring you within range.

Goat are thought of as long-range game, but I have never personally found this to be the case. They live in big, rugged country, so a long shot is always possible; but in my experience the jagged, broken country that goat love usually allows for a fairly close approach. I have hunted numerous varieties of wild goat on four continents. I don't recall ever taking a shot at more than 250 yards, and that just once; I have taken most of my goat within one hundred yards, and on many occasions I have been within twenty-five yards of mountain goat and other varieties of wild goat.

TAKING THE SHOT

Some years ago I hunted goat in the Kootenays of southeastern British Columbia in November, a perfect time to find a great goat. The valleys were still fairly clear, but the slopes were covered with snow, and it was a tough hunt. It got tougher when I just

It is easy to aim too high on the goat because the hump gives an impression of a very deep chest. Take care when placing your shot, as a bullet that hits between the lungs and the spine, or just over the spine, will likely lead to a wounded goat and a long followup. (Photo courtesy of Len Rue Jr.)

plain missed a perfectly acceptable shot at a great goat. I don't like to miss, so I don't know if it was pure nerves or if I ate something I shouldn't have, but I was extremely sick all that night. The next morning, shaky and queasy, I forced myself to the top of the mountains. It was windy and extremely cold, but we got the drop on a goat bedded on a little bench about a hundred yards directly below us. It looked to be a good billy, but it was alone, so we couldn't be certain. We held the spotting scope tripod down against the wind and finally resolved the black scent pads behind the black horns. It was a billy, and a long-horned one as well.

I don't like to shoot bedded animals, and on this goat the angle was bad. We elected to wait it out, so I shook and shivered on the top of that windswept ridge for an hour. Finally the goat stood, and I shot it on the shoulder with my David Miller 7mm Remington Magnum, not the most accurate rifle I own but one of the most consistent. Absolutely nothing happened. So I shot it again with the same hold. Still nothing, and then it took a few steps, coming perilously close to a steep chute that would take it to God knows where. I shot again with the same hold, and my goat took a couple more steps and vanished into that chute.

We found it a hundred yards down, stone dead, with a group on its shoulder and on into the heart, measuring little more than an inch. Pound for pound, I

Goats have a reputation of being both phlegmatic and tough. Mature billies tend to have a large hump, so it is important to place the shot not too high in the chest. With a well-placed bullet, Rocky Mountain goats are not hard to kill. (Photo courtesy of Len Rue Jr.)

have never encountered any animal in the world that is tougher than the mountain goat. It seems exceptionally resistant to bullet shock, with an uncanny ability to simply walk away from a hit that would flatten most animals of similar size right in their tracks.

Mind you, a short run after a fatal shot isn't unusual and in fact should be expected. But with goat this is a problem because of the incredibly rugged terrain they inhabit. Upon sensing danger—danger perhaps meaning the sting of a bullet—a goat will instinctively head for the steepest, nastiest stuff it can get to. It might be dead on its feet, but it doesn't know that, and the goat will tumble over a cliff or down a shale slide—perhaps ruining the hide and breaking the horns—and quite possibly will wind up in a spot from which you cannot recover it. So the idea with goat is to stop them and drop them.

I must tell you that I don't know exactly how to do this. Even if you're close enough and the conditions are right for a head or neck shot, you shouldn't try either because, especially with the white cape, you might destroy the trophy you have worked so hard to obtain. A spine shot is possible, but oh, so tricky. A standard lung shot is extremely unlikely to stop a goat before, with its last strength, it launches itself over a precipice. The very best option is clearly the shoulder/heart shot. Its placement is the same as with any other animal; simply follow the centerline of the foreleg into the bottom third of the body. On a broadside presentation this shot will break the on-shoulder, penetrate the heart, and, if everything is perfect, break the off-shoulder as well.

If you take out both shoulders, you have a good chance to drop the animal in its tracks, where you want it. But I want to recommend something on goat that I would not recommend on any other animal. Goat are almost always taken within a few yards of extremely steep stuff. With the last breath in its body and that final burst of adrenaline, a goat will make for the vertical slopes that are its natural sanctuary. To get there it will drive with its back legs if it is able, even if both front shoulders are broken. Place your first shot perfectly, and if your goat goes down, fine. If it's making a last run and isn't anywhere close to a cliff or chute, equally fine. But if it's still moving and trying to get into some bad stuff, shoot it high through the hips. This is definitely not a "perfect shot," nor a first shot—but it is the best way to immobilize a goat that has already taken a fatal bullet.

THE RIGHT GOAT

Under most circumstances both nannies and billies are legal game, for two reasons.

Left to right: 1) .270 Winchester 2) .270 Winchester Short Magnum 3) .270 Weatherby Magnum. To my thinking the fast .270s are the "best of the best" for Rocky Mountain goat. Mated with fast-opening bullets, the .270s will do everything you need to do and can be housed in light, easy-to-carry rifles with mild recoil.

My Browning A-Bolt .270 Winchester groups wonderfully with Winchester's fast opening and deadly Ballistic Silvertip bullet. I haven't used it for Rocky Mountain goat, but I have used it on several Asian ibex . . . taking each of them with just one shot.

It is so difficult to sex goat that it would be foolish to regulate otherwise, and goat are so prolific that taking a nanny without kids does little biological harm. The goat with the longest horns are usually nannies, so an exceptionally long-horned nanny can be a very fine trophy. To most hunters, however, the more massive bodies and thick horns of a billy are the superior trophy. Once you get past the difficulty of telling a billy from a nanny, the next hurdle is judging the length of horn. This is extremely difficult.

Any billy with horns over nine inches is an acceptable trophy, and any billy with horns over ten inches is outstanding. Depending on mass, a billy with ten-inch horns could make the rigid standards for the Boone and Crockett record book. A billy with eleven-inch horns, which is rare, should easily make it, and the world record is just twelve inches. No one, even with the best optics, can accurately judge mass at the second and third quarters, so there isn't much separating good from great. Ear length of around six inches is a reasonable guide for length, but pay attention to the curve of the horn. The extremely straight horns of most billies probably aren't as long as you think they are, and you will generally get a bit more length than is apparent from a well-curved horn. Unless you're obsessed with having your name in the record book, the best course is to try hard to find a billy goat with horns that are apparently thick and seem to be more than 1½ times longer than the ears. Match this with a thick, luxurious coat, and you will have a great trophy.

GUNS AND LOADS

Any flat-shooting, accurate, and well-scoped rifle from .270 Winchester through the magnum .30s is a fine rifle for goat. In other words, any good sheep rifle is also a great rifle for goat. The country will almost certainly be extremely steep, so gun weight is definitely a factor. Heavy rifles are difficult enough in sheep country, and they have no place on goat mountains.

BULLET PERFORMANCE

Although goat are extremely tough, I am not convinced that larger calibers are the answer. Goat are slab-sided animals, and, as physically tough as they are, they don't offer a great deal of resistance to a bullet. Thirty years ago, on a mixed-bag hunt in British Columbia, I shot my first goat with a .375 H&H. A .375 will flatten elk and big bear, but it wasn't impressive on that goat. I shot it several times, each time poking caliber-sized holes that didn't seem to bother the goat much at all. I finally finished it with my guide's .30-06, thus learning two valuable lessons: Bigger isn't always better, and bullet performance is far more important than caliber.

On goat you want a bullet that will open up quickly and do serious damage to the vital organs. Provided you're shooting an adequate caliber with a bullet that is reasonably heavy-for-caliber, goat aren't so big or heavily boned that you need to worry about failure to penetrate the shoulder. A good old .270 with fast-opening, 130-grain bullets will not only work fine on any goat but will almost certainly work better than my .375 did, firing bullets designed for much heavier game. On goat you really don't want tough, penetrating bullets. Think instead about good old conventional softpoints like Sierra, Hornady, Speer, Winchester Power Points, Federal Hi-Shok, and Remington Core-Lokt, or newer polymer-tipped bullets like Nosler Ballistic Tip, Hornady A-Max, Swift Scirocco, and Winchester Ballistic Silvertip. Bullets like these, when mated with a perfect shot, are far more likely to get into the vitals and do the damage necessary to stop a goat before it pitches off into vertical country.

MUSKOX

Beware of the hair!

The recovery of the muskox happened quietly in the far northern regions where it roams, but its recovery during the latter half of the past century is a great conservation success story. Early Arctic explorers found plenty of the shaggy beasts, but as the Arctic was opened up, hunters, trappers, and Inuit—all better armed than ever before—hunted them for meat, hides, and the soft layer of underwool called qiviut. The muskox was never really endangered, although often described as such. Its numbers declined dramatically during the latter half of the nineteenth and the first couple of decades of the twentieth century. With protection, however, its numbers have increased dramatically, especially in recent years. Today Northwest Territories alone estimates as many as fifty thousand muskox. The animals also remain plentiful in East Greenland, and transplanted populations have been established in Alaska, Norway, Siberia, and northern Quebec.

The Boone and Crockett Club's *Records of North American Big Game* is the oldest North American record-keeping system. The muskox listings are a study in hunting history. They include heads taken in 1890, 1900, and 1915, and then there are no listings until the 1930s, which reflect several entries from Greenland. There is almost nothing until 1974, when Alaska's Nunivak Island herd was officially opened to limited sport hunting. I well remember when drawing for a permit on Nunivak Island was literally the only opportunity to hunt muskox, but in the latter part of the twentieth century it got a lot better. Hunting on some of the Arctic Islands of Northwest Territories began in the early 1980s. Over time these programs have expanded to numerous native communities on both the islands and mainland. The current edition of *Records of North American Big Game* (11th edition, 1999) reflects a tremendous number of entries from the 1970s, 1980s, and 1990s. Between the lines, this doesn't necessarily suggest that muskox grow bigger than they used to; it just means that there is much more hunting opportunity.

Unless you refer to older record books, it may not be obvious that the minimum score for inclusion has been raised considerably, and the world record has changed hands a number of times in the past couple of decades. I took my first muskox back in 1981, when Northwest Territories first opened. Back then it was considered a huge bull and would have been in or near the top ten in Boone and Crockett, and for a short time it was the world record by Safari Club International standards. Today it ranks clear down in 147th place in Boone and Crockett's records, and it has slipped to eighth place in Safari Club's listings for Greenland muskox.

The muskox's Latin name, *Ovibos moschatus*, means "musky sheep-ox," and reflects considerable confusion about this animal's origin. The musk comes from facial scent glands that exude an extremely strong smell during the summer rut. The underlayer of qiviut does indeed produce fine and highly prized wool, but the muskox is much more of a wild bovine than anything else, with distant ties to the takin of southern China. Like most North American animals, the muskox crossed the land bridge from Siberia during the late Pleistocene Epoch, but for unknown reasons the Asian populations became extinct around the time of Christ. Muskox fared better in the Western Hemisphere, and during the ice ages were at one time found as far south as New Jersey.

Although fairly large on the scale of North American big game, the muskox is a relatively small wild ox; bulls normally weigh around seven hundred pounds. Their appearance is deceiving; they look much larger than they are because of the incredibly long hair that enables them to survive Arctic winters. Individual muskox hairs may be two feet long, and the animal will have at least a foot of shaggy hair surrounding the neck and shoulder area. Both males and females have horns that grow close to the head, then turn out and curve upward in sharp hooks. At first it seems difficult to tell the sexes apart, but

By habit muskoxen form a defensive circle when threatened by their only traditional enemy, wolves. These days they have been hunted enough by humans that you may not see this natural defensive posture; muskoxen are learning that greater safety lies in rapid retreat.

only the bulls have horns with heavy bosses, and the two horns are almost joined together at the top of the skull. Coloration is generally dark brown, with a lighter saddle patch on the flanks and pale legs.

Although not all authorities agree, they generally recognize that there are two subspecies: *Ovibos moschatus moschatus*, the barren ground muskox of mainland Canada; and *Ovibos moschatus wardi*, the Greenland muskox. Greenland muskox are found not only in Greenland but also on Canada's offshore islands; the transplanted herd on Nunivak Island is Greenland muskox. The barren ground muskox is definitely larger in the body, and record-book listings suggest that it grows somewhat larger horns. Boone and Crockett currently lumps the two subspecies together; Safari Club's record book separates them into different categories.

SHOTS AT MUSKOX

Along Canada's northern shores you can find muskox in open tundra, the same country where you might search for migrating caribou. This particular tundra is rich with lichen and has fingers of scrub willow. The muskox are better fed, and they grow larger. Mainland bulls are said to run up to 750 pounds, but friends who have hunted them there maintain that really big bulls are considerably heavier. The Arctic Islands are much more barren and are also fairly arid, with limited snowfall and sparse

Muskox hunting is a chilling experience, but the country is starkly beautiful in its way. I think a bolt-action rifle is the best choice because this action type will work the best when thoroughly degreased.

grass that seems insufficient to support such a large animal. Here body weights for mature bulls are unlikely to exceed 650 pounds. Wherever it lives, the muskox lives in big, open country, and unless it is hidden by terrain its dark, bulky form can be seen at vast distances.

Most muskox hunting takes place in late fall and early spring, when the landscape is white. At that time a herd of muskox can be seen from miles away, appearing like peppercorns on a white blanket. A hunter will often encounter a solitary bull, but muskox are gregarious creatures and usually occur in small herds of ten to twenty. They have a tough time making a living, especially during the long winter, so they're usually active during the day. You will often find them out on windswept flats, digging through the snow to graze. Of course, the more there are the easier they are to spot—but finding the animals isn't a huge problem. It might take a few days to find them in the huge country they live in, but, as long as the weather holds, modern muskox hunting is extremely successful, with most hunts lasting no more than five days.

Weather is the primary enemy. My first muskox hunt was in November, when the days were extremely short and the cold was incredible. It started to gray up around ten o'clock in the morning, and around midday the sun came over the horizon in a short arc. It was pitch-dark again and very cold by three in the afternoon. We came upon a fair-sized herd late in the afternoon of our first

Although rarely considered dangerous, the muskox deserves the same respect you would give any wild bovine. He can turn the tables and seriously injure an unwary hunter very quickly. The Arctic cold is no place for an accident!

hunting day. I had no idea how to judge muskox, and since I was one of the first sport hunters I doubt my Inuit guides knew, either. I figured I would pass the shot because it was too early in the hunt. When my guides realized this, they became concerned, telling me they didn't know what the weather might do and maybe this was our chance. I shot the largest bull in the herd, and it turned out to be huge. The next day bad weather set in, and visibility went to zero!

My second hunt was in April, in my view a much pleasanter time to hunt. It was warmer, with temperatures a bit above zero Fahrenheit. Even better, we had hunting light for nearly twenty hours. I think the weather is a bit more reliable in the spring, but weather is still the enemy. We left Coppermine and headed out across the Queen Maude Gulf, we hunters bouncing along in sleds behind snow machines—a backbreaking means of travel that, in the Arctic, you might as well get used to. We hadn't gone terribly far when a storm came in out of nowhere. Our guides wisely diverted to some fishing shacks at the tip of a peninsula, and we sat out a storm in relative comfort for two days. Then we crossed the Gulf and set up camp on the southern edge of Victoria Island. The next day all three of us took good muskox. The message is, on this hunt, you must make hay while the sun shines!

You will travel mostly on snow machines or on sleds behind the machines. This allows you to cover quite a lot of ground, and if the

With lots of hair just about everywhere, it is not easy to see where to aim on a muskox. If possible, follow the animal's front leg straight up to find the heart/lung area. (Photo courtesy of Leonard Lee Rue III)

weather is perfect, you may be able to look at a lot of muskox. Historically, the shaggy beast's only enemy was wolves, and the muskox would form a circle, horns outboard, in defense. When modern muskox hunting first opened, this was also their defense against humans, so it wasn't much of a hunt. The animals would circle up, and all you needed to do was walk around the herd, locate the bulls, and take your shot as soon as the chosen bull was clear.

These days you will occasionally see this, but muskox have now been hunted enough that they know the difference between men and wolves. They are much more likely to run than to stand, so today you need to glass them from farther away and make a covered approach within shooting range. Either way, muskox hunting is not difficult, nor are the shots likely to be difficult. The primary problem is the cold—but it's worth enduring to see how the wonderful Inuit hunters deal with their inhospitable environment. The muskox, too, is worth it. It is truly a spectacular and very underrated trophy.

You should also not underrate the potential danger of hunting the muskox. It is absolutely true that the primary danger is from the cold, but muskox have the equipment, the power, and occasionally the disposition to turn the tables. Their defensive circle is not static; once it is formed, individual animals will charge outward from the circle toward the perceived danger, then retreat into the press. Bow hunters especially can make the mistake of getting too close. It

There is a lot of hump and loose, curtainlike, guard hair on a muskox. This gives the animal's body an appearance of being much larger than it actually is. (Photo courtesy of Leonard Lee Rue III)

also isn't unusual for other muskox to be reluctant to leave one of their downed companions. A few years ago Otis Chandler, an extremely experienced hunter, got well and truly hammered by a muskox bull that refused to leave its buddy after Chandler shot it. He survived despite numerous broken bones—but I can imagine few things less pleasant than being badly hurt in that cold.

TAKING THE SHOT

Because the country is so open, there is certainly the opportunity for a long shot, but muskox are rarely so spooky that it's necessary. Most of the time it isn't difficult to close within a hundred yards, so there is no excuse for less than a perfect shot. Still, this isn't quite as simple as it might seem. The animals are no larger than the average bull elk and certainly no tougher, but the tricky part is figuring out where the animal is underneath all that hair.

Gravity being as it is, the heaviest layer of hair is underneath the body. This makes it almost impossible to see where the hair stops and the muskox starts. It's extremely easy to shoot too low, and I did exactly that with my first muskox. I assumed I was making a perfect shoulder shot, but I actually only broke the foreleg high. I corrected instantly, shot again, and the bull went down—but now I know better. On an animal as big as a muskox, the shoulder/heart shot is definitely the best approach. On most animals you simply come up the centerline

Muskox camp on Victoria Island. Typically the camp is carried in sleds that are towed behind snow machines, so you can travel through the day and set up wherever darkness finds you.

of the foreleg to the bottom third of the body, but on muskox there's a good chance you'll hit only hair, or at best the foreleg itself, if you take this approach. Instead, come up the centerline of the foreleg fully halfway between what appears to be the belly line and the back line. Chances are this placement will actually be low in the chest, where you want it; but it will not be too high.

Muskoxen are not large creatures, rarely weighing more than 700 pounds. The largest calibers are not required, but you do want fairly tough bullets to ensure penetration. The good old Nosler Partition is an excellent choice.

THE RIGHT BULL

Muskox are quite difficult to judge. Unfortunately, the reality of the hunt is that you may not have a chance to look over a whole lot of bulls before making your selection. If the skies appear to be clear and you're seeing a lot of animals, you can look around a bit. But the weather is very uncertain, and muskox are rarely concentrated, because the forage is sparse. The bull you see just may be the one you take home.

Boone and Crockett's scoring system and Safari Club International's are quite different. Boone and Crockett measures the length of each horn, the width of each boss, width at the first quarter, and circumferences at the second and third quarters. SCI uses total length of horns, from tip to tip across the bosses, and width of the bosses. By either measurement a big muskox is a big muskox—but neither measurement is particularly easy to judge. Look for horns that go down below the jaw before turning up, with hooks that come up as far as possible. The bosses are extremely important by either system, so look for a huge, bronze skullcap. If the boss appears to be partly covered by hair it probably isn't very big.

In spite of today's increased standards, the muskox remains one of the easiest animals to get into the hallowed Boone and Crockett records. Not all will make it, but if the weather gives you a chance to look around, your odds are better with muskox than with any other animal I know of. Record-book score, however, shouldn't be the most important thing. The high Arctic is so different that it might as well be a different planet. It's beautiful in its way, especially on a clear day, and the night skies are spectacular, especially if you catch the Northern Lights. The trophy is spectacular, too; the fabulously long hair is every bit as impressive as the horns. My first muskox is a head mount, and it's wonderful. My second is a closed-mouth rug, a great shaggy thing that is truly impressive. Many hunters do life-size mounts, and if I had room I'd have one of those as well.

GUNS AND LOADS

The muskox is a big, blocky animal, but not so big as to require extremely powerful rifles. I used an 8mm Remington Magnum on my first muskox, and it worked just fine. I used a .375 Weatherby Magnum for my second, and it was spectacular. But, in truth, any versatile cartridge from .30-06 on up to the .33s will do just fine. The rifle should be scoped, but it should also wear auxiliary iron sights because rifles take an incredible pounding on the sleds and snow machines.

The most important consideration, however, is to completely weatherproof the rifle. Liquid lubricants absolutely will freeze, so I strongly recommend a bolt-action rifle for this kind of hunting. It is the easiest action to degrease, and it will operate very smoothly with just a bit of dry graphite lubricant. Take the bolt completely apart and degrease it with alcohol or some other degreasing agent. Failure to do this invites a slow hammer fall, or failure to fire altogether.

BULLET PERFORMANCE

The muskox is a big enough animal to require bullets that will absolutely penetrate. Just how tough a bullet you should use depends somewhat on the caliber and bullet weight. If you're using fairly light calibers like the 7mm Remington Magnum or .30-06, you have enough gun, but you should use plenty of bullet—bullets that are heavy-for-caliber and tough, like the Barnes X-Bullet, Winchester Fail Safe, and Swift A-Frame. Larger calibers are much more forgiving of bullet performance, but the muskox is simply too large for light, fast, quick-expanding bullets.

BISON

A small taste of yesteryear!

The American bison, *Bison bison,* is one of the world's largest bovines. It is larger than a Cape buffalo and larger than an Asian water buffalo. Only the huge gaur of India and Southeast Asia is consistently larger than the American bison. Perhaps oddly, these bovines of Africa and Asia, and many lesser ones such as the dwarf forest buffalo and banteng, are legendary for their aggressiveness and ferocity. The myth of the bison is that it was once the most numerous large mammal on the planet, but it stood and allowed puny men to slaughter it by the millions.

The slaughter was no myth, and it was one of the most unfortunate chapters in American history. The culture of the plains tribes depended on hunting the bison in their untold number. It was widely believed—with some justification—that "pacification" of the Indians rested on eradication of the bison. Politically, the destruction of America's sixty million bison was considered a good thing. As the railroads penetrated the buffalo's domain, hunters could make their fortunes shipping buffalo robes to a ready eastern market. Add to this a sea of land-hungry settlers rolling into bison country, and our buffalo never had a chance.

Serious market hunting for bison didn't begin until the Civil War ended in 1865. By the early 1870s the great Kansas herds were gone, and the hunters turned south and north. By 1880 the buffalo had vanished from Oklahoma and northern Texas. The Montana herds were the last to go. The winter of 1882 is considered the end of the market-hunting era. So, in the space of a single bison's lifetime, the incredibly numerous species became seriously endangered. Characterizing the bison as a placid beast is grossly unfair, because it didn't survive man's onslaught long enough to become a game animal!

In the early days, before the development of centerfire rifles, bison were typically hunted by "buffalo running"—galloping alongside the herd on horseback. With prairie dog and badger holes dotting the prairie, this was an extremely dangerous pastime. Had this method continued, it's possible more bison would have survived. But the buffalo is an open-country herd animal, and it never had a chance. With the development of the centerfire cartridge, the opening of railheads, and the voracious eastern markets, buffalo hunting changed. No longer was it a wild adventure; it became a serious business for professionals who stood off at increasing distances and measured their profits against cartridges expended.

In the 1880s there were scattered remnants of bison, but by the 1890s the only viable wild herds in the United States were in Yellowstone National Park, with a few populations in Canada. As we know, the bison was saved from extinction, but very few herds are truly wild. Even the Yellowstone herd was augmented from semidomesticated herds in 1902. So we don't really know what the bison might have been like had it survived long enough in the wild to learn to fear man and pass that fear along to its progeny.

Anyone who has been around bison, wild or domesticated, knows they are not barnyard cattle. They are almost impossible to fence, they are unpredictable as hell, and they can be downright dangerous. We will never know what the Kansas prairies were like in the 1860s, when herds of bison marched from horizon to horizon, but we should not underestimate the bison. Any bovine weighing more than a ton is a formidable creature!

Ancestors of the American bison crossed the land bridge from Siberia thousands of years ago. At one time their range extended across Alaska, down the Rocky Mountain chain into Mexico, and east to the Appalachians. Although very scarce today, there is a European bison that is clearly a first cousin to ours, though smaller and woollier. Here in North America two subspecies are generally recognized: the plains bison (*Bison bison bison*) and the woodland bison (*Bison bison athabascae*). Some authorities believe there were two other races that are now extinct: *Bison bison haningtoni*, a smaller, paler mountain bison of Colorado's high country, and the eastern bison, *Bison bison pennsylvanicus*. Not enough data survives to substantiate these. The plains bison existed

Colorado outfitter Alan Baier and I with a good bull taken in South Dakota. The bison is one of the world's largest wild bovines, with mature bulls weighing well over a ton. Because of the open country they inhabit, genuine danger is rare, but an animal this large deserves respect.

from the Rocky Mountains eastward, and the woodland bison extended from the western slopes of the Rockies north to the Northwest Territories and to the west across Alaska.

The woodland bison is larger and darker, but the only pure specimens are found in sanctuaries in the Northwest Territories and Alberta. It is estimated that by 1890 fewer than one thousand bison remained in all of North America. The original Yellowstone bison were probably woodland bison, but plains bison were used for restocking. Elsewhere the reverse occurred, so most bison today are a mixture of the plains and woodland varieties. We are fortunate that the great humpbacked beasts exist at all.

The American bison is a very large, woolly coated animal, with mature bulls averaging over a ton and occasionally weighing as much as three thousand pounds. The horns are short and very thick, curving out and up from the sides of the skull. During the hot plains summers the bison appear almost mangy, but their winter coats are thick and luxurious, and they grow a long skullcap of woolly hair that, in cold climates, obscures the base of the horns.

Today there are many private herds. The North American population is believed to exceed one hundred thousand. Bison are fairly prolific, so there are plenty of opportunities to shoot bison—but there is little opportunity to actually hunt it. With very few exceptions, modern bison hunting is purely herd management, carried out under controlled conditions. The opportunity to hunt free-range

Many bison get shot in the brain or spine to ensure an instantaneous kill; however, these shots require very accurate shot placement. (Photo courtesy of Leonard Lee Rue III)

bison by genuine fair chase probably exists only in the Henry Mountains herd in Utah and a couple of free-range herds in Alaska. These hunts are available by permit draw. Whether you can have a good experience hunting herds on private land depends on the circumstances—not only the acreage but also how one goes about hunting bison.

SHOTS AT BISON

There are a few places where you must work hard to find a bison, and Utah's rugged Henry Mountains is a prime example. In most situations, taking a bison is more of a collection than a hunt. This is neither bad nor good; it just is. The reason we have so many private herds is not only that bison meat is excellent but that many hunters desire a specimen of this most American trophy. Regardless of the circumstances, eventually you must take your shot, and if you aren't somewhat awed by the size of this great creature—and the history that brought you to that moment—then you should consider taking up golf or tennis.

Bison are an open-country, grazing animal. They are not naturally wary, and today's herds are so carefully managed that flight at long range is unlikely. There are always reasons why you can't get particularly close to any game—such as wind direction and natural obstacles—but it is unlikely that you will make a long-range shot at bison, and I certainly would not recommend it on such a large beast.

A bison, often erroneously called a "buffalo," is easily North America's largest land mammal. Mature bull bison weigh more than Cape buffalo. If body shots are taken, anything considered for a Cape buffalo should be thought of for the bison. A sensible minimum would be a .375. (Photo courtesy of Leonard Lee Rue III)

Most of the time you can close within a hundred yards with relative ease, and then it's just a matter of placing the shot.

TAKING THE SHOT

Legend has it that the old-time buffalo hunters stood off several hundred yards with their big Sharps rifles and dropped bison after bison in their tracks. The real story was different. In the 1870s, when the genuine professional buffalo hunters were in their heyday, profit was the primary incentive. Teams of skinners followed the hunters, and the skinning took time and cost money. The goal was to drop as many buffalo in one spot as possible—called a "stand"—instead of stringing carcasses to the far horizon. The really big Sharps cartridges, the .50-140 and .45-120, didn't even exist until the buffalo were gone. The Sharps "Big Fifty" was popular, but it was neither particularly big nor fast. It was a .50-90 cartridge that was only a slight improvement over the .50-70 Gov't. cartridge, which preceded the .45-70. The trapdoor Springfields in both .50-140 and .45-120 chamberings were far more available and economical, and it is almost certain that they accounted for more buffalo than all the rifles by Sharps, Remington, Ballard, Bullard, and all the rest put together.

With the arcing trajectories of the black-powder rifles, "long range" was a relative figure. The idea was to stand off far enough so that the smoke and belch of the rifle didn't disturb the bison but close enough for every valuable cartridge to count. A hundred yards was too close, but two hundred yards was a long shot. The rifles were accurate, and the hunters were extremely skilled—many of them shot bison into the thousands—but this was business. They didn't try head shots, and they generally avoided shoulder/heart shots because the animal was certain to make a death run and spook the rest of the herd. Instead, they concentrated on lung shots.

Unless rutting or angered, the bison is a phlegmatic beast, not subject to bullet shock. It usually takes a bullet through the lungs quite calmly, continues to feed for a while, and then lies down and eventually dies. The old buffalo hunters concentrated on this shot: safe, sure, and least likely to cause a stampede. We modern hunters want to take our game more quickly and cleanly, so this is not the shot we want.

Under many circumstances today, the bison hunter gets the skin and trophy, but the meat goes to the market—so hunters insist on head and neck shots. The neck shot is difficult with bison. The neck is extremely deep, and within the neck the spine dips very far down as it enters the region of the body. It's hard to visualize shot placement

Penetration is absolutely essential on bison, so a case could be made for shooting nonexpanding bullets, left, to ensure penetration from any angle. If softpoints are chosen, they must be tough bullets designed to retain weight and penetrate. The center is a Barnes X-Bullet, and the right is a Trophy Bonded Bearclaw.

and altogether too easy to get it wrong. The brain shot is never easy, but it's a bit easier to visualize. On a broadside presentation, shoot just under the horn and your bison should drop to the shot. From the front it's much trickier, but you must shoot for the center of the skull just under the horns. I have to admit I fluffed this shot on a bison, shooting less than an inch too low. Then things happened fast, and multiple body shots were instantly required!

If body shots are appropriate, they are by far the safest course. On an animal of this great size, a shoulder/heart shot is the best approach, but only if you're shooting a powerful rifle with tough bullets that will penetrate. Just follow the centerline of the foreleg up into the bottom third of the body, and you will have your bison. Unless you're shooting an elephant gun, it probably won't go down instantly, but it will go down.

THE RIGHT BULL

Most bulls have fairly long horns, and a really huge bison will have horn length in the upper teens. Horn mass comes with age, and it's the mass and how that mass is carried throughout the horns that really makes the trophy. This is not easy to judge, but beware of horns that appear sharp and thin, regardless of length.

It's best to shoot bison during the winter; the luxurious coat is every bit as important to trophy quality as the horns. The long hair on the head makes judging trophies even more difficult, however. Often you cannot see the bases at all, and the hair comes up as high as the horns. This in itself is a tip-off: If a winter bull has horns that extend above the hairline, take a good look at the mass. The curve is also important; you get a lot more length along a curved horn than you do from a straight horn.

GUNS AND LOADS

Because of the relatively open country and the controlled circumstances under which bison are hunted today, you could certainly use a .30-06 with a good, tough bullet and be perfectly safe—especially if you take a brain shot. I used my old Winchester Model 71 in .348 for a South Dakota bison, and it would have been just perfect if I had made the brain shot correctly. But, as I said, I didn't. It took several body shots to correct the error, and that is the common result if you don't have enough gun. You wouldn't think of taking on a Cape buffalo with a .30-06 or a .348 Winchester, and bison are considerably

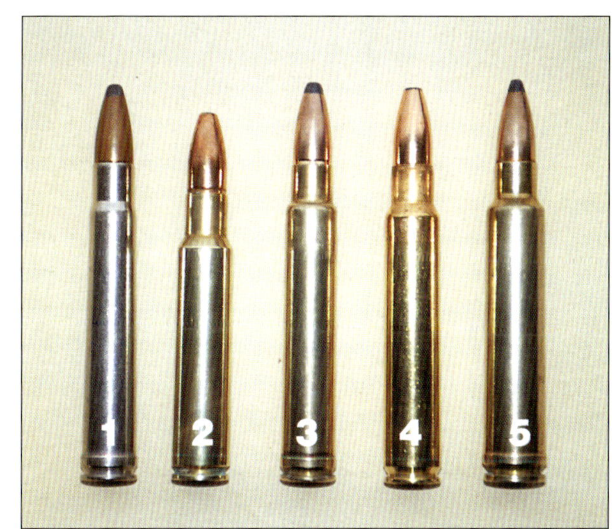

Left to right: 1) .375 H&H 2) .375 Dakota Magnum 3) .375 Remington Ultra Mag 4) .375 Weatherby Magnum 5) .378 Weatherby Magnum. Many modern bison hunters use traditional cartridges for reasons of nostalgia. However, bison outweigh Cape buffalo, so, in modern cartridges, ideal rounds for Cape buffalo are equally ideal for our American buffalo. The various .375s are just right, especially considering the open country in which bison are found.

I used a single-shot Wesson and Harrington .45-70 to take this huge bison. The hard-cast bullets worked perfectly, just like they did back in the 1870s.

larger. I think this huge animal deserves more respect.

Among modern rifles, think about the same cartridges you might use on African buffalo—the .375s and .416s. If you take a brain shot and do it right, the cartridge you're shooting probably won't matter much—but if you blow it, or you decide on a shoulder/heart shot because of distance or presentation, the big guns will deliver much more satisfactory performance.

Buffalo hunting today has a lot to do with nostalgia, so many hunters opt to use the old black-powder cartridges. The .45-70 is the most popular and most available of the old cartridges, but you must keep in mind that it's no powerhouse. Remember that the old-timers weren't nearly as concerned about clean kills as we are today. Using older cartridges certainly adds a different dimension to the hunt, but if you use one with traditional open sights, you have probably eliminated your ability to make a brain shot unless you are very close, and you aren't long on power for so large an animal.

Use heavy bullets, and, if you don't mind cheating, use modern heavy loads as well! A .45-70 in a strong, modern action loaded with good handloads becomes an altogether different cartridge, and it is far more adequate than the black-powder loads our forefathers used. In December 2001, I used a single-shot Wesson and Harrington .45-70 to take a huge bison bull with John Ray in southern Colorado. The particular loads I used were black-powder handloads behind a hard-cast bullet, pushed a good deal faster than the standard load. Performance was superb; regardless of the high-energy figures obtained with smaller, faster calibers, there's much to be said for the hitting power of big, heavy bullets! While I used black-powder loads for nostalgic reasons, modern .45-70 loads like the Garrett's (for use only in modern rifles) offer a great deal more power than anything used in the nineteenth century!

BULLET PERFORMANCE

Regardless of the cartridge you choose, you simply must use bullets that will absolutely guarantee penetration. You want tough bullets that are heavy-for-caliber and well constructed. Bullet construction does depend on velocity; at the speeds of which a .45-70 is capable, hard-alloy bullets will absolutely penetrate. If you use a modern rifle, however, you should use modern bullets like Swift A-Frame, Barnes X-Bullet, and Winchester Fail Safe—especially if you use calibers less powerful than the .375 H&H.

JAVELINA

Our smallest big game . . .

I guess you could make an argument that the javelina is the largest small-game animal. I've always considered the javelina big game because it is hunted by traditional big-game techniques: glassing and stalking, still-hunting, hunting from a stand.

When I started hunting, there were many Texas counties that had year-round seasons and no bag limit on javelina, so they seemed more like a varmint in that time and place. Today, the seasons and bag limits are much more restrictive in most of Texas, and in Arizona and New Mexico tags are required for a one-javelina limit, mostly obtainable only through a drawing.

The javelina is a fearsome-looking creature, all head and teeth, and when threatened it pops its teeth together and makes a truly frightening noise. Normally, it is found in small herds of a half-dozen to fifteen or so, but once in a while you run into much larger groups. Javelina have a fierce reputation, and there are stories of humans being "treed" for hours by large groups of these ferocious creatures. I suppose this might happen under very unusual conditions, but, despite its intimidating appearance and the sound effects of its teeth clashing together, the javelina is really a very small creature. Normal weight for mature javelina is no more than forty pounds. Males and females are about the same size, and the occasional outsized specimen will top fifty pounds.

Because of its flat snout and piglike shape, we tend to refer to the javelina as a "pig," but it really isn't. Its proper name is collared peccary. The Brazilian Indians gave it the name, which means "an animal that makes many paths through the woods." Collared refers to the light-colored stripe running diagonally from shoulder to throat, generally distinct against the grizzled gray coat. Its Latin name has bounced back and forth, but today it is generally agreed to be T*ayassu tajacu*, *tayassu* meaning "gnawer of roots" in an Indian tongue and *tajacu* taken from a native Brazilian word for this animal.

Since the javelina's proper name and scientific names stem from South America, one might surmise that the javelina is not strictly a North American animal, and this would be correct. The peccaries are strictly animals of the Western Hemisphere, although fossil remains suggest they once occurred in the Old World as well. The range of the collared peccary just touches on the United States; it is fairly plentiful in most of southwest Texas and southern Arizona, with a more limited range in southwestern and southeastern Arizona. It is well distributed in Mexico and Central America, and its range extends south to northern Argentina. There are two other species as well.

Javelina

The white-lipped peccary, *Tayassu pecari*, also touches both continents, ranging from the jungles of southern Mexico down through Central America. It is more uniformly dark in color, with the pale lower jaw for which it is named. The white-lipped peccary is considerably larger, weighing as much as eighty-five pounds. The giant of the breed is the Chaco peccary, similar in color to the collared peccary but with longer, paler hair on the ears and legs. This peccary, confined to the Gran Chaco region of northern Argentina, southeastern Bolivia, and northwestern Paraguay, can weigh nearly one hundred pounds—but this is not the most significant difference between the Chaco peccary and the collared and white-lipped peccaries. The Chaco peccary lacks the vestigial third toe on the hind feet, which is probably the reason science awards it a different genus and species: *Catagonus wagneri.*

Despite similarities in appearance, the peccaries are considerably different from true pigs. The feet are different, the stomach is different, there is no gall bladder, and the teeth are considerably different. The tusks of a peccary are elongated canines that grow more or less straight; a pig's tusks grow up and out. Javelina also have a prominent scent gland about six inches up from the stubby tail, giving the animals a strong odor that, in heavy cover, acts as a sure giveaway of their presence.

In good country javelina can be extremely plentiful, which is misleading.

We rousted a big group of javelina from this cave in Sonora. Javelina will often hole up in caves during wet weather and during the heat of the day.

They are not nearly as prolific as pigs; the females usually bear no more than two young. Although they do well in arid country, they do need water, so their populations suffer during drought years. These factors have led to the more restrictive hunting we enjoy today—and ensure that there will be javelina to hunt tomorrow.

SHOTS AT JAVELINA

Hunting techniques vary considerably, depending on where you are. In game-rich Texas the javelina receives little respect as a game animal and tends to be hunted coincidentally to deer hunting, or simply ignored. Javelina are extremely common in the brush country of south Texas, but it is very difficult to hunt them on purpose there. They are occasionally hunted with dogs, and they will respond to a varmint call. More often, however, they are taken when they wander by a deer stand. (This "wandering by" is considerably aided by the fact that baiting for deer is legal in Texas.) Shots will be close and fast when calling or hunting with dogs—in contrast, a shot from a deer stand is defined as any shot the hunter believes he or she can make!

Once you get out of the thick brush and the country starts to open up, the situation changes. Along the oak mottes of the coastal plains, the oak-studded ridges of the Edwards Plateau, and anywhere you can find prickly pear flats, you have an opportunity to glass

Outdoor writer Durwood Hollis and I are next to the Arizona javelina I took with the 6mm Benchrest Remington in a custom XP-100 pistol. Handgun hunting for javelina is so much fun that it's been many years since I've taken one with a rifle.

My buddy Duane Adams, a good Arizona outfitter, packing a javelina out of the Catalina Mountains north of Tucson. Arizona's spring javelina season is a major event in Arizona's hunting calendar, and there the javelina is definitely considered big game.

and stalk javelina. Farther west, in New Mexico and Arizona and down through Sonora, you tend to find javelina up in hilly country where glassing and stalking are the primary hunting techniques.

In Arizona most javelina seasons occur in the spring, and the spring "pig" season is a major event. Part of the reason is that wildlife resources are fragile in Arizona's arid country; virtually all big-game tags are by drawing, and many hopeful residents do not draw deer tags. Part of the reason is that the season is in the early spring, when not much else is going on in the hunter's world—and this is a glorious time to be in the southwestern mountains.

I have not hunted javelina in New Mexico, but I have hunted them in Texas, Arizona, and Sonora, and I have enjoyed every minute of it. The primary challenge is to find them, and although they are generally not scarce, they are small animals that live in very big country. When glassing, you look for small black peppercorns on a distant hillside. It doesn't take much brush to hide them, but when they step into the open they appear shiny and black and are quite easy to see.

Sometimes you hunt them by sound; although their family groups tend to be quite social, they seem to have a lot of extremely vocal arguments. Some years back, Arizona outfitter Duane Adams and I glassed a big herd going over a distant ridge. It was late morning and hot by the time we huffed and puffed our way over that ridge, and we found a system of deep canyons on the far side and absolutely no javelina. Duane guessed that they had bedded in the thick brush in the bottom of one draw or another, so we sat down in a prominent place, glassing into the brush and listening. Nothing happened for an hour or so, and then a ruckus broke out in heavy brush right below us. We closed the distance a bit, making some noise as we did so. Before long, more than twenty javelina trooped up out of the canyon bottom. We watched and counted, and I shot a nice one when it paused on a boulder just opposite us.

Javelina have extremely keen noses, and their hearing is just fine, but they can't see worth beans. This means that, provided you watch the wind, it usually isn't too difficult to close in for a shot once you locate the game. This makes them excellent game for bow hunters, and I've long enjoyed hunting them with a pistol. Depending on the country, you can also snipe at them at long range, but I've always enjoyed closer encounters—and just because you are close doesn't necessarily mean the shots are easy.

Once, in Sonora, we located a small group bedded in a cave. This isn't uncommon; javelina love to bed in caves. It was uncommon to find a particular cave with javelina in it at that particular moment. This cave was known to our Mexican cowboys, and once again it was a javelina's squeal that led us there. The mouth of the cave was tight against thick brush, so there was no way to get at it from below. It lay just below the crest of a jagged ridge. Only by leaning far out—with someone holding onto your belt—could you peer into the shadows of the cave and make out the forms of sleeping javelina. There was absolutely no way to shoot, so we sat there stalemated for quite a while. Finally, we decided we had little to lose, so we woke them up by lobbing some rocks.

This is usually not the wisest course. When the wind changes or javelina hear you, there are usually javelina exploding everywhere. A scattering herd tends to run in all directions, and this is almost certainly the genesis of many of the legends of javelina "charging." When this happens it's difficult to pick a target, just as it is when a covey of quail erupts. Also, a javelina running through the brush is an extremely difficult target. This time it worked; I hammered a nice one just a dozen yards from the cave mouth.

TAKING THE SHOT

Although small, javelina are fairly tough. If the shot is placed poorly, they can take the impact of surprisingly powerful cartridges and escape into the brush. Record-book entries are based on skull measurements, and the bleached skull of a javelina makes a really neat secondary trophy, so avoid head shots. The neck shot is OK; just shoot right into the center of the neck—but it is a very small target. The lung shot and the shoulder/heart shot are by far the best. The animal is small enough that there isn't much margin for error no matter what you do, so I recommend coming up the centerline of the leg almost halfway into the body.

THE RIGHT JAVELINA

Boone and Crockett does not have a category for collared peccary, but Safari Club International does. Trophies are accepted into the record book based on skull

Unlike its distant cousin the wild boar, the javelina is a light-boned and easily killed quarry. Any caliber from .243 on up, with sensible bullet construction, will do. (Photo courtesy of Len Rue Jr.)

measurement, but this is impossible to judge on a live animal. To me, one javelina looks much the same as another; brush usually prevents getting a glimpse of the sex organs, and without that I've never been able to tell the males from the females reliably. Fortunately, no open javelina season requires that you shoot only boars, so most of the time the goal is to find the biggest javelina you can. They are herd animals, and this is the good news, because the best way to judge size is simply to compare them and shoot the one that looks the biggest.

Again, one javelina looks much like another to human eyes—so beware the lone javelina! Many years ago, when I was in my twenties and thought I knew much more than I did, I was sitting on a deer stand on the southern edge of the Texas Hill Country. It was getting dark, and I was pretty sure I wasn't going to see a buck (at least not well enough to see the antlers properly) when a huge javelina stepped into the open. I made a quick decision—not necessarily a good one—and shot it. It turned out to be a very small boar, not even close to full-grown. I never got a buck on that hunt, but I sure took some ribbing about my "trophy" javelina!

Actually, unless you want to mount the trophy, that little boar was probably just the right size to shoot. Young javelina aren't great eating, but they're edible. The adults aren't very good at all. This creates quite a dilemma: I like hunting javelina, but I don't like to eat them, and I don't want to mount

The javelina is small with a light bone structure. Any deer caliber will result in a quick, humane kill. (Photo courtesy of Len Rue Jr.)

another one—so it has actually been some years since I've shot one.

GUNS AND LOADS

I have taken a lot of javelina with rifles, but I have taken more with handguns. Javelina are actually quite easy to hunt, and there isn't much challenge involved in killing one with a scoped centerfire rifle. Of course, you don't really know that until you've taken a couple, so I'm certainly not knocking hunting them with rifles; but alternative means—whether handgun, bow, or muzzleloader—offer a more satisfying experience.

Whether you prefer a rifle or a handgun, it's ridiculous to talk about "adequate cartridges" on an animal weighing no more than fifty pounds. Any centerfire rifle is clearly "adequate," but if I were choosing a rifle for javelina, I would use the milder .22 centerfires, from .22 Hornet up through .223 Remington. In handguns any cartridge from the .357 magnum upward will do just fine. I have shot more javelina with a .44 magnum revolver than with anything else, but that's because I like the .44 and that's what I usually carry, not because that level of power is essential. The scope-sighted "specialty pistols" chambered to rifle cartridges are also lots of fun. I have used the 6mm Benchrest Remington in an XP-100 to take a number of javelina during Arizona's HAM (Handgun, Archery, Muzzleloader) seasons, and it works just fine—but a single-shot pistol in .223 Remington would work just as well.

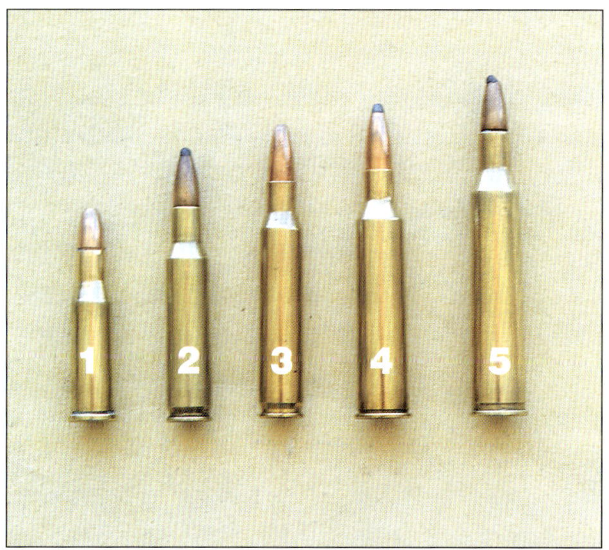

Left to right: 1) .22 Hornet 2) .222 Remington 3) .223 Remington 4) .225 Winchester 5) .220 Swift. All of the .22 centerfires are perfectly adequate for javelina, the best choice really depending on whether you prefer to get close or shoot from some distance.

BULLET PERFORMANCE

A fast-opening bullet from a powerful cartridge, whether fired from a rifle or pistol, can really make a mess of a javelina. Since adequate power isn't really an issue, I recommend using fairly tough bullets that will simply zip on through without doing a lot of unnecessary damage. In revolvers, hard-cast, flat-point bullets are probably a better choice than destructive hollowpoints; in rifles, think about controlled-expansion designs instead of frangible bullets that will blow up. I mentioned that I like the .22 centerfires for javelina, but you will get better results and less trophy damage if you use them with heavy-for-caliber bullets intended for deer-sized game instead of the more common and more destructive varmint bullets.

FERAL HOG

Not native, but
an all-American game animal just the same!

Years ago, when I was working in Los Angeles, one of the closest, easiest, and least expensive hunting getaways available was to dash up to the Central Coast region and hunt wild hog. Public land is scarce in that region, and public lands that hold wild hog populations are scarcer yet because pigs are naturally drawn to private land where there's agriculture and permanent water. An extended drought in the early 1980s changed things, but in the 1970s there were tons of wild hog in the coastal mountains, and we did pretty well. We would gather around midnight at my house in a northern suburb of Los Angeles, drive north through the wee hours, and hunt our tails off all day—often making the four-hour return trip that night. I figure we averaged about 50 percent success on those grueling "search-and-destroy missions"—not bad for one-day hunts on public land!

One time I asked an extremely experienced hunter friend of mine—whom I admired greatly—if he wanted to come along. He replied, "No, thanks, I'm not much of a pig hunter"—as if being a pig hunter were some sort of lower life form. I was crushed, but I didn't stop pig hunting. I guess it's part of human nature—the bad side—to want to think you're better than someone else, and we hunters are no different from anyone else. Many bow hunters think they're better than gun hunters, big-game hunters think they're better than small-game hunters, sheep hunters think they're better than deer hunters, and so forth.

This is unfortunate, because any day you can spend afield is wonderful. Today I live in the Central Coast region, and the pigs, which I used to drive through the night to hunt, leave their sign in my back yard. I hunt them often, and I still enjoy it. I've been fortunate to have hunted most of the major big-game species in the world, but I cannot say that I've had any better hunting days than some days I've spent in pursuit of our wild hog.

Over the years mankind has transplanted numerous species. Most of the species now hunted in both the South Pacific and South America were introduced from other continents, wild hog included. Thanks to intensive management, European big-game animals have been moved around for so long that it's difficult to tell exactly what was originally present and what was not. Even South Africa, with an incredible abundance of native game, has some populations of nonnative game.

North America is no exception. Many of our native game populations weren't exactly native where they now occur, and we have a goodly array of nonnative species as well. We have free-range ibex and aoudad in Texas and New Mexico, axis deer in

Texas and Hawaii, and scattered populations of Sika and European fallow deer. However, the wild hog is far and away our most plentiful and widespread nonnative big-game animal—and the only one that has become a truly important big-game animal almost from coast to coast.

In California the wild hog is a full-fledged big-game animal, requiring not only a license but also tags. This is somewhat of a joke; our season is year-round, there is no bag limit, and we residents buy our pig tags for $7.90 for a book of five. But they are legally a big-game animal in the Golden State and for many years now have been more important than deer in terms of both hunter participation and numbers harvested. Elsewhere this full-fledged status is rare, but there are free-ranging populations of wild pig in many parts of the country. They extend from California up into Oregon, and certain river systems in Colorado and New Mexico have them. Wild hog are extremely well distributed in Texas, with some now spilling up into Oklahoma. The razorbacks of Arkansas are legendary, and from there wild hog extend southeast—not quite continuously, but close—all the way to Florida. Most of the Hawaiian Islands also have wild hog.

In addition to genuinely wild hog there are "hunting preserves" all over the country that offer hog hunting as a staple. Some of them have breeding populations, offering a hunting experience that differs little from hunting free-range populations.

You can call them what you will, but virtually all of our wild hogs in North America are simply feral pigs, domestic swine gone wild. Hogs in some areas are strongly influenced by pure European stock, but in most places a wide variety of color variations occur.

Others, regrettably, are "put and take" situations, offering hunting that is a poor substitute for the great hog hunting thousands of American hunters enjoy.

Our wild hog is often called wild boar, European wild boar, Russian boar, razorback, and even more exotic titles. One memorable magazine story called it the Russian imperial boar. The reality is that most of our wild hog populations are just plain feral hogs, with roots in domestic pigs that were allowed to range free. This is not necessarily a bad thing. The genuine article—the Eurasian wild boar—and the good old barnyard domestic pig are actually one and the same species: *Sus scrofa*. Over the years a number of introductions of purebred European stock have been made here and there, the most famous being on George Gordon Moore's estate at Hooper's Bald, North Carolina. By the way, the same George Gordon Moore also introduced pure Eurasian wild boar in my country, California's Central Coast region.

The Eurasian wild boar is a massive animal. It is all shoulders and head, with a grizzled grayish-brown coat, long snout, ears that are short and straight, and a straight tail. The young are reddish with white stripes at birth, a telltale sign of pure wild stock in the bloodline. Domestic swine, although conspecific with their wild ancestors, have been bred into a wild array of colors. Where the primary bloodlines are from domestic swine, you will see hog that are white, black, gray, brown, red, spotted, belted, and you name it.

It seems to me, however, that the pure Eurasian bloodline is dominant. Our local hog—along with most wild populations in America—stem primarily from the common nineteenth-century practice of letting domestic swine roam and forage freely. More than three-quarters of a century have passed since a pure Eurasian strain in my particular area was known to be introduced, yet a fair percentage of our local hog show the grizzled gray color and striped offspring of the real McCoy.

Several hundred miles away, in the western foothills of Mount Lassen, there is an altogether different and historically isolated population of pigs, originally pure feral hogs that were a grab bag of all colors. A buddy of mine, Mike Ballew (now director of the NRA Whittington Center), used to manage the hunting on the huge Dye Creek Ranch, and wild hog hunting was the cornerstone of his operation. One of his management goals was to improve his pig herd, and he was a stickler about selective hunting. Whenever possible he took out the off-color animals—belted, spotted, white, et cetera. At the same time he brought in and released a few pure Eurasian animals. I hunted up there a couple of times a year for about a dozen years, and in just that short period I saw the dynamics of the herd change from a riot of color to predominantly black, with the grizzled gray of the Eurasian wild boar well represented.

In terms of trophy quality, most of us who hunt pig feel that the fairly common black boar and the grizzled Eurasian-type hog make the best-looking head mounts, but there isn't really much difference between these "good-looking" pigs and the odd-colored animals you often see. Left to forage for themselves for just a couple of generations, the domestic swine regresses quickly. The shoulders become more powerful and the fat hams streamline. They become hairier, the ears become straight instead of floppy, and the tail unkinks. All boar, domestic and feral, are capable of growing the same wicked tusks, and the boar grow a thick cartilage shield over neck and shoulders, probably protection against other boar during their vicious mating battles.

Size varies tremendously, depending largely on available food. I occasionally hear about "wild hog" that weigh in excess of six hundred pounds. This is certainly possible in the barnyard, so it is theoretically possible in the wild if food conditions are ideal. But not in my country! Our wild hog deal with long dry seasons and periodic food shortages. A nice-sized mature boar in our country starts at about 180 pounds, and a genuine 250-pound boar on good scales is big. We do get larger boar; on rare occasions boar will weigh over 300 pounds, and weights up to 350 pounds aren't unheard of. But in our area a 500-pound pig was either "guesstimated" rather than weighed—or wasn't long out of the stockyards! Elsewhere in the country, where food and water conditions are more reliable, larger weights are certainly possible. I'm pretty well convinced that Texas hog average somewhat bigger than ours, and this should be true in the Southeast as well. But anywhere, whether in Germany's Black Forest, Russia's Caucasus Mountains, or here in America, a free-ranging wild boar that approaches four hundred pounds is very, very big.

That is big enough. A mature boar, whether it weighs two hundred pounds or twice that much, is a most formidable creature. The armor plate on its shoulders

Col. Roy Chevallier and Kyler Hamman have stalked a herd feeding in a barley field, and now they are trying to select the best hog. We hunt pigs year-round in California, but late spring and early summer is a great time because the pigs can't resist the ripening barley.

This was a very unusual morning along the central coast of California, hunting with Doug Roth's Camp Five outfit. We saw exactly three pigs, but all three were truly exceptional boars. Left to right: Geoff Miller, shooting a .308 Winchester; me with a .30-06; and Jack Sundby with a .308.

may be more than an inch thick. It might have as much as four inches of razor-sharp tusk showing above the gum line—and it has no enemies save man and other boar of like size. Mountain lion and coyote take a toll on young pig, which is probably a good thing, because *Sus scrofa* is an extremely prolific breeder. Sows are also somewhat vulnerable, especially just before and after giving birth. A healthy, mature boar, however, is beyond the capability of any North American predator. Although its eyesight is poor, that wide snout is incredibly sensitive, and its ears are almost equally keen. It learns early that humans are dangerous, and its normal reaction on scenting man or hearing a strange noise will be flight. But if it's hurt or cornered, it just might fight.

In my area alone we've had two incidents in the past year where hunters were injured, one seriously, by wounded hog. This is not a high incidence: I live in San Luis Obispo County not far from the Monterey County line—the two counties that have California's highest wild hog density and largest harvests. But it can happen. Despite a lot of experience with Africa's dangerous game and a lot of experience with bear, two of my own closest calls have been with wild hog. This does add another dimension to hunting them. They aren't really dangerous unless something goes wrong, but they absolutely have the capability and disposition to turn the tables!

Despite fairly intensive hunting pressure almost everywhere they occur, wild hog are expanding their range rapidly. Our California hog decreased considerably during the drought but after a few good years have bounced back considerably. Interestingly, the drought also had the effect of expanding the population into areas that used to have no pig at all. Not all game managers, and certainly not all landowners, are happy about having pig. They are hard on fences, and where they are plentiful, their rooting can cause serious erosion problems—but they're an established fact in many areas, and in time they will be much more widespread.

The huge Tejon Ranch, one of the largest contiguous holdings in the United States, straddles the high country about sixty miles north of Los Angeles. Until recently there were no pigs there at all, but there was a small hunting preserve on the northeastern boundary that had them. While fighting a forest fire, the fire crews knocked down a portion of the fence, and it was believed that eighteen pigs escaped. The Tejon Ranch people were horrified, and issued "shoot on sight" orders to their cowboys. Over the next few weeks about a dozen pig were shot, and no more were seen for a long time. They believed the problem was solved, but it wasn't. That was just a dozen years ago, and today there are at least several hundred pigs firmly established on the Tejon. The good news is that pig hunting is now an important part of operation of their recreational and hunting division.

SHOTS AT WILD BOAR

Techniques for hunting pig vary with the area. Hunting wild hog with dogs is probably the most common technique in the southeast, and there are hound hunters in Texas and California. This means extremely close shooting, and it can be fast and quite dangerous. In areas with heavy cover, a lot of hog are taken from stands, not only incidental to deer hunting but also on purpose. In my country we have rolling coastal hills. Some hills and valleys are choked with poison oak, manzanita, and chaparral—ideal bedding cover. Other hillsides are relatively open and studded with acorn-bearing oaks. We call this "oak grassland" country, and it's ideal country to glass and stalk pig. This is my favorite hunting technique, and it's a great experience in beautiful country with typically wonderful weather.

When stalking pig you can usually get fairly close, but the shooting isn't the point-blank range common with hound hunting. Shots much beyond a hundred yards are uncommon, because you can usually get at least that close. But anytime you're stalking there may be obstacles—brush, shifting wind, moving game—that prevent you from getting as close as you would like. I usually tell hunters to be prepared for shooting up to two hundred yards, and that covers almost all sensible shooting situations.

Typically hog start moving and feeding in the late afternoon, feeding and resting through the night and then returning to bedding grounds in thick cover in the early morning. Pig tend to move along well-established trails, so in the morning we try to catch them moving from known feeding areas to bedding cover. In the afternoon we often set up closer to bedding cover, hoping the pig will start to move just before dark. On particularly good days I've seen literally hundreds of pig moving, and it isn't unusual to see several groups totaling forty or fifty in a morning or afternoon hunt. Sometimes, of course, the pig just vanish, and sometimes you only see a couple.

One June morning Geoff Miller, Jack Sundby, and I hunted about an hour north of here with Doug Roth's Camp 5 outfit. It was a perfect morning, unseasonably cool and slightly foggy at dawn. We hunted a system of high ridges above barley fields that pig dearly love, and we should have seen pig all over the place. In fact we saw exactly three pig all morning. This was enough; all three were exceptionally good boars, all three alone and traveling on separate ridges. Jack shot his at about 6:45 a.m. Geoff shot his at 7:15, and I shot mine around 8:00. Three shots, three really good boars, all shots at about 125 yards. That's about as good as it gets!

TAKING THE SHOT

Wild hog are extremely tough. They are often taken very close to heavy cover, and because of their thick hide and layer of fat, they don't bleed very much. Wounded pig are thus very difficult to recover, so it's essential to hit them very hard. Head and neck shots are certainly good options, but the long shape of a pig's skull makes the placement very tricky for a brain shot. I tend to stay away from it, but if you can hit just in front of and slightly below the ear on a broadside presentation, you will get your pig. The best neck shot is just behind and slightly below the ear, in the center

This is a really good tusker anywhere, any place. You have to work at it to get into trouble with a wild hog—but they have the equipment and know how to use it, so common sense and caution go hand in hand.

Hunters often underestimate feral hogs. They have tough bones and a super-hard shoulder plate made of gristle. The best, well-constructed bullets should be used, and most guides prefer a caliber of .30-06 or larger. (Photo courtesy of Gary Kramer)

of the first third of the neck. This is also tricky, but it certainly will work.

The standard lung shot is also a bit tricky on pig, unlike this shot on other animals. A pig's heart and lungs lie a bit farther forward than they do in the deer family, so a very standard behind-the-shoulder lung shot that would be almost immediately fatal on a deer can easily be a bit too far back on a pig. The placement is the same: Mentally divide the body into horizontal thirds. On a broadside presentation come up the back line of the foreleg into the bottom of the middle third. This will be a good lung shot, but the difference is that you have very little margin for error to the rear. Still, this is one of the better shots on a wild hog—especially if it's a big pig and you're shooting a fairly light cartridge.

If you have plenty of gun and plenty of bullets, then a shoulder/heart shot is probably better and certainly safer. Just come up the centerline of the foreleg into the middle of the bottom third of the body. This will probably take out the major arteries at the top of the heart rather than the heart itself, but such a shot will be quickly fatal and offers the greatest margin for error.

THE RIGHT HOG

There are two ways to hunt pigs. You can shoot for meat, or you can shoot for a trophy. They aren't mutually exclusive, but a young boar or, even better, a fat sow, offers much better pork than a rank old boar. In my little town we have at least a half-dozen outfitters who make much of their families' income

There is a formidable gristle plate on a mature feral hog. A heart or shoulder shot will require the hunter to penetrate that gristle for a humane kill. Unless the situation is dire, a brain shot is not recommended because the target is so small. (Photo courtesy of Gary Kramer)

hunting wild hog. They tend to call a big, old boar a "sausage pig," meaning that's all the meat is fit for, while the preferred meat comes from animals weighing about 100 to 125 pounds. I don't necessarily agree. The chops and hams from a boar can be very good, but they need to be smoked. The meat from a smaller pig is very good fresh. Actually, I think our wild hog have better, more flavorful pork than domestic pig, so most of my pig hunting these days is for "meat hogs."

Now, if you want a trophy, you have three considerations: size, tusks, and color. This is a tall order. It is very difficult to see the tusks on a live pig. Sometimes you'll catch a flash, but often dirt and brush prevent a really close look. Smaller boar can have teeth that are just as good as those of very large boar—and tusks are often broken off short. Body size is much easier to see, and, provided you get a good look in a clear spot, it usually isn't all that difficult to tell a boar from a sow. But color complicates things terribly. To me it isn't that important, but many hunters want only a dark-colored boar for mounting. This may not be the wisest course, because really good boar with thick tusks showing 2½ inches or more above the gum line are fairly uncommon. If you see a really big boar, consider it a trophy regardless of color—and if both tusks are long and unbroken, you just got a great bonus!

GUNS AND LOADS

There's a big difference between a hundred-pound meat pig and a really big boar. A .243 is just fine for the former but isn't enough gun for the latter. This doesn't mean you need a cannon. My old buddy Mike Ballew guided hunters to literally thousands of pig during his Dye Creek days. Mike hates big guns and usually carries a .243 or .257 Roberts for all his deer hunting. For backup on pigs he always took out a "big gun," which to him meant a 7x57mm or .270! My local pig-guiding buddies don't all agree. Roger Miller uses his .270 Weatherby Magnum loaded with Barnes X-Bullets. Kyler Hamman usually carries a .375 H&H. August Harden usually carries his 8mm Remington Magnum. Alfred Luis is another .270 fan, but he recently acquired a .338 Ackley Improved for his pig hunting.

Left to right: 1) .356 Winchester 2) .358 Winchester 3) .348 Winchester. In my country I really like the medium-velocity .35s for hog hunting. They have enough range, and their big, fat bullets hit hard enough to really anchor wild hogs.

Anything from about .270 on up will work just fine on even the largest pig, but I think something on the order of a .30-06 is probably the best all-round choice. For close-in hunting the good old brush cartridges, like the .35 Remington, .375 Winchester, .444 Marlin, and .45-70, are just wonderful. Personally, I like the .35s, and I do most of my hog hunting with the .348 Winchester, .358 Winchester, and .35 Whelen. My most recent "pig gun" is a light .350 Remington Magnum, also a wonderful choice. All of these cartridges will reach out to two hundred yards, which is important in the country I hunt—but they will also absolutely flatten a pig, whether up close or out there. Handguns are also great for close-range use, especially when hunting with dogs, but you should consider no less a pistol cartridge than the .44 Magnum.

BULLET PERFORMANCE

Again, there's a big difference between a small meat hog and a big boar. You never know when a huge boar with gleaming tusks might appear, so you need a bullet that will absolutely penetrate, no matter what size pig appears. I believe strongly in bullets designed to penetrate, especially if you're using fairly light cartridges (like typical deer rifles). Good bullets include the Nosler Partition, Barnes X-Bullet, Swift A-Frame, Trophy Bonded Bear Claw, and Winchester Fail Safe. No bullet is forgiving of shot placement, but all of these bullets will get into the vitals where it counts.